The Script is finished, Now what do I do?

The Scriptwriter's Resource Book & Agent Guide

K CALLAN

© K Callan 1993
ISBN 1-878355-00-7
Library of Congress Catalog Card Number ISSN 1068-5162

Other books by K Callan
The Los Angeles Agent Book.1 (The Actor's Workbook)
The New York Agent Book.1
How to Sell Yourself as an Actor.1
The Los Angeles Agent Book.2
The New York Agent Book.2
The Life of the Party
How to Sell Yourself as an Actor.2
The Los Angeles Agent Book.3
The New York Agent Book.3
The Los Angeles Agent Book.4

Cover: Barry Wetmore
Photography: Van Williams
Editor: Kristi Nolte
Copy editing: Nicholas Hormann

Thank you...

to all the writers who asked me to write this book.

to The Writers Guild of America for answering my questions,
providing me with data and generally being the most generous and
non-elitist group I have ever encountered.

to The Dramatists Guild for answers, generous support and
information.

to all the writer support groups who provided me with newsletters
and information.

to Adele Weitz for computer support.

to David Notle for design consultation.

Introduction

Read the Directions

Most of us buy an appliance and never read the instructions. We might use the equipment for years before we find out that in addition to its basic function, it also sings and dances.

Though you are eager to skip through the book to the agency listings and begin sending out manuscripts, be patient: this book also sings and dances. There is valuable information here that can enhance the effectiveness of your submissions.

Many agents complain that writers seek agents too soon. You can avoid rejction by learning what to do first. Determine if you can have a career from Peoria. If you decide to move to a big production center, learn how to penetrate the fence and get inside the system. Discover which classes can enhance your business opportunities as well as your script. Find out about contests, scholarships, The Writers Guild, The Dramatists Guild and other details before focusing on agents.

The Script is Finished deals with query letters, meetings, writer/agent relationships and how to nurture them; what the writer has a right to expect and what is too much to expect; the relative value of no agent, a star agent and discerning which is (given a choice) the agent with whom you would have the most fruitful relationship. There is a list of books you'd find helpful for your reference library, a glossary and sound ideas on when it's time to change your work habits instead of your agents; all this before you ever get to the agency listings. Each chapter informs the next so if you digest the main dish before you get to dessert, the dessert gets better.

One of the most important things I learned by researching agents for this book is how much form means to them. They do judge your work relative to whether you took the time to learn the format and do it right. Begin to practice patience and form now, by going a step at a time.

Good luck.

Contents

Who Makes the Money? 1
Focus/Homework 14
Does It Matter Where You Live? 33
Ways into the Business 41
Agents 76
What Everybody Wants 82
Query Letter 101
Conglomerate Agencies 112
Divorce 122
The Relationship 129
First Aid 145
Rating the Agents 158
Agency Listings 161
Glossary 267
Index to Agents & Agencies 271
Index to Los Angeles Agents & Agencies 283
Index to New York Agents & Agencies 289
Index to Everything Else 291

Who Makes the Money

Show biz is a glamour business. Where else can you get heartbreak, pain, disappointment and rejection, plus big time money, sex and fame all at the same time? In order to join the club and become a working writer, actor, director, producer (not even a star, you understand), you must have grit, drive, ingenuity, talent, professionalism, craft, patience, stability, wit, style, grace, faith and hope. Many get by without charity.

If you are reading this, I'm assuming you either have or can develop all the attributes described above. That being the case, before you jump completely off the cliff into the abyss of perennial temp work that encompasses anyone engaged in an artistic endeavor, particularly scriptwriting, there are several meaningful questions to ponder:

☞   What are your chances of actually making any money doing this?

☞   What kind of writing do you have in mind?

☞   Is there any market for what you want to write?

☞   How can you enter the system?

☞   What can you do for yourself?

☞   Should you study? Where and Why?

☞   Can you write from Iowa?

☞   Do you need an agent?

☞   What does an agent really do?

☞   What are agents looking for?

☞   What should you be looking for in an agent?

☞   How can you research agents?

☞   What do you have a right to expect from an agent?

☞   What does an agent have the right to expect from you?

☞   What is the best way to approach an agent?

☞   How can you have a mutually rewarding relationship
    with your agent?

Money

First things first: is it worth it to you financially to pursue a career
as a scriptwriter?   Just because Joe Eszterhas makes millions of
dollars for his script is no guarantee that you will. Don't become
intoxicated by the possibilities and ignore the realities.

•   *If we think working writers have a difficult time (and we're
only talking about the 5%-10% of Guild members who work on a
regular basis), look at all the people on the outside trying to get in
-- and they're all looking for agents as well as for job
opportunities.*

"Les Liaisons Dangereuses"
The Journal
June 1991

In 1992, only 51% of the 7,522 members of the Writers Guild, made *any money* at all. Of those who did make money, 20% made less than $4,000 and *only 10% made over $7,000.*

Who Makes the Money?

As in the other entertainment guilds, the money is made by white men. And it is made by young white men.

• *A new five-year study about writer employment in Hollywood shows that the industry is not making any great strides in terms of overcoming racism, sexism and ageism.*

> "White Male Pens Still Busiest"
> Kathleen O'Steen
> Daily Variety
> June 15, 1993

• *...while males' share of total employment has declined by just under 2%, but they still account for over three-quarters of the writers working in the industry. Women account for just over a fifth of all employed writers, increasing just slightly from 20.7% employed writers in 1987 to 22.3% in 1991.*

> The 1993 Hollywood
> Writers' Report
> William Bielby/Denise Bielby
> June 1993

• *Young males are the preferred group. It crosses a sociological line that has to do with* life-scripting *of what happens to females when they grow up in school and males growing up in school, who's allowed to do what. Boys growing up are allowed more freedom to explore and express and the girls aren't and this is the residual effect.*

> Laya Gelff
> Laya Gelff Associates
> Los Angeles

- *...the share of employment going to writers over 50 declined from 24.4% to 20.3% between 1982 and 1987 and declined further to 16.9 in 1991.*

  While just over half of the membership (52.5%) was not employed in 1990, unemployment varies by gender, minority status and age. The lowest rate of unemployment continues to be for non-minority males aged 40 and under, at 40% (up slightly from 35% in 1987). The unemployment rate is close to 50% for both non-minority women and minority writers under the age of 40. Among writers over the age of 40, the percentage of writers not employed ranges from 72% for minority writers, to 59% for non-minority writers, regardless of gender.

  > The 1993 Hollywood
  > Writers' Report
  > William Bielby/Denise Bielby
  > June 1993

- *If you are a minority, you have to be three times as good as anyone, but if you are, you'll work forever.*

  > Rima Greer
  > Writers & Artists
  > Los Angeles

Age

There's a lot of conversation these days about ageism, particularly in television. The consensus among many is that since the heads of networks these days are quite young, they prefer to hire writers in their own age group.

- *Today, in Hollywood, it is not the* Blacklist, *but the* Graylist. *Nobody in Hollywood reveals his or her age. It goes well beyond female actresses hungry for good, mature roles. Ageism is about writers not being able to write, directors unable to direct, producers not producing. It isn't always easy to prove discrimination since people aren't likely to tell you to* get lost *because you're older, any more than it's been easy to prove racial or religious discrimination.*

*According to Loreen Arbus, ageism in the industry affects
actors most, and writers second. She said directors are less
affected because producers are not often going to put young
directors in control of the millions of dollars it takes to make a film.
Studios don't want to try a hot new director to the extent they seek
the hot new writers under 40.*

Studios tend to think younger executives are best at developing
young *projects. Therefore, it is less and less a news item when a
22 year old writer or 23-year old director is working on a major
feature film. Writers and directors interviewed for this story
explained that young people feel more comfortable hiring and
working with young people. They share the same experiences and
their peers are not likely to bring up subjects they never heard
about.*

*Some directors and writers with experience have had to grit
their teeth in pitching sessions. A young executive sits stretched out
at his desk facing the gray-haired writer.* So what have you done?
the exec asks, Before or after you were born? *is the reply.*

*Then there's the one where the baby-faced producer asks for
the writer's credits and the writer says,* You first.

*Being a star, no doubt, helps keep you off the Graylist. Mel
Brooks, over 60, hasn't been affected.* I get a call a day to do
something. However, *he acknowledged,* if a director gets to be
over 55, the studios don't call unless he has a stellar career.

"Are you now or will you
ever be...old?"
Directors Guild Newsletter
September-October 1992

• *Reading that Burt Prelutzky can't find assignments at 51 and
Larry Gelbart has to defend himself for being 63 and not 43, I am
glad that I am a retired writer.*

"The Man Who Set Me Free"
David Karp
The Journal
April 1992

• *For a new writer who is older, yes, that would hurt. For an established writer, not necessarily. I represent many writers over 45 or 50 for that matter who are successful and making lots of money.*

I would think hard before taking on a television writer who is getting up in years, I wouldn't care on a feature film. I don't think there is as much age discrimination with a feature film. They don't care if my mother wrote it. Everyone wants to get their hands on a hot feature script.

There are more jobs open to the women in the industry than there have ever been. They are requesting black women directors.

Rima Greer
Writers & Artists
Los Angeles

• *Most of us know that many agents won't represent older writers because privately, anonymously, they have been informed, for a number of years, that writers of a certain age aren't welcome and won't be given assignments.*

"Ageism Revisited"
Mort Thaw
The Journal
June 1991

• *I think some ageism is legitimate. I think the perception of people over a certain age might not be relevant to the marketplace. But, I think more often than not, ageism is unfair. When they say,* How old is the writer, *if they're not in their 20s or 30s or 40s, it can be a problem.*

There's a certain place in your career where it doesn't matter, but if your last produced credit was 10-15 years ago and you're 50 something, you're in trouble.

I used to be outraged that if you're older and you want to pitch "The Encino Man" at Disney, well, they're not going to hire you. Can a 50 year old write it? Well probably, but they're going to go with a younger writer.

On television, it's even more noticeable. With Steven Bochco and David Jacobs and Steven Cannell, that's fine, but I have an older client who is trying to get her half-hour read and when they ask how old she is, I say, she's really good.

I know any number of men and women who have made a good living in television and if they get to a certain age and if they are not really successful, they have a harder go of it than people 10 or 15 years their junior. It's sad and true.

Writers that used to sell 2 or 3 episodes a year free lance making $40,000-$50,00 a year, now I can't get them an episodic assignment because most shows are staff written. Out of a 28 show series, they buy maybe one free-lance script. You get on a series, it's the key to the bank.

Lynn Pleshette
Pleshette & Green
Los Angeles

• *I think ageism is a reality. Unfortunately there comes a point where if you have no credits, it becomes a lot harder to find work. It's a lot harder to start an older writer who doesn't have credits than a young writer who doesn't have credits. There is a preference in this town for youth.*

Jim Preminger
Jim Preminger Agency
Los Angeles

• *I think there is something in the writing that gives them vibes as to who is writing it, the way phrases are used, the dialogue, the nuances of the material. I read things and say,* this is written by someone who is not in tune with the times.

Laya Gelff
Laya Gelff Associates
Los Angeles

• *Age is more of a problem in television. In film, you can be hot at any age.*

Debbee Klein
Irv Schechter Company
Los Angeles

• *It's that people making decisions are so young and I think people find it hard to give orders to people who are older than they. Even in films with a finished script, they are going to have to be working with these people for the next year.*

> Rima Greer
> Writers & Artists
> Los Angeles

Older writers may just need to reevaluate their thinking, because it's not chronological age that attracts or puts off buyers. Elliot Stahler thinks age isn't the issue:

• *Everybody is looking for what's sexy. What's sexy, almost by definition, is what is new and exciting. When someone is new to the business whether the writer is 20 or 50, that's sexy. Those new ideas inspire us to get the buyers excited to see the new material, someone who can take this new person and sell him to his superior. It's about what's new and exciting.*

> Elliot Stahler
> Kaplan Stahler
> Los Angeles

There are times however, when only experience will do:

• *I think there are many cases where producers are looking for people with a track record and you can only develop a track record with age.*

> Jim Preminger
> Jim Preminger Agency
> Los Angeles

• *I've studied the situation pretty closely, it all depends. If you are in television and the show is Beverly Hills 90210, common sense tells you they're not likely to be hiring somebody 60 years old for that show or something where it's an ensemble of kids or people in their early twenties. If it's a screenplay, hey, you can be 18 or 80, if it's good, it's good. I think that think is exaggerated, just as,* The women are hired for this and that and whatever. *I really and truly have not found that to be a problem. Someone is going to write most scripts regardless of gender. If it's a television series about guys in the tank corp, there's not going to be too many women.*

Stu Robinson
Paradigm
Los Angeles

Endangered Species: Minorities and Women

Being old is one thing, being a minority and/or a woman stacks the deck even further. There's no old boy network to mentor you and there are few role models to emulate. Minorities and women have not been allowed inside the castle walls long enough be help others waiting to be admitted.

Linda Bloodworth-Thomason, creator of "Designing Women", feels that a woman has to be strong to succeed.

• *We've got to get up earlier, work harder and go to bed later every day. We've got to have more sheer raw talent, pound for pound, than men do. Because at the end, there's no network. Women don't get put out to pasture with golden parachutes and women don't get to discuss business deals on the golf course. We don't have access to the same sort of power forms men do.*

"An English Empire"
Daniel Cerone
Los Angeles Times
September 20, 1992

The Los Angeles Times tracked the progress of Diane English, creator of "Murphy Brown", after graduating from a local state college and teaching at an inner city high school. Her burning desire to write kept English frustrated until she decided to go for it. She decided she could always return to teaching and encouraged by a college professor, she headed to New York to write.

English worked as a free lance writer, including a stint as Vogue's first regular TV columnist. She drew industry attention from her initial major TV assignment, a rewrite of a PBS movie for which she received a Writers Guild nomination. When she decided to move to Los Angeles and start a production company, she got work right away. She did exactly what she espouses:

• *Instead of wallowing in our bitterness, I think what we need to do as women is to go out and if you can't get in the front door, you have to go around to the back door. You have to find a way. And if that means making your own projects, getting your own financing and doing it your way, instead of trying to play by their rules, then do it. We can spend a lot of time getting angry about it, but it isn't going to get you what you want.*

"An English Empire"
Daniel Cerone
The Los Angeles Times
September 20, 1992

Susan Fales who wrote for "The Cosby Show" is a double minority: a woman and of color. There was an interesting feature in The Journal tracing her entry and progress in the business,

• *During my senior year at Harvard, Bill Cosby expressed an interest in meeting me through my parents who are friends of his. So, I thought, don't just meet the man, do something.*

I wrote a spoof of "Lifestyles of the Rich and Famous" and made a cassette tape with different voices on it. Bill loved it, and told me when I graduated I could be a writer's apprentice. So I joined "The Cosby Show" during its second season.

Although I was extremely fortunate to have the entree of being Bill Cosby's protege, it was still very difficult for me to break into the tight environment of a television series. I was the only woman. I was thrust upon the other writers, and they were clearly wondering: Who is this woman and what is she doing here? So I discovered there was a rite of passage to be accepted into the club.

I eventually proved myself by working my butt off. I was willing to do any research, any menial task that was pertinent to the show. I shut up, and I listened and learned. As a result, the other writers understood I was very serious about what I was doing. They realized I had a brain, and ultimately, they came to appreciate that.

I have heard of environments where men will say, point blank: You're a woman so you're never going to be a producer. I've never heard those kinds of comments, so I don't know how I would react to them. Judging from my own experience, my advice to a woman or any minority would be to do the work and not come in with a lot of defenses.

"Profile: Susan Fales"
The Journal
February, 1992

Screen Actors Guild and The American Federation of Television & Radio Artists sponsored a panel discussion titled "Blacks in the Entertainment Media: The Search for Diversity."

• *Racism is still rampant within Hollywood, especially when it comes to hiring minorities for key executive posts, but there are indications that some studio chiefs are starting mandates to add more women and minorities.*

The primary focus for black performers is still comedy...and behind the scenes, less than 2% of producers, directors and writers are black *according to Sandra J. Evers-Manly, president of the Beverly Hills/Hollywood NAACP. She added that* the Beverly Hills/Hollywood chapter of the NAACP has now turned its efforts toward helping its members get funding to do their own short films...We've got to diversify our crafts and help people get their start at writing and directing and producing, *she said.*

"Minority Hiring Lags"
Kathleen O'Steen
Daily Variety
February 19, 1993

• *...minority employment increased by 36% (from 92 to 125 employed writers), but the overwhelming majority of employment still goes to those who are not members of racial and ethnic minorities.*

*...employed minority writers in 1991 earned 79 cents for every
dollar earned by white males. This reflects a substantial increase
from the figure of 52 cents for 1987.*

The 1993 Hollywood
Writers' Report
William Bielby/Denise Bielby
June 1993

The only way that any minority makes inroads into the business is
when he stops waiting to be chosen.

Spike Lee, Robert Townsend and John Singleton (Academy Award
director nominee for his first effort, "Boyz 'n the Hood") are all
contenders these days. No one handed them their break; and all of
these men not only wrote and directed their first films, but in most
cases, raised the money for their projects as well. Robert
Townsend, who wrote and directed "Hollywood Shuffle," has
become a show business legend because he financed his successful
film with credit card advances.

Twenty-four year old writer/director/producer, Robert Rodriguez of
"El Mariachi" is an innovative entrepreneur. He not only managed
to make his first feature for $7,000 raising money by participating
in medical experiments, but landed CAA as his agent. He wrote
the script while lying in bed hospitalized for the tests. He even cast
from the hospital bed, choosing a fellow guinea pig for the film.

Because the public is unaccustomed to seeing people of color at all,
these examples appear to be great progress. And they are. But
they still represent a very small percentage of the overall pie.

Lest anyone jump to the conclusion that higher black employment
has anything to do with affirmative action, talent or fairness, let's
be clear: higher black employment reflects the growing economic
clout of the black community.

The only way other minorities are going to find work in the
marketplace is by finding ways to finance their projects. I don't

blame the white male establishment: it is their money, they get to tell any story they want. If minorities are to have success, they must have the motivation and the vision to tear down all the barriers standing in the way of their progress. Money comes to those who pursue it and believe they deserve it. With that headset, perhaps other stories will be told that will begin to reflect what happens to those people who are not white men under 50.

Wrap Up

Earning potential:
✓ young white men make the money
✓ 30 year old white men largest fraction of Guild membership and most likely to find employment
✓ opportunities increasing for women in television
✓ minorities and women make less money for same work
✓ a good screenplay is the best ticket
✓ tell your own story

Women and minorities:
✓ have no old boy network
✓ need to initiate their own projects
✓ need to raise their own money

Focus/Homework

Now that you know more about your earning potential, the next task is to become focused on your goals in a businesslike way. In tennis, no matter how great the swing, if you don't keep your eye on the ball, you may miss it entirely. This principle also applies to writing. It is not enough to say, *I want to write* or even *I want to be a scriptwriter*. In any scriptwriting area, there are subdivisions. In film there's action, drama, adventure, comedy, fantasy, etc. In television there are even more alternatives: situation comedies, daytime soaps, nighttime soaps, drama, reality and interactive programming, game shows, etc. Theater runs the gamut from one-person shows to musicals. *It doesn't matter*, you say, *I can write*.

Your objective needs to be more precise. Pick an area and focus on it. When a smart business-person starts a new business, he does research. He finds out what is already available and checks to see how his product compares in quality, price and style to others already in the marketplace. His product needs to be trend setting or so perfectly in tune with an existing product that he could go to that employer and expect to be hired instantly. Don't you consider your writing career to be a business?

* *The biggest problem with new people is that they are not prepared. People don't do their homework. I was speaking at a seminar at Northwestern. I was on the panel. I was in the information booklet, and people would raise their hands and go:* How do you spell your name? What company are you with? *Excuse me, they should know my favorite color. They should be*

nice to my assistant, he decides who I talk to.
> Rima Greer
> Writers & Artists Agency
> Los Angeles

(Rima's favorite color is green and her secretary, as of this writing, is a very charming fellow named David Higgins.)

• *If you see a screenplay and the names of the characters are justified to the left, you won't read the script because you think this person doesn't understand.*
> Howard Sanders
> Pleshette & Green
> Los Angeles

• *One of the big problems is that people look for agents too soon. There's this myth that is fueled by the exceptions. 15 years ago, actors and directors were all caught up in the Sylvester Stallone/Rocky craze. Judging yourself by that criteria, you felt like a failure. There are always students right out of school that suddenly makes a big splash. 99% of the scripts don't get sold on their first script. I think people start to look for an agent before they have a body of work. The only way you get better at writing is to write. You have to hone your skills and be able to write. Writers need to have two or three scripts with 12 rewrites on it before they show it to anyone. They need to have every friend that they know read the script until they think it's the very best they can do. They need to have three of those in each genre they're looking to move into. It's a very unusual situation where your first script gets picked up. Agents want depth. You send a script out, the agent likes the writing, you do a lot of work on it and they don't sell it.* What else do you have? *If you don't have anything else to show, you've reached a dead-end. You've done all this leg-work for this person and that's the end.*
> Anonymous Agent
> Los Angeles

• *The best thing for a writer to do is to try to get somebody who knows somebody who knows somebody who knows somebody to read his work.*

> Elliot Webb
> Broder•Kurland•Webb•Uffner
> Los Angeles

• *I got a letter from someone who wanted me to read his script. It was totally formal:* Pursuant to my conversation with your assistant *and so on* I've written an outrageous, zany comedy. We looked at this and we said how can we believe he wrote an outrageous zany comedy? *There is no interest on my part to read it. He didn't make me laugh. I have no ideas from this letter that would make me think the script is going to work. So, think about what you are doing. Position yourself in a way that reflects your work.*

> Ken Greenblatt
> Media Artist Group
> Los Angeles

• *Writers should be very careful about the story they want to tell. They should really work on the story before they even put pen to paper. They should tell their story to people they respect and are close to or are not so close to and get the reaction. It's harder to ask a friend to read a 120 page script. It's not so hard to go to lunch with them and tell them a story. See if they are still awake by dessert.*

It's not necessarily true that a story is interesting because it's true. My mother went to the store and she broke her leg. *So what?*

> Lynn Pleshette
> Pleshette & Green
> Los Angeles

• *Write and keep writing. I had one client who wrote about 8 scripts before he mastered screenwriting form. I could see the person was extremely talented. In the first script he wrote great characters and no plot, and the next script had an exciting plot and weak characters.* *Suddenly, it all came together.* *He ended up with an overall deal, including a corner office with a parking place downstairs, $100,000+ a year salary, and most importantly, the ear and the eye of all the executives at the studio.*

Ken Sherman
Ken Sherman Agency
Los Angeles

• *The inspiration for those who want to break in is to see how much second-rate material is around.* *That's a clue to the fact that there is room. The clue isn't,* Oh, I could be just as bad. *It should be an inspiration to say,* Oh, I could do better.

We have some writers who are wonderful and we have some writers who are mediocre. I don't think we should kid ourselves. The reason for that is that there are a lot of pedestrian writers and very few good ones. The best are writers who have been writing since they were young. They just write. Writers write - whatever it is, poetry, fiction. They just write and some of them have the talent and some of them just don't. People can learn the skills if the talent is there.

Lynn Pleshette
Pleshette & Green
Los Angeles

• *It's very important not to send your material to producers or studios until you have an agent. It is so important, I can't even tell you.*

Rima Greer
Writers & Artists
Los Angeles

• *The life of the writer is <u>rewrite</u>. The first draft sent to us by a new writer, should be what they consider their third or fourth draft. We want to represent the writers who write because that is what they do.*

Fredda Rose
Monteiro Rose
Los Angeles

• *For me, writing screenplays is like speed chess. A page is a minute; it's a race. You've got your pyramid, you've got five characters, you've got two hours. You can't do any dallying in the valley the way you can with a novel. When you're screenwriting, you've got to be LeRoy Neiman. You're painting a horse race from the instant they leave the starting gate and you've got to have it done before they cross the finish line.*

> "The Organizer"
> F.X. Sweeney
> <u>Premiere Magazine</u>
> September, 1992

• *As soon as they finish the first script, they should start on their second one, as soon as they finish the second one, they should start on their third. They should write and write and write. What happens too often is that a writer turns in the script to the agent and then sits on his hands and waits for the agent to call and say,* Guess what? I sold your script for a million dollars. *It doesn't work that way.*

> Howard Sanders
> Pleshette & Green
> Los Angeles

• *We'd appreciate it if writers did not call us cold. We won't take the calls if we know it is someone asking about representation. If they get to us anyway, we are nice guys so we are not curt or rude. We will chat with them and explain the situation to them. We're real nice that way, but it would be better if people would not call cold. The best thing is an inquiry letter and if we are interested, we'll respond to them.*

> Stuart Jacobs/Glen Brunswick
> CNA
> Los Angeles

• *A lot of writers think they have to sell their script right now. Although that would be pleasant and we're all spending a million hours writing it and want to sell it right away in order to eat, actually, it's much better to make yourself a part of the community and it's also important for us to support each other.*

Robin Moran Miller
New York

• *The best thing you can do is write something you truly believe in. If you spend your time trying to create what you think sells, you're dead in the water. In my case, it was only when I wrote something from the heart, something extremely personal, that people in the industry took notice. And then, lo and behold, they began to think of me for all sorts of things. They even took a second look at my old scripts they previously had thrown in the trash. You must write for yourself first.*

Jonathan Tolins
playwright/screenwriter
"Twilight of the Golds"

• *Stuart and I do all the reading ourselves which is much better than having an outside reader because you're actually getting the agent to read the stuff. The downside is that we have reading stacks that literally are a mile long. If the writer wants to follow up, he should take that into consideration and wait longer. I'm not going to get to it any sooner because of the phone call. When I read it, I will call you, if I am interested.*

Glen Brunswick
CNA
Los Angeles

Your task is to hone your craft to a particular niche in the marketplace. This does not mean that action/adventure is hot right now, so you decide this is going to be your specialty. It means isolating what it is that you are most suited to write. Once you have made that decision, then focus your material into that form and begin to do research in that area.

• *Write, write, write. Until you have made it, don't worry about guessing what's trendy, write for quality whether for series television or feature films. If you are going to write series television, try to write speculative scripts for the best shows. For feature films, try to write layered screenplays with fully dimensional characters, unusual stories, something that feels real. Real does not rule out science fiction, etc., just the reality of that.*

Jim Preminger
Jim Preminger Agency
Los Angeles

• *I find it very difficult for those writers who walk in here with a drama sample and a comedy sample and they don't really know which way to go. You must decide which way you want to attack this career and go for it 150%.*

Rima Greer
Writers & Artists Agency
Los Angeles

• *Don't second guess the buyer. Write what you have to write, then it's the agent's job to find the right venue for it.*

Jonathan Westover
The Gage Group
Los Angeles

Scriptwriter/teacher Robin Moran Miller, who was a literary agent at DGRW in New York brings special insights to the subject:

• *I always know that a writer is not very good when he/she doesn't want to tell me what his project is about because he thinks I'm going to steal the idea. Good writers know it's not the idea, it's their voice. No one can steal your voice. David Webb Peoples who wrote "Unforgiven" can say,* I'm writing this script about an old gunfighter who reformed because of his wife, and now she's dead and he's got to go back to gunslinging for the money to feed his kids. *That doesn't sound like much. It's how you tell the tale. So when a writer says,* I have this idea, but I don't want anyone to steal it, *I know from the get-go that he's not a real writer or he wouldn't even be worried about it.*

What you have to offer as a writer is your voice telling the story and the way you're going to tell the story. The way you're

going to tell "Romeo and Juliet" is different from the way
Shakespeare told "Romeo and Juliet". It's your way *of telling*
whatever story you tell. That is what makes you special.

Robin Moran Miller
New York

• *Do it. There's a great market out there for new writers, more*
so than ever before in the 9 years I've been agenting. There are no
closed doors - not to women, not to minorities. I don't even feel
it's closed to people 40 years old.

Make sure you have a nice portfolio of material that includes
one or two spec scripts, some variety sketches (because there are a
lot of variety shows right now and there will be more next season).
Make your decision as to what you write.

It's a tough business. It's much tougher in drama. There are
fewer drama shows. There are many out of work dramatic writers,
directors and producers. It's cyclical, they'll all be back, drama
will be back, but there's fewer of them and the ones that are out
there are more dramedy: "Melrose Place", "Beverly Hills 90210",
all the Spelling shows. There's less Stephen Cannell product, less
Fred Silverman product. You have to really decide which area you
are going to attack first.

Rima Greer
Writers & Artists Agency
Los Angeles

• *Know the market, know your craft. Live so you have*
something to write about. Learn the business, immerse yourself in
it. I have a major deal happening for one of my writers. He told
me, I don't want to see the deal. You just do it. *I told him to*
learn the business. To learn what's in a contract. To learn what
an agent is and how to interact with the agent. To learn what a
producer is, a network executive. To take acting lessons. To take
directing classes. To learn all the other sides.

To learn what's in a contract so that you know if you're in the
ballpark, because you know, in this town, the game for the buyer is
to get what he can for as little as he can. There's no respect in it.
You just have to be a little wiser so that you can laugh and have a

sense of humor so that you don't go home and start crying.

You have to learn to face rejection head on. To learn how to take rejection positively. Learn the elements of the industry. Learn the personality of the producer.

> Bob Hohman
> Richland/Wunsch/Hohman
> Los Angeles

• *It's a great market for new writers now. There are no closed doors. It's better for women than it ever has been. Have a portfolio with one or two spec scripts, variety sketches, original sketches.*

Don't vacillate between comedy and drama, decide what you want to write and go for it. Variety sketches are the hottest thing in town. Lots of entree through "In Living Color."

> Debee Klein
> Irv Schechter Company
> Los Angeles

• *In television, the writer is king. That's why, as an agent, only having done movies, some people still think television is a lower art form. I have definitely revised my opinion about that. I'm hopeful about that. Also, I see the economic reality.*

> Bob Hohman
> Richland/Wunsch/Hohman
> Los Angeles

• *Writers get my attention by being good. You become good by understanding every part of the business. Take an acting class. Take a directing class. When you empathize with the actor and the director, the material reflects that.*

> Debbee Klein
> Irv Schechter Company
> Los Angeles

Some agents had interesting things to say, but did not want to be quoted by name. I felt what they had to say was relevant so I am including it anonymously.

• *The best thing to do is to write. Too often, you get someone who wants to come in. Let's say they have a feature script and it's okay. Say we sign them and then we make the effort to get the script out to try and sell it, but also to use it as an introduction of this person to everybody around town.*

Then they come in, I've got an idea. I want to go pitch it. *Well, no, you need just to keep writing. You need to write and write and write and write. Realistically to sell a pitch, to sell a treatment, that comes with a track record. People do it, young writers sell treatments all the time, but to give yourself the best advantage in being able to show off your work in various areas, you have to hone your craft, you just have to keep writing. In feature films, that means spec scripts, in television, you keep writing samples (specs). As opposed to someone who has no track record and they say,* I've written a great pilot. *Who cares? Let it be a great pilot. I don't care.*

In a lot of ways, it's easier to break into feature films. If you have a feature script and it's good, people will read it. Somewhere along the way, there is such a lack of great material. Logically you'd think there is so much more television production than feature film production that they would be the ones screaming for new material...not so. It's actually (from my perspective) harder to break a new person in television. It's much more of a closed club. Let's face it, they're all scared to death and to bring somebody in that they don't know, can we trust them? will they deliver? *It's ludicrous, but that's the case.*

Anonymous Agent
Los Angeles

• *In TV doing your homework is going to WGA and if you are going to write a "Murphy Brown," you read "Murphy Brown" scripts. Everybody has friends in town. Everybody knows somebody who's working at the studios or doing part time temp work. People come in and write spec scripts and it's clear that they have never seen the show. This is not thinking. Format signifies you did your homework. It all goes back to school,* Does neatness count? *The answer to that is,* Yes, neatness does count. *If there are a ton of typos, yes, of course it makes a difference. If you*

*haven't done your homework, that makes it harder for us to take
you seriously.*

Anonymous Agent
Los Angeles

If your interest is situation comedy, begin to analyze every comedy
on television. Watch the good and the bad. Tape them and watch
them over and over. Why is "Seinfeld" appealing? Does it have
more jokes? More interesting characters? Does the story unfold
more quickly than on a show you don't like as well? Or does that
even matter? Scripts from "All in the Family," "Mash," "The
Mary Tyler Moore Show" and other classic shows that defined the
form are all available at the Writers Guild library and are a must
for any student. Watch "I Love Lucy" reruns, compare them to
"Seinfeld" and check out their similarities and differences.

• *Two friends of mine who are incredibly successful writers each
probably have 3 or 4 scripts that have never seen the light of day.
When they started out writing screenplays, the thought was never
about selling them, it was about telling a very interesting story. No
one has ever seen these scripts and no one ever will, because they
are not very good, but they are rungs to a ladder.*

Richard Green
Pleshette & Green
Los Angeles

• *Samuel French publishes screenplays. It's hard for me to
believe that you can't get hold of screenplays someplace. Also, it's
so easy to rent the films. But they should read for the form, for how
writers have professionally solved problems.*

Lynn Pleshette
Pleshette & Green
Los Angeles

Would be film writers read "Casablanca" and "China Town" and
other classic scripts. If you can't get copies of the scripts, tape
from television or rent videos. Watch them once for entertainment
value and then begin to *study* them. It's your job to figure out

what's so appealing about them. When encountering a really bad movie on television or in a theater, don't turn it off or leave; keep watching and try to figure out how it could have been better. And maybe you'll even sit down and write a scene for that film.

Just because you have written one or two or even three scripts, doesn't necessarily mean that you are far enough along for an agent to be interested in reading your material. This is not to say that there aren't some millionaires out there who managed to sell their very first script though probably not the very first draft.

Theater

• *I think a writer's best bet is not to write a script and then immediately try to get an agent which is what most writers do. In New York, there are lots of ways of getting your work read or produced and the more you do that, the more likely an agent is going to want to look at your work.*

Robin Moran Miller
New York

Robin went on to name several venues in New York that might be fruitful: Playwrights Horizons, West Beth, The Write Start. She also mentioned Matt Williams' New Harmony Festival in Indiana (Williams was the head writer on "Roseanne"). In Los Angeles, the Audrey Skirball-Kinis Theater, Mark Taper Developmental programs and PKE (Patchett Kaufman Entertainment) are just three from a large number available.

An invaluable guide for information about developmental groups that support playwrights and screenwriters is The Dramatists Sourcebook. There is valuable support material on every subject — submission guidelines, fellowships, organizations, script preparation, workshops, colonies and residencies and publishing opportunities. TDS should definitely be on your reference shelf. It is published by Theatre Communications Group, New York.

A playwright frequently goes through a long, arduous process before he's written what will be the final draft.

- *Before a play is submitted to either agents or producers, agent Susan Schulman suggests that it probably should have been through some kind of workshopping or reading process - - not for the public's benefit, but for the playwright's benefit - - to hear how the actors respond to the language of the play, how long it is, and whether or not the individual voices of the characters are clear and the way that the author intends them to be. Since it's an oral tradition, I don't see how one could possibly write without hearing it.*

> "Literary Agents"
> Ben Alexander
> Back Stage
> October 2, 1992

Although readings are an accepted procedure, many playwrights feel the practice of an endless amount of them can be disheartening and destructive. In a conference sponsored by the Audrey Skirball-Kenis Theater of Los Angeles entitled "Inventing a Future: The Playwright's Perspective", the playwrights were heard on the issue:

- *In the discussion that followed, the inevitable bugbears emerged: the need for subsidy, and the dissatisfaction with the development which the majority of writers defined as interference in the writer's work by meddling dramaturgs and auteur-directors. There was a genuine split between those writers who felt all readings and* workshopping *were useless - unless and until the theater committed to a production - and others who accepted the humiliating necessity for their plays to be* auditioned *through the reading process.*

> "Los Angeles in Review"
> Charles Marowitz
> TheaterWeek
> October 12-18, 1992

And it's not just the playwrights who think it's a bad idea:

• *Some plays do not read well and others only read well. When I ran the Back Alley Theater and we had a play we were not sure of and staged a reading, we never ended up producing that play. If we liked a play, we produced it. Readings only point up the flaws in material.*

Laura Zucker
Executive Director of the
Los Angeles Arts Council

The most fruitful avenue for a playwright involves forming his own relationship with a theater where his material is staged on a regular basis. It's advantageous for the playwright and for the theater.

Bruce Graham is an up and coming screenwriter who has managed to forge a relationship with a theater where his plays are staged annually. He has a three picture deal at Universal and has been offered a staff position on the number one on television while continuing to live in Bucks County, New York.

Los Angeles

Although New York City is still thought of as the place for a playwright to ply his trade, Los Angeles is beginning to draw its share of writers for the theater although as this article points out, the possibilities of living on royalties (if you are fortunate enough to get any) seem pretty slim:

• *Despite the fact that Los Angeles is home to a growing number of playwrights — some guess upwards of 2,000 — few actually get to see their work on stage, and fewer still make any money at their chosen craft...The Dramatists Guild alone has 1,200 members here, and there are more than 40 organized playwrights groups in Los Angeles.*

...The average playwright royalty on the Taper [The Mark Taper Forum] mainstage for a six to eight week run may range from $35,000 to $50,000, but the average royalty for the same number of weeks at a 99-seat theater is $600-$800.

...A commission at the La Jolla Playhouse is $5,000 and

generally goes to an established writer. A 99-seat theater might pay $100 for a reading or $500 for a workshop and some even ask for money from the playwrights themselves.

> "To Live and Write in L.A."
> Barbara Isenberg
> The Los Angeles Times
> Calendar Section
> February 14, 1993

Producers

It's also mutually beneficial to cultivate relationships with free lance producers who are interested in helping develop new material. As you begin to accumulate a body of work (even if only in your portfolio) that is being read by various folk in the business, *one* of those various folk will read it and take an interest. The process will then begin to include not just you alone with your word processor, but an interested second party who is either ready to buy or willing to advance money to encourage the developmental process.

Access — Easiest/Toughest

It's easier to get agents, producers, would-bes, will-bes, and anyone else walking by, to read your movie or television feature than any other area of the business. In the past, that meant preparing a treatment for submission; today, however, fewer and fewer deals are being made from treatments except for those writers with extensive backgrounds. In a precarious economy, the buyers want to know exactly what they are getting.

Although the doors are harder to penetrate, agents say television comedy is where the real money is. Since nearly twice as many writers are employed in television as in feature film (and because the mony can be staggering), the snob line between film and television writers is becoming less and less distinct.

Films for television run the gamut from disease of the week to star vehicle to thoughtful treatments of subjects that the big screen (usually for economic reasons) is too timid to deal with. The quality is as varied as the subject matter, and as more prestigious film writers are writing for cable and even for the networks, the standards are becoming higher (along with the stakes).

Isabel Nagy Storey worked in local news and reality based TV shows, but had never written until she had a maternity leave in 1991. She sent her script to producers and agents and within four days got a call from CAA:

• *People often hawk stories about real-life events but few get nods from agents and producers, said Dick Berg, a producer at Viacom Pictures, the company to which Storey sold her script. But he said Storey stood out because she took the uncommon step of not just pitching an idea but also writing a script about it.*

What she's done is extraordinary, he said. She put up her own money...she researched it and to cap it off she wrote a script with style....She spent 22 months and $2,000 on developing and marketing the work.

> "Writer's First Script
> Draws a Speedy Response"
> Walter Hamilton
> <u>The Green Sheet</u>
> February 8, 1993

Episodic Television

• *The samples for television have to be great. They almost have to be better than the shows themselves.*

> Jonathan Westover
> The Gage Group
> Los Angeles

• *In terms of television specs, they have to capture the show, they have to get the ear of the show, it's got to work for that show.*

It's got to knock our socks off, that's the only way it's going to knock their socks off.

Kirk Durham
The Gage Group
Los Angeles

• *The core of a successful TV series remains the ability to bring viewers back week after week, and more than anything else that relies on characters. Even TV's best series don't turn out gems for all 22 or 26 episodes.*

TV characters must bond with the audience in order to succeed, either positively or negatively, while film characters need only to intrigue or visually dazzle them for the two hours they're on screen.

"Character's the Thing That'll
Catch the TV Viewers"
Brian Lowry
<u>Daily Variety</u>
June 24, 1992

The name of the game in situation comedies and one hour dramatic shows is being able to write excellent spec scripts for existing television shows. There's a difference of opinion about what show to choose as a specimen. The majority of agents tell me that the best shows to write for are those that, whether or not they are garnering big numbers, have the respect of the industry — "Murphy Brown," "Roseanne," "Northern Exposure," "Seinfeld," etc., but there are other points of view:

• *Write the spec script. And don't write for the season's hot show, they already have brilliant scripts. Write a brilliant script for a show that's not brilliant. Think how happy they would be to see a brilliant script.*

Elliot Stahler
Kaplan-Stahler Agency
Los Angeles

If you write spec scripts for deceased shows, this makes people think you are not tuned into what's happening. They are right.

It is necessary to have numerous scripts to showcase your ability. Agents tell me spec scripts must be excellent writing because they are so highly scrutinized.

An article about Brandon Tartikoff (past president of NBC Entertainment), who recently stepped down as Chairman of Paramount Pictures to spend more time with his family, shows how he learned to put his career in focus.

- *There's nothing like cancer to get you focused on what's important, the first time around, I just felt that I had this bad card dealt to me. I was in my mid-20's, tremendously cocky, and what the illness did was bring a humility to the situation. I'm not saying that I'm a poster boy for humility right now, but it changed me. With no bad card dealt, I might have become a reasonably successful local television manager. I had 18 balls in the air - acting at the Second City Workshop in Chicago, writing plays, writing free-lance articles for New Times magazine.*
  Afterward I just focused. You know you're sick, and you've got to do this and that to try to get the result you want, and you put on blinders and plunge right ahead. I definitely bought into the concept that the cancer was curable and to look ahead this year and next year.

> "Tartikoff Examines"
> Bernard Weintraub
> The New York Times
> October 13, 1992

Tartikoff's words made a big impression on me. Although it is advantageous to learn all aspects of the business in order to augment our specialties, having too many balls in the air may prevent our dreams from coming true.

If Tartikoff's decision to step down from Paramount really is to spend time helping his family recover, he demonstrates the truth that none of us wants to know: you really cannot have everything. Nobody has it all. It's like going into a room with the most fabulous food in the world. You can put it all on your plate, if you want, but you can't possibly consume it all without becoming sick.

Wrap Up

Define your goals
- ✓ pick your genre and stick to it
- ✓ write to form - neatness counts
- ✓ study the classics
- ✓ find your niche
- ✓ have lots of material
- ✓ know the marketplace
- ✓ keep writing
- ✓ keep networking
- ✓ write from the heart
- ✓ determine your values

Does It Matter Where You Live?

While your brain is in focus mode, this is a good time to talk about where to focus your career geographically. Can you be a viable client without moving your life to New York, Chicago or Los Angeles? When I asked agents the first thing a writer should do when he got off the bus, I was surprised when a couple laughed and said, *Get back on.* They were joking, but there were some truth behind the joke.

Since what you are selling is primarily you and your way of looking at life, it just might be a more valuable look if it's not tainted with a show biz point of view and is still pure with the Cleveland, San Antonio or Ft. Collins air.

• *I think they should not get off the bus before they figure out what they want to do when they get here. You don't have to be in Los Angeles to be a writer. Maybe you need to stay at home and write. Everybody is looking for a new novel because it is an original voice. Writers from out of town are original voices because they are not reactive to the movie business. Sometimes novelists do not become screenwriters because it's a whole different skill. One reason buyers want novels is that they are people's experiences that are not from this particular place.*

Lynn Pleshette
Pleshette & Green
Los Angeles

Even if you want to write for television, there is no reason to leave a protected environment until your writing has reached a marketable level. You can be writing "Murphy Brown" and "Northern Exposure" spec scripts in Iowa with the same zest and much less overhead. Rejection won't be so expensive, you'll have an emotional support group for comfort and you'll be bringing a fresher outlook to the proceedings. Even if there seems to be nothing in your own environment comparable to the bright lights, those bright lights are not going anywhere and they are a lot more attractive when you have the money to pay for your own electricity.

You can write from jail, a convent, or a cruise ship. You can write from any place. If you want to be a scriptwriter, it is not necessary to incur both the financial and emotional expense of moving to a totally new environment to experience rejection; you can do it at home.

Criminal defense attorney John Grisham (who wrote The Firm, The Client, and A Time to Kill) lives in Oxford, Mississippi, coaches Little League, never studied writing and wrote his books in long-hand on yellow legal paper:

• *In the past 18 months, Grisham has accomplished the unthinkable: he has sold movie rights to three of his novels for nearly $4.4 million. Tom Cruise is set to star in one of the films, Sydney Pollock is set to direct. Julia Roberts is in line for another.*
> "A Novel Success Story"
> Robert W. Welkos
> The Los Angeles Times
> October 19, 1992

Grisham's agent Jay Garon (Jay Garon-Brook Associates) is the man writers dream of. He actually responded to a blind manuscript that arrived at his office.

David Webb Peoples, Academy Award nominee for "Unforgiven", is a perfect example. He has lived in northern California since he graduated from Berkeley in 1962. Working as a news and documentary film editor, he struggled for years to sell screenplays. His big break came in the late 1970s when his writing partner read one of his scripts and handed it over to his brother (Ridley Scott), who asked Mr. Peoples to help write "Blade Runner."

Even though "Unforgiven" and "Hero" have made Peoples hot, The New York Times reports he's not changing his style,

• *Even though Mr. Peoples said he was planning to move his office from his Berkeley home to escape the constantly ringing phone, he said he had no plans to move to Los Angeles.*
    Berkeley is home, *he said.* I have a lot of friends who are not in the movie business and that's fine with me. Although I love people in the movie business, it sometimes becomes too much. It's like you don't want the whole meal to be one thing, one big piece of cake. You want other things in your meal, too.

"In Screenwriter's Life,
the Script Features Privacy"
Bernard Weintraub
The New York Times
October 6, 1992

Peoples' agent Martin Shapiro has been his representative since 1982 when another client introduced them. Shapiro has several clients who do not live in Los Angeles. Other agents have similar stories.

• *I get a lot of writers from out of town, they first communicate from out of town looking for an agent. There's no difference in the quality in town or out of town for new writers. First, I want to see their script. It has worked out with a client or two that way. They can function out of town. Of course, if it is a staff position or a project gets going, then they have to come to town.*

Laya Gelff
Laya Gelff Associates
Los Angeles

• *A writer should do his or her homework before he comes to town with a script. Learn the industry format for scripts. Go to the library. Get samples. Font, length of script, even covers are important. Don't try to make the script look different. Don't try to reinvent the wheel because it only makes you look like a novice. The most experienced and professional writers work within a certain accepted format.*

Barbara Alexander
Media Artists Group
Los Angeles

As mentioned earlier, Bruce Grand has managed to be successful in both theater and film and to be offered a top staff position on the number one television situation comedy. Even so, he says that it was a lot harder to make things happen from where he lives. It was difficult to turn down the money possibilities from the sitcom, but Bruce said that his most important consideration was living with his wife and children on the same street on which he grew up.

It took him a long time to get to a place where he could give up his day job teaching college and make a full time living as a writer, but he says that it can be done and he is happy with his decision.

Some agents, on the other hand, think a writer <u>must</u> come to town:

• *Although it is possible to have a career from out of town, it's difficult. I won't represent anyone from out of town. I did it once and I won't do it again, unless they are a very major player. I represent New York people. You can get them meetings in New York and they can fly out here for specific things. It's a lot tougher when they are sitting in Timbuktu. So much of what our writers do to get work and to jump-start a career is not just me sending their work out, but them following up with meetings.*
    What often happens is that a producer will call me up and say, That was a great piece of writing. What a wonderful writer, does he have any ideas to pitch? We can't do that story, it's too close to something else, but this is a writer that I really must be in business with. *So they go in and they have a meeting for two hours and*

maybe they end up developing a project together.

Then, again, it's possible that they can go in and have a meeting and hit it off and they don't have anything, but two months later, the producer will call me up and say, you know that writer that we were talking about? I have a project that's right for them. *If that meeting had never happened, I would have never gotten that phone call. So by a writer being in Timbuktu, you can't make that happen.*

Glen Brunswick
CNA
Los Angeles

• *If someone wants to be a staff writer on a show and they are in Timbuktu, you can't get them a meeting with a producer or with the network. They need to be in town. It needs to be on the page, but relationships count, too. A producer is not going to hire someone as a staff writer unless they think they are going to work well with them, they're going to be an asset to the team and it's going to be a pleasurable experience.*

Stuart Jacobs
CNA
Los Angeles

Make a Home for Yourself

If you do leave your roots for the big city, one of the most comforting things you can do for yourself is put together a cozy light place to live and make it your own. Spend money on a coat of paint, if it needs it: you need a place of shelter from the storms. Living a free lance life, as most artists do, requires that you build into your life a routine, a support group, financial security, decent food and an atmosphere that nurtures you.

If you intend to write every day from 9 to 3, do it, but also, be sure to go to the gym or walk from 7:30 to 8:30 or participate in some other activity that includes both exercise *and* regular contact with people. If your writing habits dictate that you write before all else fine, just don't skip the all else. Fight the temptation to eat junk food. It is more convenient, but your mind and body both pay for it later. If all you have in the house is carrots and celery, that's what you'll eat. At least make it harder on yourself to get candy and Fritos by not keeping any on hand.

If you don't have a nest egg to tide you over for a while, get some kind of job, preferably in the industry. Even if you do have enough money to survive for a while, a job puts you in the company of other people, gives form to your life and enables you to keep your forward motion (or lack of it) in perspective:

Success is reached over time. Great success begins with a series of little successes starting with getting situated in town and being financially secure. That doesn't mean you have to be rich, but you do have to have a job.

If you are in an impossible relationship or if you have any kind of addiction problem, the business is only going to intensify things. Deal with these things first. Show business takes even balanced people and chews them up and spits them out for breakfast unless they remain extremely focused and provide another life for themselves. Daily Variety recently recounted the rise and fall of ex-superagent, Bill Tennant,

• *When it came time for Tennant's life to crash, it happened big. Cocaine addiction cost him his marriage, his savings and ultimately, even shelter. The man who once owned a beautiful home replete with tennis court now lived on the street, trading even the gold inlays in his teeth for a fix.*
 I know I was my own worst enemy, *he reflects.* Hollywood has always been a magnet attracting incomplete people who think that money and glamour can somehow make them complete. It can't, of course. You get consumed by it, not completed.

> "Exec comes full circle
> after descent into despair"
> Peter Bart
> Daily Variety
> February 5, 1993

If you are balanced, tenacious, driven, and talented, take time to get your bearings before you attack the marketplace and vice versa.

Build a Support Group

Life is easier with friends. Begin to build relationships with your peers. There are those who say to build friendships with people who already have what you want. Although I understand the thinking, it's not my idea of a good time. It's a lot easier to live on a shoestring and/or deal with constant rejection if your friends are doing the same thing. If your friend is already on staff on "Murphy Brown" or already has her feature optioned and has plenty of money while you are scrambling to pay the rent, it is going to be harder to keep perspective about where you are in the process. It takes different people differing amounts of time to make the journey. Having friends who understand that will make it easier for all of you.

Whatever else you do, commit to being positive. It's one of the most important things you can do for yourself.

Actress-writer Ruth Gordon had great perspective,

• *Life is getting through the moment. The philosopher William James says to cultivate the cheerful attitude. Now nobody had more trouble than he did — except me. I had more trouble in my life than anybody. But your first big trouble can be a bonanza if you live through it. Get through the first trouble, you'll probably make it through the next one.*

> "The Careerist Guide
> to Survival"
> Paul Rosenfield
> The Los Angeles Times
> April 25, 1982

You create your life by the choices you make in how to spend your time. You can be happy or depressed. There is no value judgment. If you choose to spend your time being depressed, which takes more energy, that's your business. It is beneficial to note that this is *your* choice. If you don't get something out of being depressed, you will take some action to change that state.

If you are already a member of the Writers Guild, check for support groups and/or become involved with one of their committees to help someone else. This will engage you in a productive activity with your peers on a regular basis.

Chapter 11 lists some support groups and resource ideas. Check them out when you get to that part of the book.

Although you may be one of the lucky people who begins to work immediately, it is unlikely, so prepare yourself for a challenge, whether you are staying home or moving.

Wrap Up

Reasons to stay home
- ✓ protected environment
- ✓ cheaper to live
- ✓ emotional support group in place
- ✓ may end up with better material

Home away from home
- ✓ get a place to live with good light
- ✓ cultivate a routine
- ✓ get a job
- ✓ exercise and eat well
- ✓ see people every day
- ✓ get involved in a support group

Ways into the System

If you've decided you <u>can</u> make money, you know what you want to write and you've decided that you and/or your material is moving to the big city, you will now have to be more than an ingenious writer because other than saving Mike Ovitz from getting run over by a bus or being related to someone in the business, it's very difficult to get agents and/or producers to read your material. Although this part of the process is extremely frustrating, if you can bear to look at it from the agents' perspective, you'll be more understanding and appreciative once you have made it into the exclusive club of represented writers, knowing your agent's attention is on you and not on searching for your replacement.

• *Writers shouldn't get angry with agents because they won't read their material. Busy agents already have a full time job keeping their present clients serviced.*

Daniel Ostroff
The Daniel Ostroff Agency
Los Angeles

Though your writing may be the best thing since "Casablanca," "Death of a Salesman" or "The Mary Tyler Moore Show," if you can't get anyone to read it, no one will ever know.

Getting your material into the hands of a buyer is not an insurmountable task, you just have to do it properly. There are various ways to put yourself in a position to pass your material on to someone in the business who counts. You've arrived in Los

Angeles from Podunk and don't know anyone who counts? There are still ways.

• *Be as aggressive as humanly possible. Don't waste your breath giving your whole pitch over the phone. If it's an office you really want to be with, go after everyone there until it's read. Find out each agent's name. Find out the assistant's name. Call him up. Send him a script. The eager assistant may try to sell the script.*

Raphael Berko
Media Artist Group
Los Angeles

The most successful method of entry is to get *any* kind of job at any studio. Many studios have temp pools of over qualified people to call when an employee calls in sick. Your assignment could be anything from picking up an actor at the airport and delivering him to the set, to working in the mail room, being a production assistant or driving a producer to appointments. I know of several people who worked as drivers who managed to pass their material on to staff writers who became their advocates.

There are temp agencies that specialize in providing workers for networks and studios. Although there is much more opportunity for these kinds of jobs in Los Angeles, there are jobs in New York as well. You can end up working at WMA, ICM, paradigm, CAA or any of the big agencies, production companies or networks. You don't get to choose where you are going to work if you go through an employment agency, of course, but any destination will be illuminating.

Check the temp ads in the trades or call a studio yourself and ask if there is an in-house temporary employment pool. Many temp jobs work into regular employment if you strike the fancy of your employers and are clearly motivated. In that case, not only do you have a chance to pass your material around, but you will begin to meet other writers who are already in place, as well as producers, directors, and actors, the very people you want to be doing business with. I don't want to imply that getting a studio job is a piece of cake, but if you apply yourself, you can do it. No matter what city you live in, there is some kind of show biz community of work. Check out your local opportunities.

Pam Veasey, the head writer/coproducer of "In Living Color," got her start by working as a receptionist for "Gimme a Break."

• *Veasey wrote a script for another half-hour show and submitted it to the "Break" producers* - just so they could tell me if I was even close.

She was close. They fired her as a receptionist and hired her as a writer, and she went on to write for "Break," "What's Happening Now!!" and "The Robert Guillaume Show" before linking up with Keenan Ivory Wayans on an earlier CBS pilot that didn't pan out. She later submitted sketches for "In Living Color."

I camped out in Keenan's office for thirty minutes without an appointment so I could say, Please hire me or let me submit some other work, *laughs Veasey. He said,* I've already hired my staff this year. *I went,* Great, *and came back again and said,* Here are some more sketches. *And ultimately, I got hired.*

"Below the Line"
Rip Rense
Emmy
October 1992

Producers/Lawyers/Professional Colleagues

Producers are easier to contact than agents because producers can't make a living if they don't have scripts to produce. Even though the producer may have 200 projects in development, he can always use one more. Connected show biz lawyers have entree and are easier to contact. If you paid agents every time you queried them, they'd probably be happy to take your calls, too. So, if you have money, a lawyer might be your answer. Just make sure he really is in the system. Many charge just to read your material. That always makes me suspicious. Do some research. Define his avenues of access.

Robin Moran Miller was head of the literary department at prestigious DGRW in New York. A writer herself, she finally quit in order to focus more of her attention on her own work. In addition to writing, she teaches master scriptwriting classes in New York. Clearly part of the community, Robin loves writers and extends herself in their support. She thinks the most logical alliance for a writer (other than with a bankable name actor) is with a director. You'll see several quotes from her throughout the book.

• *A lot of my friends who are screenwriters got their foot in the door through a specific director that they may have met at some school or along the line, who has liked a script of theirs. When the director got development money, he said* I want to do this script.
> Robin Moran Miller
> New York

There's Always Subterfuge

Zak Penn and Adam Leff are two resourceful scriptwriters who dug their own tunnel into ICM.

• *Having failed to grab an agent's attention by more conventional means, the writing team had brazenly orchestrated a plan to transform their screenplay into a hot property and get themselves an agent.*
> "Well, They Wanted Action"
> Terry Pristin
> Los Angeles Times
> May 16, 1993

Penn and Leff created their own buzz using low level studio or agency employees they knew who also knew the agent in question. Each friend called (supposedly unbidden) to recommend the script. By the time the agent learned the truth, he had already signed the writers and the script was hot. Retitled and rewritten by several other screenwriters and without screenwriting credit, Penn and Leff still got to take home $500,000 and a less prestigious writing credit (story-by) for their idea for the Arnold Schwarzenegger film, "The Last Action Hero."

Even though they made money and sold their script, the experience was far from perfect. There were lots of disappointments and the two no longer write together.

- *Having a kid come into a movie awakened certain fantasies I had as a kid in Austria. What would it be like to sit on John Wayne's saddle, or have him come with this huge horse right out of the screen? The script had a great concept, but it wasn't executed professionally.*

"Five Writers + One Star
= A Hit?"
Aljean Harmetz
The New York Times
May 30, 1993

Commitment

The success of these writers was the outcome of their being very serious about their task. Once focused on a goal, that work paid off.

- *...Penn and Leff decided their idea was good enough to warrant a full-time commitment. Quitting their jobs that spring, they set about viewing 45 action movies, analyzing them with the zeal of cineastes dissecting the oeuvre of Hitchcock or Fellini.*
  Holing up in Penn's bedroom near Hancock Park and sharing a desk, they wrote a screenplay but were dissatisfied with it, so they pounded out a highly detailed 80-page treatment before completing another draft.

"Well, They Wanted Action"
Terry Pristin
The Los Angeles Times
May 16, 1993

So, although these guys were outrageous in their approach, they committed themselves totally to the outcome. Their research into the action genre paid off by moving them ahead in the business very quickly. Even though Leff and Penn didn't get the whole enchilada, their *story-by* credit is still worth a lot,

• *Mr. Leff and Mr. Penn, with only their* story-by *credit, now have the cachet of being hot screenwriters. They have a deal at Fox and New Line has bought "Central Park," their screenplay about the giant rat.*

> "Five Writers + One Star
> = A Hit?"
> Aljean Harmetz
> The New York Times
> May 30, 1993

Jonathan Tolins

It was my pleasure recently, to attend the opening of a play written by Jonathan Tolins. I met Jon when he stage managed a play at The Matrix Theater in Los Angeles. A year later, he produced his own first play. Today, his second play, "Twilight of the Golds" is on it's way to Broadway via The Kennedy Center and has been sold as a film. Tolins is only four years out of college and his name is all over the trades. Here's a guy who was not only talented and motivated, but very, very smart:

• *Even at 26, Tolins clearly knows the business. His "Twilight" script was rejected for a reading at one theater, he concedes, but he also turned down possible productions in small local houses. He put up $500 of his own money for a reading of "Twilight" last July to widen his producer net:* I really felt I had something that might have commercial potential.

> "Tales from the Front"
> Barbara Isenberg
> The Los Angeles Times
> February 14, 1993

Tolins graduated from Harvard in 1988 with an impressive theatrical university resume. A triple threat, Jon had acted, directed and won a major literary award. When he got to Los Angeles, he got a job writing questions for a game show. He says he wrote "Twilight" while temping at studios. When we were working at The Matrix, he showed me one of his plays. Jon managed to do all the things the agents tell you to do: write all the time, be visible and work in the industry. Oh, and be talented.

Readers

Another avenue that provides entree plus an important overview and some visibility in the business is getting work as a reader.

• *A job as a reader is a good way to get into the system. The club is a big club. You can get in any which way.*
> Elliot Webb
> Broder•Kurland•Webb•Uffner
> Los Angeles

Because the number of scripts submitted to agents, producers, and others who routinely traffic in the written word exceeds their available reading time, readers are employed who read scripts and make recommendations about the project's viability. These folks decide whether the material will move up the food chain to the ultimate buyer.

Although being a reader en route to being a writer sounds like a good idea, when I called the readers union (called Screenstory Analysts), the woman I spoke to said, *if you want to write, then write.* She said becoming a reader on the Industry Experienced Roster is such a hard thing to do and there are so many union members already in place, that your energy would be better served using it to write.

Union readers are paid a range of prices from the low end ($750 weekly) to *whatever you can negotiate.* Some people get jobs from producers who are not signatory to the union and are paid by the script. $50 per script is the going rate for someone with no experience. Depending upon one's reading and comprehension skills, it can take about two hours to digest one script.

Being able to digest, discern and be articulate about your conclusions can give you enormous entree — depending upon your employers — since your name is then the first thing the producer sees when perusing the script. Readers are sometimes called story analysts.

• *If you're well read and willing to work at a job that is unforgiving sometimes in its boredom because you are reading so much junk, being a reader is an invaluable way to get to understand the business better than most people. You will hone up on your writing and reading skills (you will actually get to use your education if you have one to use) and you will get the attention of people in the business. If you can put your thoughts down on paper coherently, you will learn what people are looking for, what is good and what is bad, and you will learn to write your thoughts in a concise and educated form. These papers are not only read by your superiors, they are passed around and your name is the first thing these people see.*

> Sidney Iwanter
> Director Children's Programs
> Fox Children's Network

Script Analysts

There are two points of view about script analysts: theirs and everybody else's.

The WGA looks unfavorably on those who charge scriptwriters to read their material. So does every professional scriptwriter I queried. All seem to feel charging to read is exploitation.

Analysts counter that if you can get a professional eye to read your material and critique it in a professional manner, you will revise your script appropriately and have a better shot at success.

The sticking point is that if you couldn't get anyone to read your material <u>before</u>, why would it be easier to get this unseen *better* script read <u>now</u>. It may have been great before, but you just didn't have entree.

• *There are people who are experts in the field who are screenwriters and teachers who do a combination career counseling and reading. If you find someone who has been really recommended and is going to work with you on the script and you are <u>totally new to this business</u>, then it can be a good idea, but check their references.*

Barbara Alexander
Media Artists Group
Los Angeles

Career Guidance

Donie Nelson is a prime example of just what Barbara was describing. Donie is a credentialed professional who has worked with film companies and independent production companies for feature film and television in the creative developmental area. A problem solver by nature, Donie's industry background brings not only insights into the creative process, but practical career guidance for both novice and established writers and producers.

As of this writing, Donie's fees are much less than a script analyst (less than $200 for a first read with reduced rates for subsequent readings of the same material). The initial fee includes a read plus an hour and a half career and/or script conference. Hourly rates are less than $50.

Donie Nelson
5035 Overland Ave.
Culver City, CA 90230
310-204-6808

As you read the agents' quotes throughout this book, you'll notice a recurring theme: keep writing. Do good work. Somebody who knows somebody who knows somebody will read it — for free. You will be found. <u>Everyone</u> is searching for a good script. Whether you are a playwright or a screenwriter, you must be persistent and creative in your thinking:

• *If you have one reading and send a postcard, people aren't going to come, but if you get two or three and keep informing agents, after enough time, the agent says,* Gee, this guy is getting done a lot, he must be good *and they go.*

Robin Moran Miller
New York

• *It's your job to get that screenplay on the desk and get it read. Try to get an internship or get a job somewhere in the industry. You've got to know someone to get it on the agent's desk unless you want to wait a year, and maybe not even then. Referrals do help. Get into a writing block. Anything. If you get a job in production as an assistant, there are professionals around that you can show the script to. Of course, you always risk getting ripped off, but referrals help.*

Anonymous Agent
Los Angeles

• *As a writer, you never know where offers are going to come from. The more out there you are, the better the possibilities. You can't just sit there in your room writing, you need to go to things.*

Robin Moran Miller
New York

• *Find out everything you can about the agent. Write him a letter. Call him by name. Demonstrate that you know who he is. Agents have big egos. I throw away everything that says* Dear Agent. *Tell him you have been following his career. We're all susceptible to flattery.*

Raphael Berko
Media Artist Group
Los Angeles

• *Writers who want to get an agent should identify agents who are young and just starting out in their career. Most of my clients and I grew up together in the business.*

Daniel Ostroff
The Daniel Ostroff Agency
Los Angeles

• *I just sold a script last week. My literary department had turned it down, but the writer got the script to me and I fell in love with it. That's why I was able to sell it. It's all subjective.*

Anonymous Agent
For Obvious Reasons

• *If you write for film, go to film festivals and it's not to go around going,* Here's my script, *but going around saying,* Hi, how are you doin'? I really liked your film. *And then chatting about the film and that's it. Meet people so that a little later on you can say,* Oh, I met so-and-so. *He might be interested in that.*

Robin Moran Miller
New York

• *Be persistent without being obnoxious. If someone gives you any encouragement to see your second script, don't forget, follow up. Let them know when it's going to be ready and remind them in your cover letter that they asked to see it.*

Barbara Alexander
Media Artists Group
Los Angeles

• *Even before you get to Los Angeles, you should investigate the film schools (AFI, USC, UCLA) and the colleges that have communications departments. Besides the craft-skills to be gained from their programs, internships are invaluable. The best interns I've worked with have been from the communications department with film emphasis from Cal State Fullerton. The smart ones are the ones who say,* I want to be a screenwriter and I hope you'll read my material along the way, but in the meantime, I want to learn everything I can about the business. I just want to learn.

I always say, if you want to work here, it's better than working in a smaller or medium size production company or studio job where you'll end up filing all day and you'll have little or no contact with other interns, writers, producers, etc.

I let interns sit in on meetings, read contracts, go through appropriate files and read my clients' work. Anyone wanting to get into the business should take a job, any job, to get in the proverbial door, so that they're not imagining what people do who are writers in the business, but are seeing what they do, first hand, and that it's hard, serious work.

If you just arrive in town, take an extension course at UCLA or USC. They have major writers, producers and directors in the film and television industries teaching classes, major writers. I've taught at UCLA and at SC, both through extension or respective masters-of-professional-writing department. At least that way, a student can get into the mix. I found one client in one of my classes although I said I wouldn't read students' material.

Ken Sherman
Ken Sherman Agency
Los Angeles

• *There are a lot of classes in New York for playwrights. A good portion of them aren't geared to how you learn to write plays, they are for practicing playwrights to meet with their peers. You meet once a week and everyone brings in material. You discuss it and you have a group of intelligent people whose opinions you trust, but also you don't worry about showing them something that might not be as perfect as it should be.*

Robin Moran Miller
New York

Another way into a connected environment is to get into an acting or directing class either as a participant or an auditor. As you join in the collaborative experience that produces theater, film and or television, experiencing the problems of actors and directors, your writing will unconsciously reflect the information and begin to solve those problems.

• *Go to a lot of theater, meet a lot of people and when you meet a director whose work you really like, contact the director personally, because directors are always looking for material.*
Robin Moran Miller
New York

Screenwriting Contests

Although it's handy to pick up prize money, many feel the greatest value to contests is that your material will be read by people in the business. Others feel that since most contests charge a fee to enter, this is just another instance of paying someone to read your script.

Some contests not only charge, but put in writing that if they like your script, they have first option. Some are production companies that use this approach to canvass material. The contest keeps them in scripts and is self-supporting. You could get your material optioned. On the other hand, you might not want to just sign everything away blindly, so be sure to do research on who you are doing business with.

The newsletter from the Scriptwriters Network has some helpful advice regarding contests:

• *Overall, script contests can be an effective shortcut to making strong industry contacts if you have the funds to enter them and if you are prepared to lose. And the truth is many of the runner-up and semi-final scripts still get a great deal of attention and read. If you can afford to enter the major contests (really a small amount when compared to totals spent on classes, computer hardware, etc.) they can be a great help in getting through the door.*
And what are the major contests? The Nicholl Fellowships is still the most prestigious around. The Malcolm-Vincent and America's Best are also very high profile and worthwhile. The Diane Thomas Contest technically costs nothing to enter, but two overpriced UCLA extension courses are now a prerequisite. In terms of numbers, however, the chances of winning are better since generally less than a hundred submissions are made each year,

opposed to the thousands in other contests. The Chesterfield Program run through Universal Studios is not bad, but despite protestations to the contrary, they prefer younger writers and ask far more questions than the other contests. There is a new contest run by Hanover Square Productions, but this is only their second year and its impossible to accurately judge it's benefits to writers.

"Spotlight on Features"
Jonathan Kimbrough
Scriptwriters Network Newsletter
March 1993

The Nicholl Fellowships
The Academy of Motion Picture Arts and Sciences
8949 Wilshire Blvd.
Beverly Hills, CA 90212
310-247-3000

America's Best
The Writers Foundation
1801 Burnet Avenue
Syracuse, NY 13206

The Diane Thomas Contest
UCLA Extension
10995 Le Conte Avenue #313
Los Angeles, CA 90024-2883
310-825-9415

The Chesterfield Program
c/o Universal Studios
100 Universal City Plaza Bldg 447
Universal City, CA 91608
818-777-0998

Hanover Square Productions
7612 Fountain Avenue
Los Angeles, CA 90046
310-288-6326

Malcolm-Vincent
Screenwriting Competition
505 S Beverly Drive #17
Beverly Hills, CA 90212

Writer's Aide

The most comprehensive and up-to-date source for information
regarding screenplay contests and fellowships is Writer's Aide.
Published and written by screenwriter, Andrew Johnson, his
Screenplay Contest Package contains information, entrance forms
and interesting items for writers. Andrew decided that contests
were the best way for those outside the system and outside
Hollywood to access the producers. SCP costs $20.00.

Writer's Aide
1685 South Colorado Blvd., #237
Denver, CO 80222
303-430-4839/fax 303-782-0704

Support Groups

Whether you are in a formal writing class at a connected institution
or gathered with a group you have pulled together yourself, support
groups not only provide comfort and a place to blow off steam, but
they are conduits of information and access. Some groups are more
tied in to what is going on than others, but whenever you enlist
others on the same journey, you open the door for possibilities.

More support groups, scholarships, fellowships and contests are
available to writers than any other group of artists in theater or
film. Although much writer support is available in Los Angeles
ar.d New York, there is also help for writers all across the country:

Independent Features Projects

One of the most connected and effective support groups for
filmmakers is Independent Features Projects. IFP's 2000-plus

members across the country include grips, writers, sound technicians and anyone involved or wanting to be involved in independent film. This non-profit group sponsors seminars, classes, screenings, producer series, The Spirit Awards and an eclectic collection of industry related resources.

It is not necessary to be a member in order to attend events, but the regular newsletter is only available to members. It's full of information regarding free screenings, get togethers, resources and ads from people wanting scripts. The fee for membership is $40 for students, $95 for individuals and higher fees for corporate sponsorships. IFP has branches all over the country.

IFP West Los Angeles 213-937-4379
IFP New York 212-243-7777
IFP Northern California San Francisco 415-431-5890
IFP North Minnesota 612-338-0871
IFP South Miami 305-531-7621

Scriptwriters Network/Los Angeles

Scriptwriters Network is a consortium of writers who gather to give support, share information and rub shoulders with successful writers and producers who come to speak and shmooze. A prime motivation of the group is to give writers an understanding of how it *really is* in the business. They meet once a month and sponsor an annual contest called "The Door Opener Derby." Prizes include guaranteed script submissions to producers, heads of development and agents. The membership fee is $60. Members are admitted free to all lectures and non-members pay $10 and must make a reservation. Send *sase* for information to:

Scriptwriters Network
11684 Ventura Blvd., #508
Studio City, CA 91604
213-848-9477

Freelance Screenwriter's Forum

A national organization for screenwriters dedicated to improving the craft of screenwriting. FSF provides six 60 page magazines a year for the $38 yearly dues and endeavors to procure special rates for members for various screenwriter programs and services. The Forum sponsors contests and directories to enable members to be seen by producers and agents. FSF was founded in 1989 by two Davids (Grow and Geatty) who are writers.

The Freelance Screenwriter's Forum
P.O. Box 7
Long Green Pike
Baldwin, MD 21013-007

Chanticleer Films/The Discovery Program

The Discovery Program is a program for beginning directors. It is is specifically designed to give working professionals in the entertainment industry an opportunity to direct a short film. Whether you are a writer, actor, musician, art director or exist in any other position in the business, you are eligible for consideration for this program. The Program is designed to offer directing opportunities to those who need it most, therefore, prior directorial experience is very limited. Many writers become frustrated with directors who do not share their vision and seek to direct their own material. If you are one of these folks, write to Chanticleer for particulars. If you are chosen, Chanticleer will furnish up to $60,000, some production services and the chance to have your work shown to at least one major studio.

Chanticleer Films
1680 Vine St., Suite 1212
Hollywood, CA 90028
213-462-4705

Theater

Playwrights Horizons/New York — One of Manhattan's most prestigious Off-Broadway theaters is instrumental in presenting new playwrights on a regular basis. It takes two to four months for them to read your material, but it will be considered.

Playwrights Horizons/Tim Sanford
416 West 42nd Street
New York, NY 10036
212-564-1235

Ensemble Studio Theater — If you're a playwright, EST could be one of your best friends. They produce many new plays, sponsor new play festivals and have ongoing playwrighting groups.

Ensemble Studio Theater/Wendy Freed
Literary Department
549 West 52nd Street
New York City, NY 10019
212-581-9603

The Public Theater — New York's most famous off-Broadway theater has helped develop such plays as "Sticks and Bones," "A Chorus Line" and "Hair."   Connected and fearless, The Public also has ongoing playwright groups.

The Public Theater
425 Lafayette Avenue
New York, NY
212-598-7100

Organizations

New Dramatists — New Dramatists has been described by John Patrick Shanley as *the Fort Knox of playwright talent.* As their literature proclaims, ND is dedicated to finding gifted playwrights and giving them the time, space and tools to develop their craft, so that they may fulfill their potential and make lasting contributions to the theater. This full service non-profit group offers the following programs:

Readings and Workshops — stagings of members' plays, ranging from cold to rehearsed, public or private.

Director-in-Residence — a program sponsored by the Menasha Corporation in which a resident director aids in the dramaturgy and development of new plays. Lisa Peterson is the current director-in-residence.

Musical Theater Development — a series of intensive composer-librettist studios in which playwrights are introduced to the craft of musical theater.

Scriptshare — a subscriber service in which various film producers and theaters nationwide solicit member scripts.

Seventh Heaven — the third floor of New Dramatists where space is used for 'artists' workplaces as well as overnight facilities for visiting members. Endowed by the John Golden fund, the space is free of charge.

The Brooks Atkinson Playwright Exchange — a program in which member writers are offered the opportunity to workshop their plays at the Royal Court Theater in London.

Free Ticket Program — member writers are given the opportunity to see Broadway and off-Broadway shows free of charge.

New Dramatists also houses a library which is open to the public that includes members' scripts and a collection of theater materials.

Other programs include workshops on puppetry, screenwriting and writing for soap operas. Computer and printing equipment are available on the premises and unlimited script copying is offered at no charge. The intent of the organization is to provide a safe and supportive environment in which to develop material.

In order to apply for membership, New Dramatists requires that the playwright submit two full-length works (no screenplays), a resume and a letter of intent. Applications are available:

New Dramatists
424 W 44th Street
New York, NY 10036
212-757-6960.

The above material about New Dramatists has been excerpted with permission from The Dramatists Guild Quarterly, Summer 1992.

International Information

International Information Resources — The International Theatre Institute is an organization started in 1948 by UNESCO committed to foster theater communication with 82 centers around the world. Not only a conduit for information, ITI provides entree for artists of all kinds (actors, writers, directors, etc.) who are either going abroad or considering it. ITI puts out a quarterly newsletter that's yours for a contribution and maintains an extensive research library that is available to anyone doing serious research:

The International Theatre Institute
ITI of the United States
Louis A. Rachow (pronounced Rock-Oh)
220 West 42nd St. #1710
New York, NY 10035

Louis turned me onto the following publications:

The Original British Theater Directory

Richmond House Publishing Co. Ltd.
9-11 Richmond Buildings London IV5AF
telephone 44-071-437-9556
telefax 44-071-434-0200

The British Alternative Theatre Directory

edited by David McGillibray
Rebecca Books
Ivor House, Suite #2
1 Bridge Street
Cardiff CF12TH Wales
telephone 44-022-237-8452
telefax 344 022-223-8690

The Performing Arts Yearbook for Europe

Arts Publishing International, Ltd.
4 Assam St.
London E17QS
telephone 44-071-247-0066
telefax 44-071-247-6868

Price listed on the cover is in pounds sterling with no US
equivalent, but Louis says PAYE is roughly $50.00 and the other
books listed are about $30.00 each.

Scholarships and Grants

I'm not going to try to impinge on the territory of The Dramatists
Sourcebook. Their information on this subject is quite complete;
they list about 36 pages of grants, scholarships, contests and prizes
for scriptwriters of all kinds. As I mentioned elsewhere, I think
The Dramatists Sourcebook is an invaluable tool. The 1992 edition
features an introduction by Tony Kushner who won the Pulitzer
Prize for his play, "Angels in America." The Dramatists

Sourcebook is available in good bookstores and from

Theatre Communications Group
355 Lexington Avenue
New York, NY 10017
212-697-5230

Study

As mentioned earlier, besides possibly improving your writing,
studying can provide other avenues into the system. Some people,
however, feel it's not worth the risk:

• *You'd be better off taking a minor in screen-writing and a*
major in literature or psychology or politics or history or anything
because a screenwriting program is essentially just going to teach
you the format. A lot of professors are doing this to make a living.
My advice to students is to take the part time professors. They are
the ones who are working in the field and are able to express what
is takes to make it in this town.
The value of the film schools is primarily in networking. I
entered the business through an internship program.
Of course, you can work in any menial job at any studio and
begin your journey through the system where you meet people and
hand your work around. You hopefully meet the right people. You
meet people who are all going to be moving up at the same time.

Anonymous Agent
For Obvious Reasons

Even those who think that writing can't be taught agree that if
nothing else, being involved in a writing program at least
disciplines you, compels you to actually turn out product, and puts
you in the company of your peers and good role models. Staff,
guest speakers and other writers will be sharing information.
You'll learn where things are happening and ways other writers
have of coping with some of the same problems you are having.

• *There are the major film schools (UCLA, USC, NYU, AFI, Columbia) and then there's everybody else. Every other school has put in a film program and a screenwriting program and frankly, most of them are very high profit centers for the universities because you get predominantly white moneyed people going because it costs a lot of money.*

Many of the screenplays that you read out of the film schools (even the good ones) are bad because it becomes a process of homogenization, the school process. There was a time when I felt I could pick out not only what school they went to, but which professor they had. A lot of young writers try to second guess the marketplace. Then all you get is a derivative of the last hit that they saw as opposed to trying to write something original or put their own original values on something.

Not all situations are homogenized, but let's face it, there's only a certain number that come out of the programs that do well. It's a very few. 2% of the material is unreadable garbage. You get this enormous segment that's got a beginning, a middle, an end, it's in the right format. It's competent. Then you get this 1% that knocks you stupid.

Anonymous Agent
for Obvious Reasons

• *I guess classes can't hurt. I wouldn't say,* This is how you are going to be a success, go to class. *I've had successes with people who are AFI graduates and from UCLA and USC film school and I've had success with people who were plumbers and bus drivers and whatever. I would say, generally, that college educated people have a higher percentage of scores.*

Stu Robinson
paradigm
Los Angeles

• *A good play is a good play. Oftentimes the last thing I know about is the background of the writer.*

Fred Gorman
DGRW
New York

Although there are valuable screenwriting classes and seminars held all across the country, two schools that immediately get agent attention on a resume are New York University's Tisch School of the Arts Graduate Film Division and the University of Southern California.

The Creme de la Creme

• *NYU - In 1987 there were 497 applicants. In 1992 there were 890 applicants. The number admitted in each of those years was 52.*

USC - in 1988 there were 583 applicants, in 1992, there were 864. In 1988, they admitted 110, 1992 - 188.

Graduates of USC's school of cinema have received 30 Academy Awards.

The Guinness Book of
Movie Facts and Feats
Patrick Robertson
Guinness Publishing
Great Britain

Richard Walter is Screenwriting Faculty Chairman in the Department of Film and Television at the University of California at Los Angeles. Not only that, he is a novelist and a successful screenwriter. Many of the agents I interviewed mentioned Mr. Walter by name. If you are considering university training in screenwriting and were admitted to his program, you would be well served. If you are intent on staying in your own backyard and/or don't want to go the university route, at least get his book: Screenwriting, the art, craft and business of film and television writing.

Novelist/screenwriter Richard Price ("Sea of Love," "The Color of Money," "Clockers") was asked if he ever studied with Syd Field or any of the other screenwriting gurus:

- *All I ever studied was the movie executives. What soothes them, what scares them.*

> "The Organizer"
> F. X. Feeney
> Buzz Magazine
> September 1992

On the other hand, John Mattson did all the right things and they paid off:

- *A graduate of UCLA Film School, Mattson worked for three years as a freelance reader and HBO story editor before setting out to write for himself. Last November, his "Milk Money" sold for $1.1 million to Paramount Pictures, marking one of the year's biggest spec sales.*

> "Scripter Mattson
> signs at UTA"
> John Evan Frook
> Daily Variety
> May 12, 1993

If You Leave Home to Study

Agents think highly of The University of Southern California at Los Angeles and always answer phone calls from any UCLA or AFI teacher who recommends a promising student. The proximity of these schools to the world's movie capital ensures participation of the most famous screenwriters, producers and directors as guest speakers and guest teachers in the extension program.

- *I'm more likely to look at things from writers from UCLA or USC or NYU film school. I went to film school. I was studying to be a screenwriter and had to write ¾ of a screenplay every quarter at UCLA, so that helped. I'm a frustrated writer and consider myself an editor when I read a script.*

> Howard Sanders
> Pleshette & Green
> Los Angeles

• *Get into a class at UCLA or USC. Robert McKee's classes are good. Richard Walter at UCLA is a fine teacher of writers. When he calls me about someone, I listen.*

Rima Greer
Writers & Artists
Los Angeles

A connected film school not only puts you in the company of the greats and their material, but has a line to the industry and the ability to get your material read by important agents and producers.

• *What percentage of 1987 screenwriting majors at UCLA had agents? 67...it's now almost 80.*

Premiere Magazine
September 1992

Staying Home

It's not necessary to leave home to study. Many hot Hollywood screenwriting teachers take their shows on the road. I am mentioning the names of teachers who have reputations within the business. There are undoubtedly more.

Syd Field

The man who has written the *bible* for screenwriters is Syd Field. His book, Screenplay The Foundations of Screenwriting, sells almost as well today as it did in 1979 when it was first published. A native of Los Angeles who grew up around the business, Syd began his career as a writer-producer for David L. Wolper Productions, was a free lance screenwriter and became head of the Story Department at Cine Artists. Syd conducts classes around the world as well as in Los Angeles.

Syd Field
270 N Canon Drive #1355
Beverly Hills, CA 90210
310-271-7975.

Robert McKee

Robert McKee, a well regarded screenwriting teacher, not only travels to Dallas, Chicago, Washington, Cleveland, etc., but to London, Brussels and Toronto. I don't have a complete list, but the list I have suggests that no matter where you live, McKee is near. His weekend seminar costs $400. The fee covers classes from 9:30 a.m. to 8:00 p.m. Friday, Saturday and Sunday.

McKee is recommended by people as diverse as director Mark Rydell ("On Golden Pond"), novelist/actor Kirk Douglas, and screenwriter Patricia Resnick ("9-5," "A Wedding"). McKee has an impressive portfolio as a writer ("Colombo," "Quincy") and as an actor (Broadway, London, rep). I'm told by writers and agents who have attended that the seminars are worthwhile and exciting.

Robert McKee/Two Arts, Inc.
12021 Wilshire Blvd. Suite 868
Los Angeles, CA 90025.
310-312-1002 or 212-463-7889.

Michael Hauge

Michael Hauge is another Los Angeles based high profile story editor and script consultant who takes his show on the road. Author of the best selling book, <u>Writing Screenplays That Sell</u>, Michael not only teaches in LA, but you can catch him in San Francisco, San Diego, Detroit, Seattle, Phoenix, Boston, Washington, D.C. etc. Tuition is $195 for two full days (Saturday and Sunday from 9:30 to 5:30). 800-477-1947 or 818-995-8118.

Dave Trottier

Dave teaches seminars on all aspects of writing including what seems to me to be the most practical: "17 Ways to Make a Living as a Writer." The author of a respected format guide, Dave teaches across the land, in Los Angeles and by mail. You can't get more flexible than that.

Dave Trottier
22034 East Lincoln Avenue, Suite 300
Anaheim, CA 92806
714-251-1073.

Playwrighting

High on the list of schools known as major sources for playwrights are Yale, Columbia, Carnegie Mellon and NYU. There are also programs run through New York theaters (see Chapter 11). Paula Vogel at Brown is well thought of and particularly supportive of women. Anne Cantaneo (The New School, New York) was also mentioned as part of the elite group whose names draw respect from agents.

There are important writing programs of one kind or another at the Universities of Iowa, Utah and Missouri, as well as Syracuse University, Carnegie Tech and University of California, Irvine.

• *Minneapolis has a playwrights group (Midwest Playwrights Labs) and Chicago has a really good theater community. If you are near a university town, you're lucky, because you can tap into film through the university. If you aren't, you may have to make your own support group. People who want to form a support group should put an ad in the paper as well as places like art film houses in their community. Then have meetings and try to cull out the people who say they are writers, but are actually not. A lot of really important writers' groups grew out of somebody's living room.*

Robin Moran Miller
New York

Gotham Writers' Workshop/New York

David Grae and Jeff Fligelman are writers and teachers who decided to start a business and fill a niche for writers in Manhattan. The Gotham Writers' Workshop provides the longest class (14 weeks) in town. Not only that, it is taught by working screenwriters and playwrights. Writers of all ages and levels participate in classes geared to their progress in the process. Classes meet once a week for three hours and cost $400. And the first 3-hour class of each section is free. You get to meet the teacher, the other students and participate before you commit yourself. Sounds pretty good to me.

Although GWW appears focused primarily on screenwriters and playwrights, there are fiction writing classes as well. Besides the large number of classes available, students are invited to participate in their *Friday Night Events* attending films, or theater and getting together afterwards. This group of people seem not only knowledgeable, but amiable. Even if you don't end up taking their classes, send for their clever brochure.

Gotham Writers' Workshop
P.O. Box 1994
Cathedral Station
New York City, NY 10025-1994
212-662-9673.

Robin Moran Miller

Robin Moran Miller teaches at the Marjorie Ballentine Studio. A prize winning playwright, Miller teaches workshops for beginners and for advanced playwrights. Writing exercises are given weekly and guest theater directors and playwrights are invited to share their expertise and experience.

Since The Marjorie Ballentine Studio includes a resident Company of Actors dedicated to producing plays by their writing students, The Studio is an avenue of possible visibility by the theater community in New York.

The Marjorie Ballentine Studio
115 MacDougal Street
New York, NY 10028
212-861-9172

Be Informed

Wherever you are, it is imperative to understand who your buyers are and recognize the current trends. If drama is in and you are a comedy writer, you'll realize the rejection is not personal, you're just not where the business is right now. The pendulum will be coming your way again in the future. For film and television writers, I recommend that you subscribe to one or both of the daily Los Angeles trades as well as the monthly magazine of The Writers Guild West.

Daily Variety	The Hollywood Reporter
5700 Wilshire Blvd.	5055 Wilshire Blvd.
Los Angeles, CA 90036	Los Angeles, CA 90036
213-857-6600	213-525-2000

The Journal of The Writers Guild of America West
8955 Beverly Blvd.
Los Angeles, CA 90048-2456.

The Journal is indispensable for the up-do-date monthly material available. On pages 72 and 73, there is a sample of the kind of information you will find. It is reprinted with their permission.

Your Reference Library

Books that have the credits of directors, actors and producers should also be part of your reference collection. I strongly suggest you begin assembling a library stocked with books that give you an idea of what the business is really like. It's not that the business is so bad, but it is tough. Biographies of successful people will provide role models in your quest for achievement and may even inform your goals. Big success requires big sacrifices. Don't find out later that the cost was too high. Denial is said to be even more potent than cocaine; neither drug enhances your marketability.

Here is a list of books that will give your library a good start:

Adventures in the Screen Trade/William Goldman
The Complete Directory to Primetime
    Network TV Shows/Tim Brooks-Earle Marsh
Creating Unforgettable Characters/Linda Seger
The Devil's Candy/Julie Salamon
Dramatists Sourcebook/Theatre
    Communications Group
The Directors Guild of America Directory of Members
The Film Encyclopedia/Ephraim Katz
The Filmgoer's Companion/Leslie Halliwell
Final Cut/Steven Bach
Halliwell's Film Guide/Leslie Halliwell
Hollywood Agents Directory/Hollywood
    Creative Directory
Hype & Glory/William Goldman
Making a Good Script Great/Linda Seger
Indecent Exposure/David McClintock
Insider's Guide to Book Editors, Publishers and
    Literary Agents/Jeff Herman
The Last Great Ride/Brandon Tartikoff
The New Screenwriter Looks at the
    New Screenwriter/William Froug
NY Times Directory of Film/(Arno Press)
NY Times Directory of Theater/(Arno Press)
Playwright's Companion/Mollie Ann Meserve
Reel Power/Mark Litwak
Saturday Night Live/Doug Hall/Jeff Weingrad
Screen World (current edition)/John Willis
Screenwriter's Workbook/Syd Field
The Screenwriter Looks at the
    Screenwriter/William Froug
Screenwriting/Richard Walter
Screenwriting Tricks of the Trade/William Froug
The Season/William Goldman
Selling a Screenplay/Syd Field
Theater World (current edition)/John Willis
TV Movies/Leonard Maltin

TV MARKET LIST

Please Note: The TV Market List Hotline has a new phone number: (310) 205-8600.

Please note that this is the most current information we have available, since we have not received definite pick-up or cancellation information.

SHOW	TYPE/LENGTH	SCRIPT STATUS	COMPANY	CONTACT	NETWORK
A Different World	EC/30 min.	★	Carsey-Werner Co.	Susan Fales (818) 760-5657	NBC
Baywatch	ED/60 min.	★	Baywatch Prod. Co.	Michael Berk or David Braff (310) 302-9135	SYN
Berlin Break	ED/60 min.	▲	Berlin Productions, Inc.		SYN
Beverly Hills, 90210	DC/60 min.	▲	Spelling TV Inc.		FBC
Big Brother Jake	EC/30 min.	★	Family Prods. Inc.	Ali Marie Matheson or Jon Cooksey (804) 523-7883	FAM
Blossom	EC/30 min.	★	Witt/Thomas Prods.	Don Reo (213) 468-3250	NBC
Bob	EC/30 min.	▲	Paramount TV		CBS
Bodies of Evidence	ED/60 min.	▲	Lorimar TV	Hiatus	CBS
California Dreams	EC/30 min.	★	NBC Prods.	Susan Metrick (818) 840-2251	NBC
Camp Wilder	EC/30 min.	▲	AKA Productions		ABC
Class of '96	ED/60 min.	▲	Empty Chair Prods.		FBC
Civil Wars	ED/60 min.	★	Steven Bochco Prods.	Dayna Flanagan (310) 203-2400	ABC
Coach	EC/30 min.	▲	Universal TV		ABC
The Commish	ED/60 min.	★	Stephen J. Cannell	Steve Kronish (213) 465-5800	ABC
Dark Justice	ED/60 min.	▲	Magnum Productions		CBS
Delta	EC/30 min.	▲	Universal TV		ABC
Designing Women	EC/30 min.	★	Columbia TV	Blanca Conches (818) 954-3494	CBS
Dinosaurs	Ec/30 min.	★	Walt Disney TV	Jeff McCracken (818) 760-5303	ABC
Doogie Howser M.D.	DC/30 min.	★	Steven Bochco Prods.	Dayna Flanagan (310) 203-2888	ABC

F.Y.I.

F.Y.I. listings are provided by those persons or organizations who declare they are willing to provide FREE information to WGAW members. While every attempt is made to insure that F.Y.I. listings are purely informational and accurate, the WGAW does not endorse any of the following listings or the information they provide.

Government Departments

Air Force	310/575-7511
Air Traffic	805/266-0260
Army	310/575-7621
Board of Education	213/625-6766
Coast Guard	310/575-7817
F.B.I.	213/477-6565
Marine Corps	310/575-7272
Navy	310/575-7481
Police Department	213/485-3586
Parole	213/897-1001
Probation	213/940-2554
Sheriff	213/974-4228
Veterans Admin. Film Office	213/824-4497

Medical Authorities

Adolescent Sexuality/AIDS	310/559-5700
AIDS/AIDS Project L.A.	213/962-1600
Amer. Med. Assoc. (AMA)	312/464-5000
Anesthetic Surgery	617/735-3334

Religious Information

Catholicism	818/846-8141
Christianity	800/883-3883
Hare Krishnas	310/559-2143
Islam	213/659-4211
Judaism	213/852-1234
Mormons	213/475-7018
Protestant Media Council	800/883-3883

Social Services

AIDS/AIDS Project L.A.	213/962-1600
Amer. Humane Assoc.	818/501-0123
Amnesty International	213/388-1237
Behavior/Psychosocial Issues	310/456-2458
Medical Info. (MPTF)	818/876-1888
Hunger	310/454-3716
Literacy	916/324-7358
Self-Help Group Info.	213/825-7990
Sexuality/Sex Therapy	310/838-3776
Social Issues (N.C.N.)	310/456-1082

WGA Departments   310/550-1000

Administration	205-2598
Agency	205-2502
Claims	205-8663
Contracts	205-2501
Credits	205-2528
Dues	205-2531
Film Society	205-2502
Finance	205-2586
Human Resources	205-2580
Industry Analysis	205-2576
Journal	205-2542
Legal	205-2521
Library	205-2544
Membership	205-2532
Public Relations	205-2574
Registration	205-2540
Residuals	205-2503
Signatories	205-2514
Credit Union	213/649-1712
	818/840-9220

You'll Never Eat Lunch in this Town Again/Julia Phillips
Who's Who in the Motion Picture Industry/Rodman Gregg
Who's Who in Television/Rodman Gregg
Who's Who in American Film Now/James Monaco
Wired/Bob Woodward
The Writers Guild of America Membership Directory
Writing Screenplays That Sell/Michael Hauge

The *Who's Who* books by Gregg (Packard House Books, Beverly Hills, CA) are particularly helpful; they list directors, producers, producing companies, their credits and contact addresses.

Both The Directors Guild and The Writers Guild membership directories are free to members, but are available for a fee to non members through the guilds and some bookstores.

Directors Guild of America West 7920 Sunset Blvd. Los Angeles, CA 90046 310-289-2000	Directors Guild of America 520 North Michigan Ave. Chicago, IL 60611 312-644-5050
Directors Guild of America 110 West 57th St. New York, NY 10019 212-581-0370	
Writers Guild/West 8955 Beverly Blvd. W Hollywood, CA 90048 310-550-1000	Writers Guild/East 555 West 57th St. New York, NY 10019 212-767-7800

Writers can besiege the marketplace from home and never leave. Of course, if one of the reasons you are writing is that you want to leave home and move to the land of palm trees or subways, then it may be time to buy your plane ticket.

Wrap Up

Ways into the system
- ✓ industry job
- ✓ classes with connected instructors
- ✓ writing groups
- ✓ acting classes
- ✓ directing classes

Film support
- ✓ Independent Features Project
- ✓ Scriptwriters Network/Los Angeles
- ✓ Freelance Screenwriter's Forum
- ✓ The Discovery Program

Theater support
- ✓ Playwrights Horizons
- ✓ The Public Theater
- ✓ Ensemble Studio Theater
- ✓ The New Dramatists

Formal study/benefits
- ✓ exposed to role models
- ✓ discipline
- ✓ networking
- ✓ learn form and structure

Formal study/detriments
- ✓ can lead to homogenization of product
- ✓ can make your vision too narrow
- ✓ real life sometimes thought to be more conducive to good writing

Keep informed
- ✓ reference library
- ✓ read the trades
- ✓ DGA Membership Listing
- ✓ WGA Membership Listing

Agents, Finally

You've been very patient. I know you have been dying to jump to this part of the book from the moment you bought it. Getting an agent takes on enormous significance in the quest for a writer's credibility. Not being able to get an agent hurts our feelings, makes us hostile and undermines self confidence.

It seems you can't do business without an agent, and unless you are already making money, it's impossible to get an agent to talk to you, take a meeting or in any other way validate your existence. Some feel you can make an entire career out of getting an agent.

• *Not long after their 1990 college graduation, the pair — Leff is from Chicago and Penn is from New York City — moved to Los Angeles. Their first goal was to get an agent, perhaps the hardest task a writer ever has to face.*

"Well, They Wanted Action"
Terry Pristin
The Los Angeles Times
May 16, 1993

Even though the quest for an agent can become a full time job in itself, untried people still manage to get an agent and enter the business hourly. These new people may be related to others in the business or otherwise connected giving them entree. Those without this benefit need to be driven, clever, ingenious and of course, very talented. Many are all of the above.

This book exists for all of you neither related nor connected. The quotes are gleaned from interviews with scores of agents in Los Angeles and New York who represent writers for the theater, film, and television. The agents reveal their ideas on how neophyte writers might enter the marketplace, help themselves, attract agents and move toward their career goals in the most timely and intelligent manner.

Agents exist because there is a need. The buyers could not possibly cull through all the scripts with which new and existing writers inundate the marketplace on an hourly basis. In fact, for legal considerations, most studios, networks, and television shows won't even accept a script unless it is submitted through an agent.

What Is an Agent Anyway?

The dictionary, which knows very little about show business, has many definitions for the word *agent*. By combining a couple I've come up with:

A force acting in place of another, effecting a certain result by driving, inciting, or setting in motion; a go between.

What does an agent do? Where do I find one? Do I need an agent? How can I get an agent to talk to me? What would I say to an agent? Are there rules of behavior? How can I tell if an agent is a good agent? When is the right time to look for an agent? What if they all want to sign me, how can I choose the right agent? What if no agent wants to sign me, do I have to go back to Iowa? What will I tell my family?

Tell your family that you are writing and learning the business. Tell them that when you get an agent you will let them know, but that whether or not you have an agent has nothing to do with the fact that you are pursuing your dream. Being a writer is about writing, not about being employed. Tell them that writing is making you happy and that making money will only be icing on the cake. Civilians (those who have never pursued a job in show business) and would-be writers who are still in school, can't possibly empathize. They have no idea what any artist goes through in pursuit of employment and/or an agent. They're not going to understand anything except your name up on the screen in big letters where it says, *Written by*.

What Does An Agent Do?

In its simplest incarnation, the agent, acting on your behalf, sets in motion a series of events that result in your having a shot at a job. He gets you in the door for meetings, interviews and pitch sessions. He sends your work around and gets people to read it. Once your material begins to sell, he conceives a plan for your career. He gives you credibility by his interest in you.

Do I Need One?

Most writers possess neither the contacts, information, nor the appetite for representing themselves over the long haul. In most instances, however, it is necessary to be your own first agent: finding your own first job(s), getting to know producers and directors, sending out flyers about your work and keeping up to date on what kinds of projects are being done.

Once you have a body of work, you'll have the option of concentrating on your writing and letting someone else shoulder the major portion of keeping your work visible. You will undoubtedly want an agent's help with your career, but if you are smart, you will keep your hand in.

How Did He Get To Be An Agent?

Most of us have no idea how agents train for their jobs and therefore no basis on which to evaluate an agent intelligently. Do agents attend Agent University or something?

Actually, some of them do. Those universities are the training programs (mail rooms) of the conglomerate initial agencies: CAA (Creative Artists Agency), ICM (International Creative Management), WMA (William Morris Agency) and UTA (United Talent Agency).

Whether or not he/she is involved in such formal training, the agent I want has been getting to know the business, reading every screenplay, television script, play, novel; the written word in any form that might interest a buyer or teach an eager mind. He's watched the development of writers, actors, directors, and producers. He's apprenticed under some connected role model at another agency or at a studio. He's been meeting people on all levels of the business, networking, staying visible, and communicating. He's met producers, directors and vice presidents of development and he's cultivated relationships with them.

He only represents those writers whose work he personally knows so when he tells a prospective buyer that he's found a brilliant new writer who is perfect for an upcoming project or who has written the next "Unforgiven" or the new "Seinfeld", the buyers will pay attention. Just like a writer, an agent builds his credibility slowly, one step at a time.

• *It's really very simple to describe what agents do - they work for their clients. They look for material, they read their clients' material and they set up deals for their clients. To do those tasks effectively, they also need to know everything that's going on around town.*

> "Les Liaisons
> Dangereuses"
> Charles B. Slocum
> The Journal
> June 1991

Time

The relationships agents build take time. To get people out and introduce them and get their material read takes a lot of time and effort. To follow up on it takes more time. It's a large investment. An agent who has done his homework is probably not going to be interested in you until you have done yours.

Make It Worth An Agent's While To Talk To You

Why would an agent talk to you? Have you spent years perfecting your work, reading, writing, writing, writing, watching films, television, reading classic screenplays, devouring television scripts, learning who you are, focusing your goals? Do you read the trades? Do you know who the buyers are who might be interested in what you specifically have to sell? Have you digested the written form of whichever kind of script you want to sell? Do you have the vocabulary with which to discuss the business with your prospective business partner?

No? Well, get to it.

• *My reputation is as good as the writers I send from my office. My reputation relies upon my clients, so I have to be careful about what I send out.*
>Ken Sherman
>Ken Sherman & Assoc.
>Los Angeles

Besides getting the writer's work read, the agent must be prepared to negotiate a brilliant contract when the material sells. That entails knowing all the contracts and all of the rules and regulations of The Writers and Dramatists Guilds, as well as having an understanding of the marketplace and knowing what others at similar career levels are getting for similar jobs.

He must then have the courage, style, and judgment to stand up to the buyers in asking for what is fair without giving in to the temptation to sell the writer down the river financially in favor of his future relationship with the buyers or without becoming too grandiose and turning everyone off.

Franchised Agents

A writer who is a member of The Writers Guild can represent himself anytime he wants. An agent conducting business for a writer must have a license from the state and have signed an agreement with the WGA. That agreement is called a *franchise*. To be a franchised agent, the agent must have a license to operate issued by the state, agree to abide by the Agency Rules and Regulations of the WGA and have experience as an agent. Just because an agent is franchised by the Guild is no guarantee that the agent is ethical, knowledgeable or effective. He probably is, but since this is an important decision, check him out.

Wrap Up

Agent
✓ a force acting in place of another, effecting a certain result by driving, inciting, or setting in motion; a go between.

Agent's job
✓ to become *connected* to the buyers
✓ to get the writers' work read, arrange meetings, and interviews
✓ to negotiate salary and billing
✓ to have credibility, taste and courage

What Everybody Wants

Before a smart business person confronts the marketplace with a new product, he takes the pulse of the buyer to determine how his offering will fare. If he is looking for an agent, it makes sense to find out what is on the agent's wishlist. What is he looking for? Do you have to be a WGA member to arouse his interest? Is it enough to be industrious? Does your personality enter into the equation? Is he going to read several of your scripts to decide whether or not he thinks you can write and/or sell?

• *The ideal writer is the one that has a great concept, a great story and can execute it. Usually, you get one of those things.*
> Candy Monteiro/Fredda Rose
> Monteiro Rose
> Los Angeles

• *Of course, we prefer WGA members. It makes life a lot easier. As far as the material goes, material that is compelling, exciting, provocative and that fits within a certain structure and form of the genre that they are writing, fits form in terms of creating climax points and anti-climax points.*
> Laya Gelff
> Laya Gelff Associates
> Los Angeles

• *Most of what we see is on the Bell Curve, written by intelligent people and it's all about C- to C+. In the C to C+ range, we try to help them. We may send them off and tell them to come back with another script. There are very few where it's clear they should be in another field. The other ones who jump off the page, where it's clearly special that it's superstardom, that's rare.*

Elliot Stahler
Kaplan Stahler
Los Angeles

● *You can tell if somebody is funny in three pages. You recognize it when you see it. It's just sincere and genuine.*

Bob Hohman
Richland/Wunsch/Hohman
Los Angeles

● *What everyone wants to see is a script they haven't seen before. If you are new in town and your script has been covered by every studio, it's worthless to your agent.*

Rima Greer
Writers & Artists
Los Angeles

● *I look for someone who is very talented, who works at their craft even when they are not employed, who is serious about his career and will work at the career as well as the craft. He or she do that by going to parties, taking classes, having lunches and generally trying to make themselves visible. It's important to just get out there and meet people. I'm interested in someone who will take a hand in his career instead of just calling his agent every two weeks as well as writing every single day.*

Anonymous Agent
Los Angeles

● *We like our clients to have as small a resume as possible with one entry every several years because that means that people want you back. If you spend one year on this show and one year on that show and the next year on show #3, something is wrong. We like to have a small resume where you start as a term writer and then you're a story editor and then you're an executive story editor, then you're a producer, then you're a supervising producer and then you're an executive producer.*

The keys to this business are continuity and consistency and you don't get that from jumping around. I want to be able to show the network that he's moved up in class, and that says something. That says much more than if he's had 20 entries in 5 years. If you've done that many shows, nobody thought you were good enough to ask you to stay around. When somebody comes to me with a resume of 10 shows in 10 years, I don't respond to that.

Elliot Stahler
Kaplan Stahler Agency
Los Angeles

• *There's a difference between writing and trying to write. It's just elegant.*

Bob Hohman
Richland/Wunsch/Hohman
Los Angeles

• *There's no mystery about writing. You can read one page and know. You know if you are in good hands by how somebody writes. Good writers have an ear for how people use language. With most new writers, all the characters sound alike. You can tell by the density of pages sometimes. If the descriptions go on forever instead of one line. If a writer needs a half page of prose to describe the scene, generally speaking, you are in trouble. Not to mention that it can be really boring.*

Lynn Pleshette
Pleshette & Green
Los Angeles

• *I won't look at treatments. We won't look at outlines. If we look and when we look, it's really at finished material. You almost never sell an outline or a treatment unless you are selling a big name writer. There's no money in just selling an idea and it doesn't help anybody's career.*

Martin Shapiro
Shapiro-Lichtman
Los Angeles

• *Oh, I probably look for the same things that producers are looking for; good writing, a good story, well developed characters, something that feels real, something that feels unusual and not too familiar.*

Jim Preminger
Jim Preminger Agency
Los Angeles

• *Whether it's a great script or not is secondary. The first evaluation is the writing. How good is the person? It's really a subjective thing. I can say they're not good and they can go across the street and someone else can say they're brilliant. I can be wrong or it can go the other way.*

Martin Shapiro
Shapiro-Lichtman
Los Angeles

• *I look for originality, passion, an individual voice, as well as someone who is a craftsman and is not afraid to be different.*

Ken Sherman
Ken Sherman Agency
Los Angeles

• *A great screenplay - 118 pages or less in correct format, with paragraphs no more than 4 lines long with castable parts with a story I've never heard before.*

Rima Greer
Writers & Artists
Los Angeles

• *I read it on two levels. I read it in terms of my pure emotional reaction to it, but at the same time I have to read it with the overlay of its practicality and reality to the market. That doesn't mean that if I'm absolutely captivated or blown away, even though it may not appear to be commercial, that doesn't mean that I'm going to be scared off and I give you as examples: "Driving Miss Daisy," "Chariots of Fire," "Fried Green Tomatoes," none of these are what you would call slam-dunk commercial vehicles. If you have a passion for something, that can be fun, too. I may not expect to sell it, but if I think it's going to be a great calling card of this person's ability, it can lead to other employment. We've had that happen a number of times where the original script that got me turned on is still on the shelf, but in the meantime, it has resulted in 10-11 other jobs as a result of somebody reading the script.*

> Stu Robinson
> paradigm
> Los Angeles

• *Money is not one of the top five considerations ... more important is that they are realistic about where they are in the continuum of their career and they can't be insane. All anyone really wants is that they feel they are not going to be in the same place in their career in six months as they are now.*

> Bob Hohman
> Richland/Wunsch/Hohman
> Los Angeles

• *Most of us gravitate toward those clients who are easy to talk to because that communication helps to maintain our energy to fight the true battles.*

> "Les Liaisons
> Dangereuses"
> The Journal
> June 1991

• *One of the reasons why we have successfully mined theater is that the training playwrights get is character first. All you have is the stage and the people. We can all fix a story or come up with a twist on a story or fix the plot, but if the characters are not there, you don't have anything. Great writing is character.*

> Jonathan Westover
> The Gage Group
> Los Angeles

• *Most good literary agents will request the script before even sitting down with the writer. I try to do that. I prefer reading just*

*because I don't want any prejudices about really liking the person.
I want to see the material. I might be charmed as can be, talking
with you, but then I read the material and then I think, oh, I'm not
the agent for this person, how am I going to say that? It doesn't
mean you can't write, it means that I don't respond in a personal,
gut manner.*

> Ken Sherman
> Ken Sherman Agency
> Los Angeles

• *An adult who is psychologically sound that you can spend 10
hours a day with.*

> Bob Hohman
> Richland/Wunsch/Hohman
> Los Angeles

• *I want to know what kinds of personal and professional
maturity they demonstrate.*

> Elliot Stahler
> Kaplan Stahler
> Los Angeles

• *If you have a difficult personality and they want you, they'll
take you. The choices do get dimmer and slimmer, however.
Charm will help you, but ultimately, it's in the script.*

> Lynn Pleshette
> Pleshette & Green
> Los Angeles

• *We find that we are attracted to writers that we like as
individuals. I think writers select agents frequently based on the
agents' personality.*

> Jim Preminger
> Jim Preminger Agency
> Los Angeles

• *I evaluate off the work, but I won't take someone who behaves
antisocially. When one of my clients goes in, they represent my*

agency. They represent me, it's my name that goes in on that letterhead. It has to be someone I feel I can work with. I am not looking for the one shot, it has to be someone for the long haul.

> Ken Sherman
> Ken Sherman Agency
> Los Angeles

What *You* Will Want to Consider

If you have your life in a fairly balanced state; have an apartment, have several scripts in your bag, have at least a nodding acquaintance with the economic perils of life as a scriptwriter, have some of the traits described by agents as being attractive, and are involved with other writers, it's time for you to begin serious research to determine the agent who is right for you.

Unfortunately, agents do not send out resumes in search of clients. Even if they are looking for clients (and they are all looking for the client who will make them wealthy and powerful beyond their dreams), agents don't send out a list of their training, accomplishments, and/or a personality profile. Beyond their list of clients (which is not, by the way, posted on their door), there is no obvious gauge of their worth; it is up to you to conduct an investigation of your future business partners.

You have already taken your first step; you bought this book giving you the benefit of my interviews with a cross-section of agents. I've asked about their background, looked at their client lists, queried clients, and in general conversed with anyone and everyone in the business who might have something informed to say about literary agents. I've also read everything I could get my hands on regarding agents and the way the business is conducted.

You have probably already begun having agent-conversations with every writer you come in contact with. If you are just beginning in the business and your writer contacts are limited to your peers, they will probably be just as uninformed as you. Never mind, ask anyway. You never know where information lurks.

• *Ask any other screenwriter you can meet, any writing professors at universities, anyone you know. One of the jobs of writing professors is to refer their students to agents. Because the best agencies are constantly seeking to renew themselves by scouting new talent, they stay in touch with the universities. Agents attend screenings from time to time to see new writers and directors who come out of film school.*

Jim Preminger
Jim Preminger Agency
Los Angeles

To help you make a more informed choice, I recommend a book called <u>Reel Power</u> written by Mark Litwak (William Morrow, New York). I endorse it for information about *how it really is* to survive in the film and television businesses and for insightful reporting about what it takes to be an agent:

• *First, an agent must have the stamina to handle a heavy workload and be able to endure the frenetic pace in which business is conducted.* It's like working in the commodities pit, *says William Morris agent Joan Hyler.* It's hectic, *says agent Lisa Demberg,* because you can't do your job unless you're always on the phone, always talking to someone, or socializing with someone or trying to do business, or following up on the projects you've discussed.

Great agents, *says agent-turned-executive Stephanie Brody,* have enthusiasm and tireless energy. And they must be efficient. The agent is juggling 30 phone calls a day. He has to send out material, and follow up. You have to be extremely well-organized.

Second, agents must be able to cope with the vicissitudes of the business. In a certain sense it's like Dialing for Dollars, *says William Morris agent Bobbi Thompson.* Each call may be the big money. You never know. It's all a roulette wheel.

Third, an agent must be an effective salesman.

Fourth, agents must be able to discern talent.

Many top agents are very aggressive in their pursuit of deals, some would say ruthless. Says a former CAA agent, In order to be an extraordinarily successful agent you can't have any qualms about lying, cheating, stealing and being totally into yourself.

Mark Litwak
Reel Power
William Morrow, NY

I was particularly struck by what Joan Hyler said about agenting being like working in the commodities pit. Frequently there is no tangible reason why the commodities market goes up or down, just as there is frequently no tangible reason why one property sells and another one doesn't. It really is "Dialing for Dollars." Is it the same way when we choose an agent? Is it all just kismet?

Maybe, but just in case planning, intelligence and knowledge can inform your luck, let's consider a few things that affect the hierarchy of representation.

Size

The ratio of agents to writers is more crucial to successful representation than the size of the office. One person cannot effectively represent 100 people. It's like going to the store and buying everything you see. You can't possibly use everything, you're just taking it out of circulation. Many agents believe a good ratio is one agent to 20 to 25 clients. An agency with four agents can do well by 100 or even 140 clients, but that really is the limit. Look closely at any lists that are extravagantly over this size. It's easy to get lost on a large list.

• *We have managed to keep the size of the client list relatively small so that we can give a great deal of attention. I think for us, a ratio of 20 clients to one agent is actually a lot. Although I know that there are plenty of literary agents who represent 60-70 clients, I find for the kind of quality work that we do, that 20 each is a lot. We currently do have about 20 to 1, but we'd prefer less.*

Jim Preminger
Jim Preminger Agency
Los Angeles

Access

The dictionary defines access as *ability to approach* or *admittance*. Because the conglomerate agencies have so many star writers on their lists, they have plenty of *ability to approach*. If the studios, networks and producers do not return phone calls, they might find the agency retaliating by withholding the important actors that add credibility to the writer's projects. Mike Ovitz's real talent is not the deals he swings for Bo Goldman, Neil Simon and David Jacobs, it's *attracting* those successful writers.

Those agencies that get *A* for access — The William Morris Agency (WMA), International Creative Management (ICM), Creative Artists Agency (CAA), The Agency for Performing Artists (APA), and United Talent Agency (UTA) do not usually offer career-building services. These large corporations are there to cash in once credibility has already been established. Although it is true that star representation enhances some careers, it is not true in all cases.

In making your agent selections, make sure you are seeking an agent you have the credits to attract. Michael Tolkin's agent is probably not going to be interested. Make sure other clients on the agent's list are your peers. It's all very well and good to think big, but you must walk before you can run. Don't expect an agent who has spent years building his credibility to be interested in someone who just got off the bus. You must effectively agent yourself until you are at a point that a credible agent will give you a reading.

Stature

You don't have to be CAA to have stature. The dictionary defines it as *level of achievement*. So, Stu Robinson and Maggie Field surely have more stature than some lowly agent at William Morris, but possibly not as much muscle — although once you have strong clients, you can beef up pretty fast.

- *An agent is only as strong as the clients he or she represents.*

> Elliot Webb
> Broder•Kurland•Webb•Uffner
> Los Angeles

Style

It's all very well to have stamina, discern talent, have a short list, be a great salesman, have access and stature, but the attribute that can make or break the decision is style. Will you be able to stand talking to this person?

- *There are some agents about whom you would say, this person is never going to be able to help me because I would never want this person going into a studio representing me. And yet, there are some major agents in town you wouldn't want to have a cup of coffee with. Every agent works in his own way.*

> Ken Sherman
> Ken Sherman Agency
> Los Angeles

A friend of mine left her agent because she felt he had not been doing a good job of negotiation. She switched agencies and got a hefty raise on her show. Unfortunately, she lost rapport and communication in the process and ended up leaving that agent as soon as her contract came up for renewal.

Some things are more important than others. Because writing is such a solitary occupation anyway (unless you are on staff), it's worthwhile to have someone you can bounce things off of, so don't sell this attribute short.

Education

Just as some agents evaluate your unseen material by whether or not you have studied at UCLA, NYU or USC, finding out an agent's background and training can give you initial insights into who he/she is and what you might expect from him. Getting in on the ground floor with an agent ambitious enough to survive the grueling training at the large conglomerates may be an important way into the system for you.

Absorbing articles on this subject are: "Slaves of Wilshire Boulevard" by Andy Marx in the November/December 1991 issue of Buzz magazine; "The Players" by Lynn Hirshberg, Vanity Fair, January 1993; and "Is This the Next Mike Ovitz?" by Johanna Schneller, GQ, May 1992.

The articles are not only chilling reading, but they give a feeling for the vulnerability of beginning agents and insights into how to approach the literary power brokers of tomorrow.

I asked agents to switch places with the writers and tell me what they thought writers should be looking for in an agent:

• *Honesty. The agent works for you. You don't want an agent who is conning you. You want someone who is honest. A lot of agents aren't. A lot of agents are. I don't want to ever get in a position where I have to figure out what I said yesterday. If you tell the truth, you don't have to do that.*

> Marty Shapiro
> Shapiro-Lichtman
> Los Angeles

• *I think that if you are a writer that you want to feel that there is someone who is not just selling you on himself or herself to sign you and to keep you off the market, but that you have someone who is generally going to take an interest in you and your work for a long time.*

   I would also pick someone I could stay with for a long time not someone I can see, going into the relationship, that I'm going to outgrow in two years' time.

> Jim Preminger
> The Preminger Agency
> Los Angeles

• *I think first of all you have to evaluate does the agent understand the work? Is he simpatico in practical or abstract ways? You don't have to be crazy about your agent, after all, this is business; more important, does the agent understand your writing? Does he understand you? Does he/she understand you as a person? Is this someone you can feel comfortable calling? Who will you (hopefully) feel comfortable talking to on a regular basis?*

> Ken Sherman
> Ken Sherman Agency
> Los Angeles

• *Evaluate the agent for rapport. Are they comfortable talking to the agent? Be sure they are going with someone who has the time for them. Someone that doesn't have a lot of other new people at the same time because you can only walk in with a certain number of new people at a time. You have to make that decision partly based on the accomplishments of the agency with other people in the past who have been in similar situations. If someone has the kind of track record where they have taken other brand new people and been with them when their careers have been made, then that becomes a plus. What they have to be terribly concerned with is that they don't get snowed and go with someone who is just giving them a line. Of course, they may never get to the point of having to do that because it is difficult at best for them to get into that door.*

> Marty Shapiro
> Shapiro-Lichtman
> Los Angeles

• *My idea of success is sustenance. It's making it last and challenging yourself. You can have all the short term success in the world. You need a plan and you need a partner. My role is varied with each client. I'm not best friends with my clients, I'm very friendly with all of them, but we don't go on vacation. My relationship with some of them is quite formal and professional.*

> Bob Hohman
> Richland/Wunsch/Hohman
> Los Angeles

• *Choose the agent who has the highest enthusiasm for you. A company with five people is probably going to be stronger than a company with one person. But a company with 50 people is not necessarily stronger than a company with five people. The real question is,* Is your agent going to be saying your name every single day? *If the enthusiasm level is there, you are better off with the not-quite-so-important agent. If you are a brand new writer, you are probably better off with The Gersh Agency than with Mike Ovitz.*

Rima Greer
Writers & Artists
Los Angeles

• *If an agent turns you down, don't be depressed. It means that agent would not have been able to sell the project anyway because you can't sell a script unless you have a passion for it. Once you get a passion for a script, you don't put it down. You don't put it down until it's sold. You should only want an agent who is passionate about your work. If you have passion, you can't stop.*

Raphael Berko
Media Artist Group
Los Angeles

Be Patient

Read the agent quotes and statistics carefully before you make judgments about which agent you might seek or even your readiness to attract an agent. Since the information is enhanced by an overview, make sure you have one. Then, go back and read the agent listing section of the book again, taking notes. You'll learn their lineage, education, credits (clients), the size of their list and get some idea of their style.

If an agent interests you, check the index to see if the agent is quoted elsewhere in the book. Those quotes can give you a further clue as to how the agent conducts business, views the world and how compatible you might feel.

If all the names on the agent's list are stars and you are just beginning, that means this agent is too far along for you. If you read his dossier and don't recognize any of the clients' names, they may well be respected working writers whose names you don't happen to know. Ask questions. Perhaps it's an upcoming writer who has not yet sold. Maybe the agent is just starting and is building his list. If you are a beginning writer, perhaps you and the agent can build credibility together. It's worth a shot.

Once you have a list of agents, go by The Writers Guild of America at 8955 Beverly Blvd. in Los Angeles or at 555 West 57th St. in New York and spend an afternoon leafing through the listings of agencies. You can see that CAA has 500 clients and that Broder•Kurland•Webb•Uffner represents The Charles Brothers and James Burrows.

You can access similar information by writing the WGA for The Writers Guild of America Directory ($15.00 plus $2.50 tax and postage). WGA members are listed with representation and key credits. You will begin to get an overview of the agents and also become more knowledgeable about your fellow writers. Look for those agents you have noted. See who their clients are. You'll see famous writers with famous agents, but also some well known clients represented by agents you might not have considered.

If you are a writer of stature, you will be looking for an agent that lists some of your peers. Some fine agencies have opened in the last two or three years whose names may not be as well-known as older agencies, but who nonetheless are quite important. Usually they are agencies started by agents who interned at larger offices, learned the business, groomed some clients, and left the agencies (frequently with some of the agency's choicest clients).

As you look at these lists, you are probably having fantasies about the large conglomerate agencies, but read Chapter 8 on conglomerate/star agencies before you form your final opinion. There are many pros and cons to star representation at various levels of one's career.

While you are salivating, remember that most stars come to star agencies after a struggling independent agent helped the writer achieve enough stature and access of his own so that the conglomerate agent felt his interest was financially justified.

A friend of mine made her decision another way; passing an open door on the way to another agent's office, she overheard the following telephone conversation:

• *If my client's check is not on my desk by 5 p.m. this afternoon, I'm going to come over there and* burn your office down.

The writer decided then and there that this was the agent she wanted.

In making your agent selections, be sure you are seeking an agent you have the credits to attract. Are the other clients on the list your peers? It might be nice to be on the list with William Goldman, but realistically, such stars command larger fees and more devoted attention from their agents than you would. If you are successful in acquiring such an agent, your competition will only make you feel dissatisfied with your results. Remember, one step at a time.

Any agent?

If no credible agent will give you the time of day, is it better to have just anybody? Opinions vary, some subscribe to the theory that although your ego may be fed — *I have an agent* — it may only take you out of the marketplace.

• *A hard question to answer. I'll confine the* any agent *to a real person that the buying community recognizes as a valid agent. Not someone who has an office on Moorpark and charges to read. Even if you are a beginner, you could call the Writers Guild and ask what they know about this particular agent. Or if you know anybody in the business that you can call and say,* Do you know anything about this person? *And if they say,* He's a nice person/she's a nice lady, but she doesn't have much clout, *then you'll have to decide. It all depends on how desperate you are. If it was me personally, if I had faith in my own ability, I'd wait until there was somebody with more credibility, someone that the community recognizes as a valid agent who has been able to sustain and earn a living for whatever, 10-20 years. That should say something for them.*

> Stu Robinson
> paradigm
> Los Angeles

•   *If you have no one else wanting you to sign, carefully evaluate the situation. Does this person seem to be in a situation where he or she can help you? Look around the office. See what some of the names are on the scripts. Check out the writers a bit with the work or with other writer friends. You can say to the agent,* Do I know any of your writers? This is exciting to me, who would be I be with? *It's all in how you present yourself.*

> Ken Sherman
> Ken Sherman Agency
> Los Angeles

•   *Just to get your foot in the door, somebody's got to know somebody somewhere. Even if you are doing the peddling. First of all, most studios won't look at a script without an agent's submission because the town is so litigious. Logistically, it pays to have somebody, a show business lawyer, somebody to represent you.*

> Lynn Pleshette
> Pleshette & Green
> Los Angeles

•   *Well,* hold out *for what? They could* hold out *indefinitely. What are they going to do while they are holding out? All they can do is to continue to write. The writer's interest is in trying to sell something so that he can find someone who is willing to work with him. The writer won't find entree in the marketplace because the studios and the production companies won't talk to him without an agent, so any agent is better than no agent.*

Marty Shapiro
Shapiro-Lichtman
Los Angeles

• *What do you have to lose? You can't accomplish anything without an agent because no one will look at your material.*

Debbee Klein
Irv Schechter Company
Los Angeles

• *Any agent who is signatory to the Writers Guild is better than no agent. Keep writing and keep after the agent. And don't send your own material around to studios and/or producers. Everyone wants to see new material they've never seen before.*

Rima Greer
Writers & Artists
Los Angeles

If you are in the position of choosing, the question to answer is: who will provide the best opportunity for you to be gainfully employed in the business and beyond that to build a real career?

When you have finished this book, you should have some idea of which agents appeal to you. Some names will keep coming up. Make a list. Even if you know you are only interested in Gary Salt or Lucy Kroll, target at least five names. You can't intelligently make a choice unless you have something to compare. You may not be in a situation where more than one agent will see you, but if you are, you can only choose Agent A after you have compared him to Agent B and Agent C.

Ask advice from any show biz insiders (other writers, producers, development executives) with whom you have formed relationships. Explain that you are agent shopping and that you would like advice about the names on your list.

Ask for any names they might like to add. Listen to their opinion but remember, producers and network honchos have a far different relationship with an agent than you will have. Make your own decision.

Wrap Up

The ideal client
✓ has talent
✓ displays a singular personality
✓ exhibits professionalism
✓ maintains mental health
✓ is a WGA member
✓ writes well
✓ is realistic about his career

The ideal agent
✓ is aggressive
✓ has stature
✓ has access
✓ is enthusiastic about your work
✓ shares your vision regarding your career
✓ has an optimum ratio of writers to agents
✓ has integrity
✓ communicates with you
✓ gives you guidance

Research
✓ carefully read the information in this book
✓ check WGA Agent/Client Lists
✓ check The WGA Membership Directory
✓ consult your friends in show business
✓ don't underestimate word of mouth

Query Letter/The Meeting

7

You've finally settled on a list of two or three agents that appeal to you. Since you don't have a connected industry job and you don't know anyone who knows anyone to give you entree to an agent, it's time for your secret weapon: the query letter.

Although many agents do not accept unsolicited scripts, most will respond to query letters. If your letter is interesting or clever enough or incredibly well written, they might ask to see your manuscript. If they don't ask to read something, it's probable that you are not ready yet.

• *The approach is all important. I'll say,* I'm not going to look for anybody else right now, *then the letter or communique is so well done or so well written that we'll say,* let's take a look *either because the writing is so good in the presentation or because they are so clever in their approach. It also depends on what their piece of material is. Invariably, they will say, I've just written this thing about - and then put in a one paragraph synopsis and you realize that none of this sounds as though it's anything, whereas someone coming out of UCLA will say,* I just wrote three "Cheers" or I have a sample script for "Cheers" or "Northern Exposure" *or whatever or they are in a Masters program at UCLA and you might say,* Hey, let's take a look at it.

I would generally ask, How many agents have you gone to before you came to me? *If they have been to agents, then we may try to qualify it and say,* well, we'll look at it, but not in competition with anybody else. If we like it, we want to be able to sign you.

> Martin Shapiro
> Shapiro-Lichtman
> Los Angeles

• *Although 90% of the writers we see are through referral and we are inundated with query letters, it never hurts to try. A clever note or a clever package gets our attention. We have a writer with a spec feature who came to us from SC film school [via a recommendation].*

> Debbee Klein
> Irv Schechter Company
> Los Angeles

• *When you write a query letter, take the time to find out who you are writing to. If you are writing a letter to* Dear Sir *or* Madam, *you haven't taken the time to find out enough about the company you are hoping will represent you. Why should that person take two hours of* their *time to read your script? Names are important and very easy to get. Simply call the agency and ask for the name of the person you should write to.*

> Barbara Alexander
> Media Artists Group
> Los Angeles

• *The shorter, the sweeter, the more successful. And make it easy on the agent. If you want a reply, send a card with a sase envelope with the agency's return address written on it so the agent doesn't have to write that in.*

> Candy Monteiro/Fredda Rose
> Monteiro Rose
> Los Angeles

• *Calling an agent who doesn't have time for you is wasting everybody's energy. Somewhere at some agency, there is some guy who doesn't have any clients. An agent at a mid-level place or a*

young agent at a big conglomerate like ICM are prime agents to target. Four senior agents and one shlepper who would like to have someone to call his/her own. That's the person. There are people there who would take a pocket *client.*
>   Daniel Ostroff
>   Daniel Ostroff Agency
>   Los Angeles

I talked to a writer just the other day who told me he had sent his material to CAA and received a letter in reply asking to be kept abreast of new material. It was signed and there was a phone number. The writer assumed it was some low level person who didn't count, he said. That low level person is only beginning, he will not be on the bottom rung of the ladder long. This is the kind of contact that Ostroff was describing. Don't be put off thinking you have no entree. If you have a feature script, there is always someone who will give it a look. Particularly at big conglomerates. What do you care if it is someone in the mail room who is writing back to you? People in the mail room are Harvard law school graduates and the like who will be moving up.

An anecdote to give everyone heart concerns writer, Isbel Nagy Storey.

• *Storey sent her script to agents and producers in November and within four days got a response from powerful Creative Artists Agency.*
Of the 14 production companies to which Storey sent "Stolen Love: A Child of Her Own," 10 wanted to make it and four agencies vied to represent her.
>   "Writer's First Script
>   Draws a Speedy Response"
>   Walter Hamilton
>   <u>The Green Sheet</u>
>   February 8, 1993

It's not as though Storey was a rank beginner in the business. The article didn't say this, but it's my guess that her submissions to production companies and agents were not *blind submissions*, but were *walked or talked* in by people she knew since she was already in the business.

• *We don't accept any unsolicited material. If you send us an unsolicited script, it'll go into the recycling bin, which in our case is not the garbage can, it's actually a recycling bin. It will only be sent back if there is a self addressed stamped envelope. It's okay to send a short treatment or a synopsis though I probably won't read that either. The thing I will read is a letter. If in that letter you have a one or two paragraph synopsis of the story, that's good, so I know what it is that you are trying to send me. If the subject matter really interests me, I might read a treatment if it's enclosed or I might contact you to send me one. Anything beyond that will not be read, will not be returned.*
  Stuart Jacobs
  CNA
  Los Angeles

• *Anything over the transom, not requested, we won't read. We will call them to come get it, we don't like to dump it. We do take query letters.*
  Jonathan Westover
  The Gage Group
  Los Angeles

• *Always try to get an introduction or a name of somebody in your inquiry letter. Don't fabricate it, it's too small a town. The key that is going to get attention is good writing. That's the truth. I wish I could show you some of the things we get in in the wrong format. You know immediately, it's a first script and no one's bothered to do his homework.*
  Barbara Alexander
  Media Artists Group
  Los Angeles

Jonathan and Stuart are not the only agents who feel this way.
Most not only prefer a letter, but place great stock in it:

• *If people are just going to write letters, a letter is a letter, I
get hundreds of letters. The only reason I called the one team I
have signed from a query letter was because the letter they sent put
me on the floor, it was so funny. It was as funny as anything
you've seen on television and when I read it, I laughed so hard that
I said,* these guys are worth talking to. *That's why I met with
them.*
> Stuart Jacobs
> CNA
> Los Angeles

• *For legal reasons, we look at no unsolicited material. We do
respond to query letters as long as they come with self-addressed-
stamped envelopes. Nine times out of ten, we're not going to take
material that comes from a query letter, but occasionally I do. I
have two scripts now that first came to my attention through a
query letter, but the query letter outlined a script I was interested in
reading. But that's unusual.*
> Gary Salt
> The Kohner Agency
> Los Angeles

• *They can send a mailing out to agents, not a manuscript, but a
description of the material and a brief resume. [They should say]
whether they have written for cable, magazine articles, school
plays, student films or a graduate film.*
> Lynn Pleshette
> Pleshette and Green
> Los Angeles

• *There are a lot a query letters that I do like, but I don't make
the phone call. I have a file of maybe 100 letters about scripts that
I actually like, but if we called every single one of them, we'd have
no room on our floors or time to do our jobs. Who knows when we*

will get to them? But there are certain letters that stand out, that make us say, There's something cool here.

> Anonymous Agent
> Los Angeles

• *There has to be something in the letter, not just a synopsis of the script or a tag line, but something about them, either an educational background or a career background. Something that says,* okay, this person knows how to write and has something to say.

> Jonathan Westover
> The Gage Group
> Los Angeles

• *I respond to the idea, to how well the letter is written, the letter itself. I think if they can't write a letter, they can't write a script.*

> Lynn Pleshette
> Pleshette and Green
> Los Angeles

Whether you live in the large production centers or not, the query letter is an essential component to your acceptance to the system. When you consider how carefully agents read your letters, you will unquestionably want to take just that much care in how you write it. The letter should be brief, articulate and informative. Tell them who you are, list your most important credit (if you have one), give a three or four line synopsis of your story or idea (look to see how TV Guide does it) and ask if they would be interested in reading it. The more you tell, the more they have to reject. Be brilliant and/or witty, and above all, be <u>brief</u>. Mainly, be businesslike.

The Meeting

If you have entree to meet with several agents, by all means do so.

- *It's not that easy to get an appointment with an agent and get read, but if a writer has entree, I think he should meet with several agents.*

  I tell clients that I am signing, You should go and you should meet with these other people because they may be better for you, they may service you in a way that I hadn't thought of. You guys may click in a way that we're not going to. *I think it's really about forming relationships that are going to last where both the agent and the client feel that their needs are being met.*

  Certainly, I would advise anyone to shop around so that you will be happy signing with me. I don't want them to have to worry that in 3 or 4 or 5 months, they'll think, Gee, that other agent seemed so great, I wish I had at least taken a meeting. *Take the meeting and feel comfortable with that choice or at least try and work on the relationship that they are in.*

  Stuart Jacobs/Glen Brunswick
  CNA
  Los Angeles

For starters, be on time and look terrific. This is a job interview, after all. Choose clothing that makes you feel good and look successful and that suggests you take pride in yourself. Bright colors not only make people remember you, but they usually make you feel good, too. Remember, in today's world, packaging is at least as important as content.

- *I read every letter that comes in to me. If there is a sase envelope, I will respond with a form letter. Of the 100s and 100s of letters I have received, I think I have responded twice and one of them, I signed. These writers came in unshaven and in shorts and weird shirts and I fell in love with those guys, but that is who they are.*

  If somebody comes in and they haven't showered in three days and they are cantankerous and you just don't want to be in the room with them, then, yes, I would have felt better about them if they had showered and shaved. If it's your personality, if you only wear t-shirts and Reeboks, then be who you are. When my writers

*go into meetings with people, I want them to be who they are, they
are selling their mind to people and it's really about that rather
than an Armani suit. If someone is comfortable wearing a suit and
tie, I'd love to see them in a suit and tie for the meetings.*
    Stuart Jacobs/Glen Brunswick
    CNA
    Los Angeles

Go in and act like yourself. Be natural and forthright. Don't
badmouth any other agents. If you are leaving another agent, don't
get into details about why you are leaving. If he asks, say it wasn't
working out. Agents are all members of the same fraternity.
Unless this agent is stealing you away from someone else, he will
be at least a little anxious about why you are leaving. If you
badmouth another agent, the agent you are meeting with is
wondering — subconsciously, at least — when you will bad-mouth
him.

Don't talk too much. Give yourself a chance to get comfortable.
Adjust to the environment. Notice the surroundings. Comment on
them. Talk about the weather. Talk about the stock market, the
basketball game, or the last play you saw. That's a great topic, it
gives you each a chance to check out the other's taste.

If you do discuss a play or a film, don't just agree with him, say
what you think. If you hated it, be tactful (the writer may be his
client), just say it didn't work for you. Remember, this is a first
date. You are both trying to figure out if you are interested in each
other.

If you admire one of his clients, say so. Don't be afraid to ask
questions, but use common sense. Phrase questions in a positive
vein. Discuss producers that you know and have worked for. Tell
the agent what your plans are and ask him if they seem realistic.
Are you on the same wavelength? How does he see your career
progressing? Don't just *send out* make sure you are also *receiving.*

Find out how the office works. If you are being interviewed by the owner and there are other agents, ask the owner if he will be representing you personally. Many owners are not involved in agenting on a day-to-day basis.

Find out office policy about returning phone calls. Are you welcome to call? Does the agent want feedback after each meeting? What's the protocol for dropping by? Will they consistently read your work? Will they consult with you before turning down work? Explore your feelings about these issues before the meeting.

If you need to be able to speak to your agent regularly, address that issue. If these conversations turn the agent off, better to find out now. This is the time to assess the chemistry between the two of you.

During the meeting, be alert for subtle things that define a person, how he treats his employees, whether he really listens. Notice his body language and how he is with people on the phone. How you feel when he's speaking to you. What's the subtext?

Ending the Meeting

When the meeting is over, be the one to end it. No one can be fascinating forever so get the hell out of there before the agent finds that out. Schedule a trip to your dentist immediately following to give you the urgency needed to depart.

If the agent tells you at this point that he would like you for a client and you don't feel the need to think it over, swell. More than likely, he will need to discuss the matter with the rest of the office so don't be downhearted if things seem a little vague. Let him know you were pleased with the meeting. Even if it was not your finest moment —or his— be gracious. After all, you both did your best. Tell him you've enjoyed meeting him, but that you have another appointment. Let him wonder where. Leave.

My advice is to hurry home and write down all your perceptions and feelings about the meeting and put them away for 24 hours. Then write your feelings down again and compare them. When I was interviewing agents for this book, I found that I would have signed with almost all of them on the spot. They are all salesmen and they were charming. By the next day I was more objective about it all. By then, the hyperbole seemed to have drifted out of my head and I was able to hear more clearly what had gone on.

If the agent says he will call you and doesn't, leave it. There are others on your list. If he forgot you, do you want him as your agent? If he is rejecting you, don't insist he do it to your face.

If he does call, be circumspect in your decision. You are choosing an agent. The qualities you look for in a pal are not necessarily the qualities you desire in an agent. There are very successful writers who deal with brusque, self-centered agents that have masterminded brilliant careers.

Many artists feel anxious about choosing an agent. They feel their whole career is on the line. It's not. The agent is your business partner. Your writing is the basis of your career, not your agent.

Wrap Up

The query letter
- ✓ must be interesting, clever, brief and innovative
- ✓ needs to demonstrate you've done your homework and understand how the business works
- ✓ needs to include self addressed envelope and postage

Tools to set up meetings
- ✓ referrals
- ✓ credits
- ✓ awards
- ✓ resume
- ✓ great writing

The meeting
- ✓ be punctual
- ✓ act intelligently
- ✓ be sure to dress well
- ✓ focus on what you want
- ✓ ask for what you want
- ✓ end the meeting

Conglomerate Agencies

If you are really hot and Mike Ovitz is buying your dinner, perhaps you want to consider life at the top of the agency roster with one of the big conglomerates. Could you resist? Should you? After all, Creative Artists is the most powerful agency in the world. Wouldn't everybody rather have CAA?

When my friend Mary, first begàn to make some real money as a writer (about $150,000 a year), she succumbed to the seductions of one of the big three. Though happy with her change in status, she found she didn't have money to pay her bills since the agent was not making sure that her checks came through in a timely manner. When she called to complain, the agent was irritated and said: *I wish you were more successful and made more money so you wouldn't be calling me about money all the time.*

It didn't take her long to call up her old agent, admit she had made a big mistake and return home. She's even more successful now and her rising fortunes are the result of her excellent writing and the efforts and courage of her prestigious independent agent.

- *A lot of the people that I am representing were at bigger places (CAA, William Morris, etc.). Let's say that your agent left the business and you have been at a nice small place for a long time where you have had lots of attention. All of a sudden, you are faced with a decision, you weren't unhappy with your represent-ation, but that person no longer exists.*
  The dog and pony show that these big places do is (and I was

at a big agency and I used to do it), Here we are, we are all powerful and all connected and look at all the information we have *(and they pull out reams of paper)* and we represent all these movie stars and we'll package you with our people and we'll use our clout to get you this and that.

For 75% of the list, that's heinous bullshit, because it's impossible to spread that wealth around. It's clout because it's only used on a few people, that's why they call it clout. It's impossible to service 150 directors well. CAA has a gigantic directors list and I would say they do an incredible job for about 25% of that list. The rest of them, I hope it works out.

The point is that with some people, they wake up one day and say, Gee, I'm here at this big agency and I keep getting shuffled from one agent to another. How do I access that *clout? And they decide they need a little more personal representation. Large agencies give very personal representation to about 25% of their clients. The rest of them are dangling.*

A lot of the people that I've gotten into business with aren't seduced by the clout thing. I've been here at the party long enough, I can get anybody on the phone and frankly if a client of mine is a long shot on a project, he has a much better chance with me because I'm only calling about him, I'm not calling about 10 people with bigger names or 10 equally long shot names.

Most people in the business are not operating at the highest levels. They're having good careers and making a good living off it. What you need to make sure is that you are maintaining that level and that you have someone who is keeping you fresh and keeping you out there. It takes very personal focused representation.

I don't represent Bernardo Bertulucci and I don't represent Sydney Pollock. While I would love to represent both of them, I probably never will. I'm very realistic about who I am as an agent. I represent a very nice high end writer and director base, but they are all people that I feel some sort of parity with as people. I'm very proud of and very comfortable with the people I represent and I think we deal with each other as equals. I always approach it that I'm able to give them the time that they deserve or I wouldn't have taken them on.

Bob Hohman
Richland/Wunsch/Hohman
Los Angeles

• *We're a small agency that's been able to take people all the way. We always have people at every level from the lowest level, from the writer looking for his first job to people who are writing their own series.*

Elliot Stahler
Kaplan Stahler
Los Angeles

• *There are certain kinds of clients who want to be with us. The thing that separates the wheat from the chaff is that I think we are with a very realistic group of people. We have very few virgins, we've all been around for a while. We are in the business with a lot of adults who know what representation is all about. We have a relatively small practice. We are not in the volume business. We don't take people on just for money. It wouldn't be worth it. We have to have a real affinity for the person's work.*

Bob Hohman
Richland/Wunsch/Hohman
Los Angeles

• *Obviously I've chosen to spend my life in a small setting, part of that is based on the fact that I'm most comfortable in a smaller setting, so if a writer chooses to go with us, they probably choose us because they think they <u>won't</u> get lost here. It's a matter of individual choice, some writers like the razzle dazzle of the larger agency with just the sheer amount of activity and the access to whatever those resources are.*

Jim Preminger
Jim Preminger Agency
Los Angeles

• *I'm real opinionated about the agency business. I know a lot about it, it's the only thing I've ever done...I'm very happy being in a small agency environment. The primary difference between a big agency and a small agency is that it's impossible for a big agency not to have its own agenda. Some portion of the clients end up serving that agenda whether that is in their best interests or not. Small agencies are generally about the clients' interests and desires. It's far more client driven. The big agency has a big overhead, whereas we have a very contained, intelligently drawn overhead which is fairly easy to meet. We are recession proof whereas a big agency isn't. My partners and I feel that we have enough successful clients and that there is always enough prosperity that if you say,* You know, I want to take off a year and write a book, *we're able to say* good for you *assuming that you have the financial wherewithal to do that. It really is a marriage relationship where it is, hopefully, two adults trying to behave like adults with each other. If you want to do something that isn't financially remunerative, then that's your decision. It's far more about your desire than it's about us needing to use your talents.*

Bob Hohman
Richland/Wunsch/Hohman
Los Angeles

What's the Best Decision?

I guess we've all heard the joke about the writer who killed four people, stole a baby, bombed a building, then ran across the street into The William Morris Agency, and was never seen again. It's the quintessential story about the wisdom of being signed by a big conglomerate agency.

The whole question of whether the large star-level conglomerate agency is the best place to be is pretty heady. Both sides of this issue have validity. In the end, as in all other important decisions (who to marry, which doctor or lawyer to hire, whether or not to have elective surgery, etc.), you can only collect data and then, using your research and instincts, decide.

I hate to say it, but research leads to the conclusion that the star agencies (CAA, ICM, WMA, UTA, APA) have the most power, the most information, and the best likelihood of getting you in for meetings and ultimately, jobs, if someone there who is powerful and/or hungry believes in you. It's a fact that the conglomerates have more power and information. The questions are:

What will they do with it? And do power and information compensate for lack of personal attention?

The fact is that the power of the large agencies comes from the star actors, writers and directors. When you have Joe Eszterhas, Diane English, Neil Simon, Joshua Brand and John Falsey on your list (plus hundreds of other big names) you have the attention of the buyers. The Catch-22 is, if you are Eszterhas or English, you really don't need those agencies (because you are the power) and, if you're not one of those folk, you are mainly filler.

I did a film a couple of years ago with a young director, who, as a result of his good work on the film, managed to land CAA as his agent. He ended up leaving them because he said all the bigger name directors (almost everyone else) got all the good scripts. He is now with a prestigious smaller agency and is finally working again.

• *When I was in a one-room office on 57th Street in New York, I was as powerful as anyone, if I believed in someone. I could get them in anyplace, because I wouldn't take no for an answer. I believe if someone works out of a phone booth on Hollywood and Vine, if they believe in you, they can get you in as quickly as the strongest agent in town.*

> John Kimble
> William Morris Agency
> Los Angeles

Gene Parseghian (WMA), even confessed to me that there are days he wishes he still had a small office with three or four people and 20 clients, tops.

As mentioned elsewhere in the book, conglomerates are not equipped to handle clients who are not making a lot of money. They have a big overhead. They are usually not interested in building careers. They take you while you're hot and drop you when you're not.

I found UTA and APA (both in Los Angeles and New York) to be approachable, in spite of their being conglomerates. ICM, WMA, and CAA are all very close mouthed, so the historical background I provide on these agencies is from the trades and the popular press.

Tracking the machinations of the power struggles among the conglomerates is fascinating. The following is quoted from a chapter devoted to CAA ("The Rise of CAA") in the excellent book by Mark Litwak called Reel Power.

•   *More powerful than Sylvester Stallone, Steven Spielberg or Barry Diller, the most influential person in Hollywood is not a star, a director or a studio head. While his name is rarely in the news media and he never gets a screen credit, everyone who matters in the industry knows who he is. He is assiduously courted by producers and studio heads alike, because they need his cooperation in order to gain the services of the best writers, stars and directors in the industry. He is Mike Ovitz, the president of Creative Artists Agency.*

CAA does not have the bureaucracy of William Morris or the bickering of ICM. It has restrained its growth and has carefully chosen its agents with an eye toward their ability to work well together. CAA partner Martin Baum says his agency is successful because its agents put the welfare of the agency ahead of their own interests. The policy of this company from its inception has been that we all profit if one succeeds. *It has been the first time that there has been a total sublimation of the individual ego for the betterment of the group.*

The rise of CAA is a particular sore point with William Morris, where the original CAA partners learned the business. The partners were considered the best and brightest and when they left Morris, it was a traumatic experience for the proud agency. It was like their sons left, *said WMA agent Debra Greenfield. There had never been a mass defection before.*

Mark Litwak
Reel Power
William Morrow & Co.
New York

I heartily recommend Reel Power for insights into the motion picture business.

In 1991 and 1992, there was an enormous shifting of power among the star agencies. CAA became even more powerful when Mike Ovitz besides representing seemingly all the big writers, directors and actors in the business, acted as the power broker in the buyout of Universal Films by the Japanese company, Matsushita, and most recently stirred up a storm of controversy by signing on as consultant to France's powerful Credit Lyonnais Bank.

The other earth shattering event is detailed in the August 1991 issue of Premiere magazine.

- *It didn't sound like big news at first—just a terse announcement in the trades that senior William Morris agent Toni Howard had ankled her post for International Creative Management, taking with her such star clients as Anjelica Huston, James Spader, and Jason Robards. But a week later, when Elaine Goldsmith and Risa Shapiro joined her, taking Julia Roberts, Tim Robbins, and Andie MacDowell, it began to look serious.*

"The Case of the Ankling Agents"
Premiere Magazine
August 1991

Get hold of a copy of Premiere and read the whole story. It is fascinating. ICM now has a much more even standing with CAA in the quantity and quality of their stars. Name actors are only the first line of ammunition for a conglomerate agency. If you've got the star actors, you make it a point to have the star writers and directors.

In the Fall of 1992, seeking to recover from its previous losses, The William Morris Agency finally consummated the long rumored acquisition of Triad. At the same time, boutique powerhouse InterTalent threw in the towel when its president, Bill Block, returned to the fold at ICM. The other principals from InterTalent fanned out to various other agencies, most notably United Talent.

• *Capping a historic week for Hollywood's agencies and ending four months of secretive negotiations, the 95-year old William Morris Agency has acquired Triad Artists in an aggressive move to help resuscitate its motion picture business and reinstate its image as an entertainment powerhouse.*

"William Morris Bulks up on Triad"
Claudia Eller
Daily Variety
October 10, 1992

• *After protracted negotiations, International Creative Management officials confirmed yesterday that InterTalent Agency topper Bill Block and 12 of his associates have joined ICM as expected.*

The 38-year-old Block — who is returning to ICM after four years of running his own shop — has been installed as head of the agency's West Coast office, with day to day responsibilities for the motion picture and television areas.

After heading the agency's literary department for four years, Block ankled ICM in February 1988 to launch ITA (InterTalent) with Creative Artists Agency counterparts David Greenblatt and Judy Hofflund.

Just over a week ago, in order to bolster its agent and talent ranks, mid-size United Talent Agency signed deals with former ITA partners Hofflund, J.J. Harris and David Schiff.

"Block, 12 Others Join ICM"
Claudia Eller
Daily Variety
October 23, 1992

The big three in order are: CAA, ICM, and WMA. Although William Morris is currently #3, they are closing in fast. Every day WMA acquires some new filmmaker from one of their prestigious competitors. Next in line are APA and UTA. United Talent's most prestigious ancestor was the powerhouse literary agency Bauer Benedek).

You'd probably be thrilled to be in the company of the names on any of these lists. There are, of course, name writers at many other agencies in town, other than the conglomerates. Check The WGA Directory.

If They Want You

If one of the star/conglomerate agencies beckons, you can be sure they will do it with great style: limos, fancy restaurants and other appealing lures.

What do independent agents think of all this? During the interviews, I kept hearing agents saying over and over, *I got this person started. Just when it was all paying-off, CAA or ICM came with the limos, the flowers. The client left. Why?*

I'm reminded of something Elliot Stahler said when I asked about writers changing agents: *Some clients demonstrate a certain amount of immaturity through their susceptibility to other agents telling them what they will do for them, etc.*

He's right, of course. It is immature. It's hard to be balanced in the face of luxury. But, when all the wine is drunk, the dinner at Maple Drive is over and the limos have gone home, you're going to have to make your decision based on what is important to you. Do you want a family member or do you want a corporation?

So there you are. My final vote is for a prestigious, successful, tasteful mid-size agency. Of course, no one has plied me with limos and flowers yet, either.

Wrap Up

Conglomerates
✓ have more information
✓ command more power
✓ have access to more perks
✓ can package effectively
✓ provide less support in times of duress
✓ give advice that is corporate, less personal
✓ have a big overhead
✓ lose interest when you are not in demand

Divorce?

It's difficult to decide where to place information about relationships that don't work out. When I first started writing about agents, I began the book talking about this painful subject and vigilant folk pointed out that you have to have an agent before you can leave him.

That is true, but some people reading this book may already have an agent and are contemplating leaving. Even if you've never had an agent, you might find a discussion of relationship difficulties enlightening. The writer may be leaving just because he's not selling any material and that may not be the agent's fault.

If your agent won't return your calls, if he's been dishonest or is not getting your material around, you have good reason to leave your agent.

In the rules of The Writers Guild, if a writer has had no work in 90 days, he can void his contract with an agent by sending a letter to the agent plus copies to the Guild dissolving the partnership citing Article 7. Maybe you and your agent have different ideas regarding your potential. This is something that should have been ironed out before the contract was signed, but sometimes that conversation comes later in the relationship.

Sometimes careers change and writers feel they can be better serviced by agents with a different sets of contacts.

• *The writer/agent relationship is usually a temporary relationship, and we mustn't wear our hearts on our sleeves. We've got to do the job as well as we can, knowing that the client, with some justice, will leave eventually.*

"Les Liaisons Dangereuses"
<u>The Journal</u>
June 1991

Perhaps your level of achievement in the business has risen. You have now, through brilliance or possibly a lucky break, become a writer of greater stature than your agent. (Very possible if fortune has just smiled on you.)

There are different points of view, but the bottom line is that writer/agent relationships are just like any other relationship: as long as it's mutually rewarding, everyone is happy, when it's not, things must change.

Writers and agents seek each other because they see money-making potential. 35 perfectly credible agents may pass on you and then agent number 36 will fall in love, send your material to the right place with the right director, and you are suddenly a star.

It can happen the other way, too, of course. One minute you're hot and the next moment you're not. You didn't necessarily do anything so differently to get un-hot (frequently getting hot works the same way).

• *The business is high stakes. It's easy for another agent to whisper in a client's ear,* I could do better for you. *It was done as far back as the apocryphal story about Swifty Lazar telling Humphrey Bogart,* I could get you four deals in a day *and he did and he got Bogart as a client. Even then, there was a tremendous amount of competition to represent talented people because that's where the strength is.*

Elliot Webb
Broder•Kurland•Webb•Uffner
Los Angeles

At a smaller agency, being *warm* or even *cold* won't necessarily make you persona grata or non grata, but at the big agencies, it might be difficult for you to get your agent on the phone.

The larger agencies are not in the business to handle less profitable jobs, so they either drop you or their lack of interest finally tells you that you're no longer on their level. The reality is that representing someone is very time consuming. And time is money. Answering calls and being on call. They end up being rude to you because they can't afford to take the time to talk to someone they can't sell anymore. This is the moment when you might be sorry you left that small agent who worked so hard to get you started and engineered the big break for you. Will he want to see you now? He might. He might not. It depends on how you handled it when leaving.

I asked agents if they ever dumped clients and if so, why?

• *Drop clients? When it's a mutual thing. We try for a period of time and if we haven't been able to do it. We have a responsibility to the writer and if you feel that you'd like to get someone else, we'd certainly understand. We wouldn't throw somebody out.*
We have dropped people when they have been abusive. We are in a highly charged business and we really don't have to tolerate that.

> Martin Shapiro
> Shapiro-Lichtman
> Los Angeles

• *I would only get rid of a client for two reasons: if they don't keep writing (18 months without a new script) or if they are unpleasant to deal with. Life is too short.*

> Rima Greer
> Writers & Agents
> Los Angeles

• *There are some agents that clean house at the beginning of the year. If the client hasn't made x amount of money in a year or two, they automatically sever the relationship. I tend to think if I liked a writer once, that it's going to work eventually.*

Barbara Alexander
Media Artists Group
Los Angeles

• *Sometimes there are hard decisions that need to be made if someone's career is foundering. Sometimes we really have to say it's time for the writer to sit down and do something that he hasn't done before, which is to write a spec that is more in line with what the marketplace wants now.*

"Les Liaisons Dangereuses"
The Journal
June 1991

Maybe you want to leave your agent because the magic has gone out of your marriage just as the magic can go out of a traditional marriage if both partners don't put energy into it. And just as in marriage, it's always a better deal to try to rekindle the relationship, if possible. You were in love once, what went wrong? If you are both willing to save the relationship, that process will take a lot less energy and resourcefulness than the just learning to get to know each other period involved in any new relationship.

• *The first thing a writer thinks of that needs to be changed when they are not doing well is his agent. Rather than look on the outside, you have to look inward: examine what you have been doing — the quality of your work. Are you a good communicator with the producers you have been working with and with your agent? Have you burned bridges? Is your work as good as it should be? All these things should be examined before you change agents. There are good agents and bad agents, but you carry your problems from one place to another.*

Fredda Rose/Candy Monteiro
Monteiro Rose
Los Angeles

Don't Wait Until It's Too Late

If something is bothering you, speak up. This comes easily to very few people. We all want to be liked and it's hard to confront the situation. If you are unhappy and feel you will never sell anything again, call your agent and tell him you are concerned. He knows as well as you that you are not selling. Ask him if there is anything you can do. Ask if he has heard any negative feedback.

Whatever you do, don't just start interviewing other agents. You owe it to yourself and to your agent to talk before you get so angry that it is impossible for you to continue the relationship. If you have a conversation early on, perhaps both of you can find some way to remedy the situation. If not, at least he will have some idea of where you are coming from later when you are ready to leave.

- *We don't want clients not communicating, sitting at home, stewing and brewing. I don't mind if a client calls once every two weeks and says,* hey, what can I do?

  Stu Robinson
  paradigm
  Los Angeles

- *You should be able to talk to each other and understand where you are each coming from. There may come a time where you are at a crossroads where the agent's experience and belief is that this is not the right thing for your client to be doing. If both the client and agent have differing thoughts about direction, then you have to go your separate ways because the client isn't going to be happy until he finds out if his ideas are correct.*

  Candy Monteiro/Fredda Rose
  Monteiro Rose
  Los Angeles

Telling/Shopping

Before you start looking for a new agent, you must make a decision about telling your current agent you are going to leave. Most writers are hesitant not only because they are embarrassed and guilty, but also because they feel the agent might stop submitting their material. The writer would be left unrepresented while he is shopping. First of all, I doubt the agent would want to forego the commissions due on any new jobs. Every agent I questioned said he would never leave a writer without representation while he was shopping. Secondly, if he wants to keep you, this is his chance to demonstrate you are making a mistake and he really is the best agent in the world, after all.

Another plus for telling your agent that you are shopping is you don't have to worry about word getting back to him prematurely that you are doing research or actually interviewing. Not only that, any producers you contact during your search will note you are a person of integrity.

Leavetaking

If it is too late for a talk or you talked and it didn't help, at least leave with a little class. Even though it might be uncomfortable, get on with it. There is no need for long recriminations. No excuses. Not *My wife thinks* or *My manager thinks*. No, it's *I've decided that I am going to make a change. I appreciate all the work you have done for me. I will miss seeing you, but it just seems like the time to make a change. For whatever reason, it's just not working. I hope we'll see each other again.*

You don't need to be phony. If you don't appreciate what the agent has done and don't think he's done any work, just skip it. Talk about the fact that you think the relationship is not, or is no longer, mutually rewarding. Be honest and leave both of you with some dignity. You may see this person again. With some distance between you, you might even remember why you signed with him in the first place. Don't close doors.

If you are leaving because your fortunes have risen, it is even harder. The agent will really be upset to see you and your money leave. Also, your new-found success has probably come from his efforts as well as yours. But if you are really hot and feel only CAA or ICM can handle you, leave you must. Tell your agent you wish it were another way but the vicissitudes of the business indicate that at a certain career level, CAA and their peers have more information, clout, and other stars to bargain with, and you want to go for it.

If you handle it well and if your agent is smart, he will leave the door open. This has happened to him before and it will happen to him again. That doesn't make it hurt less, but this is business, he will probably just shake his head and tell his friends you have gone crazy.

This isn't the same Mary I always knew. It's gone to her head.

The agent has to find some way to handle it just as you would if he were firing you. It will not be easy for you to begin a new business relationship, but you are hot right now and the world is rosy.

Wrap Up

Grounds for divorce
- ✓ dishonesty
- ✓ writer abuse
- ✓ agent not reading your work
- ✓ agent not getting your work read
- ✓ sudden career change
- ✓ lack of communication
- ✓ differing goals
- ✓ personality differences

Ethical, smart professional and personal behavior
- ✓ speak to agent before shopping
- ✓ don't burn bridges

The Relationship

All your good work has paid off and you have now been proposed to and you have accepted. You and your agent are going to sign the piece of paper — you now have representation.

Setting Up Shop

The next stop is your new partner's office to sign contracts and meet and fix in your mind all the auxiliary people who will be working for you. If there are too many to remember on a first meeting, make notes as soon as you leave the office as to who is who and where they sit. Until you become more familiar with them, you can consult the map before each subsequent visit.

Now the real work begins. If this agent is a replacement for an old partnership, perhaps you are leaving your old agent because you felt he didn't work hard enough. Maybe your expectations were out of line. Maybe you were lazy. Maybe you didn't keep his enthusiasm high enough. Maybe he was a goof-off. It doesn't matter now. What matters now is how well you and your new agent are going to function together.

90%-10%

The agent only gets 10% of the money so you can't really expect him to do 100% of the work. The concept of 90%-10% is intriguing. How many of us have resented our agents when we have been requested for a job and all the agent had to do was negotiate? In fact, if all our jobs were requests, would we just have a lawyer negotiate and do away with the agent altogether? Or is the support and feedback worth something?

Maybe our whole thought process about agents is incorrect. In our hearts, we really think the agent is going to get us a job. Based upon my years in the business and my research, I finally really know that the agent does not get my work. He gets my appointments, but my work gets me work. Not only by my ability to function well in my profession, but also by my successful (or not) adjustment to the vicissitudes of my own life.

The times I have not worked as steadily have been directly connected to my rise and fall as a person. Life processes must be endured. We can change agents and mates and clothes sizes, but we can't alter reality, we must experience it. Those realities are reflected in our work and enrich us as artists.

As in all relationships, each party assumes certain responsibilities. And as in all relationships, things go much smoother when both parties are putting energy into the union and have mutual expectations.

Be pragmatic regarding what you have a right to demand of an agent, what you can realistically expect of an agent, and what your contribution is to the mix. A novice writer's expectations of his agent should be far different than expectations of the writer who is paying a major portion of the agent's rent.

In the interest of keeping you from feeling paranoid about your agreement with your agent, I asked several agents what they felt were reasonable expectations in the writer/agent relationship.

• *You have a right to expect the best professional judgement I can give you. The best professional opinions that I can give you with respect to your work. That within the limits of normal business practice and within the normal limits of working days that the agency is looking out for your interests, promoting your work, subject to a general consensus between writer and agent that the work is promotable.*

Gary Salt
Paul Kohner, Inc.
Los Angeles

• *Writers have a right to expect their agents return their phone calls, tell them the truth and work hard on their behalf.*

Maggie Field
The Maggie Field Agency
Los Angeles

• *The writer has a right to expect that the agent earns his 10%. He should pick up the phone and at least say* hello *and give the client an update on his material.*

Debbee Klein
Schechter Company
Los Angeles

• *Frequent, honest open communication. Support for their dreams. If you are not in sync with each other about what the goals are, why bother? Also, it's a writer's prerogative to expect a great deal of patience. If it doesn't happen with the first round of submissions, some agents think it's over. Your agent should be your best professional friend.*

Candy Monteiro/Fredda Rose
Monteiro Rose
Los Angeles

• *You have a right to expect your agent to work for his 10%. You should be able to speak to him every week. Just hello and an update is fine* and *the agent should attend your tapings.*

Debbee Klein
Irv Schechter Company
Los Angeles

• *As a client you have a right to expect an honest, open relationship. With a brand new writer, there's not a lot you can do, but the agent should be sending out your material and trying to introduce you to the community as a new talent so that people get to know you.*

> Martin Shapiro
> Shapiro-Lichtman
> Los Angeles

• *The agent is your link to the outside world. It's helpful if your agent is thinking of you enough to pick up the phone and call you, even if I just say,* there's nothing happening right now, it's a very dry time of the year, but never fear because in 6 weeks or 13 weeks, staffing will begin.

> Rima Greer
> Writers & Artists
> Los Angeles

• *The agent is not an editor, but if he has been doing the job for any length of time, he or she does have the advantage of having read more material than any writer will ever read...ever. I've probably read more material and consumed more material, books of any fashion than any five writers will ever do. Right or wrong, when represented by an agent, you are banking on their experience and their opinion. It doesn't mean that it's gospel, it just means it's the best they can give you at this time. They can be wrong and sometimes they are wrong, but more often than not, they ought to be right and so, long term, you want to feel that the agent is a sounding board for you and a better professional sounding board than your relatives or your friends or your wife or your kids or your next door neighbor.*

> Gary Salt
> Paul Kohner, Inc.
> Los Angeles

• *The writer has a right to expect that the agent will be very honest about the work: every script we get from our clients, we look at as though it were a piece of gold. We are our clients' biggest fans. Nobody wants it to be better than we do, so it's very difficult for us to criticize it, if it's not good, but in order to service the client, we have to.*

Fredda Rose/Candy Monteiro
Monteiro Rose
Los Angeles

• *I can't speak for all agents at all agencies, me personally, the way I like to do it, I talk to every single one of my clients every day. With actors you are filling jobs, with writers, you are creating jobs. At least a writer can go home and write a spec.*

Rima Greer
Writers & Artists
Los Angeles

• *What we try to do is to successfully maximize a client's career over a long period of time which will help him or her become both financially and creatively secure. Being financially secure provides a certain power, the power to say* no *to a project or having a range of work options to choose from. An agent's power is in his ability to say* no *or* yes *on behalf of his client.*

Elliot Webb
Broder•Kurland•Webb•Uffner
Los Angeles

• *Communication. I constantly hear horror stories from would-be clients discussing their old agents. Either the agent won't return the phone calls or the new spec script sits unread for three months. That to me is absurd. Clients have the right to hear the good news as well as the bad in terms of why it got rejected. Is there a consensus? Is there a flaw in the script that none of us saw or is it something in the marketplace?*

Jonathan Westover
The Gage Group
Los Angeles

• *It's most important that you'll be told the truth about what's going on. People should remember that unlike lawyers who get* *their $300 per hour whether their advice is right or stinks, the agent doesn't get anything unless he's successful. People should bear that in mind. That doesn't mean that you can't ever say anything because the guy hasn't made any money off you. I think if I were a client I would say,* Look, I'm entitled to honest direct communication, I'm entitled to having my phone call returned. And I'm entitled to occasional evaluation periods as to, Are we doing the right thing? What can we do to change it? *Stuff to me that is common sense.*

Stu Robinson
paradigm
Los Angeles

• *The writer should be able to ask where his material is at all times and within 24 hours have an answer. If you call me today, I should be able to give you a list tomorrow of where your stuff has been. If the agent can't answer that, get a new agent.*

Your agent should be able to get you meetings. If your agent isn't getting you one meeting a month, get a new agent.

Rima Greer
Writers & Artists
Los Angeles

• *Show their work. Answer their phone calls within a day. Give them good advice. Not lie to them. Read their work. An agent has to be careful how he responds. A person's work is very personal to them.*

Lynn Pleshette
Pleshette & Green
Los Angeles

• *It's not a given that just because you sent me a script that I am going to do it. If you send me a script that is absolute rubbish and I say it's rubbish and I try to convince you it's rubbish and that it needs work, I'll either win that argument or I won't. You'll either see my point or you won't. You'll either agree to do some work on it or you won't. What happens if you insist that you're the writer and I'm the agent and I've gotta send this out? Well, the answer is,* I don't gotta send this out.

It happens sooner or later. It happens with good writers, indifferent writers, old writers, young writers. It happens that people take a fancy to a certain script, a certain story and just go and do it and insist that this is going to be a good thing, a turn around thing, this is going to be a breakthrough movie. But, what they don't take advantage of is the agent's overview. While the writer is off isolated for three months writing the script, the agent is getting up every morning, every day, every afternoon, every evening, plowing through the town, going through buyers, plowing through scripts, rights, trade papers and everything else and has at least a reasonable feel for what's out there.

> Gary Salt
> Paul Kohner Agency
> Los Angeles

• *To accurately assess where the client is in the continuum of their career. To honestly tell the person where they are. To evaluate whether the person heard you. To figure out how to get from where you are to where you want to go. To keep the client growing. If you don't do 1-2-3, it won't work. You need a plan.*

> Bob Hohman
> Richland/Wunsch/Hohman
> Los Angeles

• *If the writer says,* I'm gonna write a script. I'm thinking of a subject. *Tell me what it is. Because if you're telling me that you're going to write a story inspired by latest headlines, I'm going to tell you that in about two weeks, CBS is going to put it on the air and ABC is going to put it on the month after that, so go on to another subject because it's already lost to you. So the first thing you can expect from the agent is a certain knowledge of the market.*

He ought to be able to tell you (within reasonable limits) what's going on out there. Not so much trends, there is always the flavor of the month, but long term, what's around the networks, what's around the studios, where they're going to go. If you're going to engage in specing out something that can take you weeks and months of time and effort for no money, you don't want to find out later on that somebody's already doing it. So it seems to me that if I were someone's client, the first thing I would want from him is, I want to pick your brain every once in a while. I want access, I want to know what you know about the market.

That may have a tremendous effect on my story selection. I believe that the biggest mistake that the writer makes is story selection. Not about the quality of the work. It's about picking something that's isn't going to sell or is already being done.

That's one thing you should expect. You ought to be able to pick the agent's brain about material.

> Gary Salt
> Paul Kohner, Inc.
> Los Angeles

• *The power in Hollywood is money. It's true. Every powerful person in Hollywood is wealthy. There is a certain power in the ability not to be needy.*

> Elliot Webb
> Broder·Kurland·Webb·Uffner
> Los Angeles

I also asked what was too much to expect:

• *Too much is calling three times a week to ask the same question. I'd call the agent every two to two and a half weeks just to say* Hello, here I am. What? Tell me something, anything?

> Stu Robinson
> paradigm
> Los Angeles

• *I deeply resent being made to feel responsible for their rent. That's the bane of my existence. Sometimes you are successful at getting them work and sometimes you are not, but you are not their mommy and you're not their daddy. It is a free lance market, after all and there are no guarantees.*

> Lynn Pleshette
> Pleshette & Green
> Los Angeles

Of course, it goes both ways, agents have expectations, too:

• *We expect a partnership. Some agents sign a client and then expect the client to go out and get a job so the agent can commission it. Sometimes clients expect agents to work hard and they wait until the agent calls them with a job.*

We expect our clients to do as much work as we do and vice-versa. Cultivating relationships in the industry. Meeting with people, pitching ideas, continuing the relationships they do have, following up on that and even calling us to make sure we follow up on specific things.

We are meticulous about following up on things, but we do have a lot of clients. It doesn't hurt if a client just calls me up and comfortably reminds me, Have we heard on this? *or* Have we followed up on this?

Maybe I was planning on calling next week, but maybe it's a good idea that I call this week anyway. I like that kind of rapport with a client. I think it is as much their responsibility as mine. It's a two way street.

Sharing information is also very important. If they hear something, a job, an assignment, whatever, we expect them to come to us immediately so we can work on that and the reverse is true. If we work on a project and we either remember or have written down that our client has a relationship that's one, two, or three years old, we may say You make the call to this friend *and we'll hit them from both sides and see if we can coordinate this. You get a lot further using a partnership.*

Stuart Jacobs/Glen Brunswick
CNA
Los Angeles

• *That the client is continually turning out spec material, otherwise he's no use to himself or to me.*

Martin Shapiro
Shapiro-Lichtman
Los Angeles

• *We expect* full time *writers. We're* full time *agents. We're not interested in dilettantes. If they are going to be writers, they should write. We understand that in the beginning of their career, they may have to wait tables — they have to eat. But, we are not interested in people who do something else* and *also write. Writer-dentist doesn't work for us.*

Fredda Rose/Candy Monteiro
Monteiro Rose
Los Angles

• *If you are my client, I expect you to continually write new material. I expect you* not *to embarrass me when you go to meetings. Not that this happens that often, but it does happen. You've got to be prepared for your meetings. You've got to be on time for your meetings, generally have good attitude.*

Rima Greer
Writers & Artists
Los Angeles

• *To listen to what the agent has to say because the agent is out in the marketplace and knows what is going on. Some people are hell bound to write scripts about things that will not sell, we'll tell them up front not to write about that, but they must and they do and they don't sell.*

For instance, we had a client who wanted to get into half-hour prime time. We told him for four years that if he wanted to do that, he would have to write sample scripts. He never wrote one and could never figure out why we were not getting him work in this genre.

Candy Monteiro/Fredda Rose
Monteiro Rose
Los Angeles

• *Someone that has taken the time to know his/her craft and is able to utilize it in a way that works best for what he wants to do.*

Barbara Alexander
Media Artists Group
Los Angeles

- *That the clients do professional work in a timely manner and not call me every day. That's not a good way for me to spend my time. My worst days are the days when I have more calls from clients than buyers. How can I sell your script if I am on the phone with you?*

Maggie Field
The Maggie Field Agency
Los Angeles

A Synergistic Relationship

Synergy is one of my favorite words. The thought that in some instances two plus two can equal five because two components complement each other elegantly, appeals to my feelings that anything is possible. The possibilities that exist when an agent and client are both motivated above and beyond the call of duty is actually a necessity if you want to be one of the 5% to 10% of the WGA that works regularly.

- *A lot of talent doesn't understand their relative importance to the business. We believe that this is a business like any other business and that our job is to focus and manage the career, to explain the business to the talent.* Yes, we recognize you have talent. Now, what do you want do with that?

Elliot Stahler
Kaplan Stahler Agency
Los Angeles

- *We service our clients in many different ways. It varies enormously from client to client. One thing we encourage our clients to do whether they're established or not, is to write speculatively. We find that whether they are in the feature film business or the television business, that speculative writing is the most powerful tool to expand a client's contacts, enhance employment possibilities and generally open new doors.*
  Also if a writer is trying to up-grade a career, let's say he's working on television shows that are not particularly prestigious, but wants to work on the A shows. If he's making good money, he

may want to write a spec script for one of the high quality shows; sometimes that can be the means to moving onto one of those shows. Or if someone has been working in the half-hour field and wants to work in the hour field and vice versa, they can write a spec script for the genre they want to move into.

Also, spec features, I'm sure you have read in the trades (as we have here) of the big sales that have occurred over the last few years of original screenplays written speculatively by writers of all levels of experience. Our agency sold one of those scripts just a few weeks ago by a young woman who was referred to us by one of our clients. This is a script that she researched and wrote while one of our agents worked quite closely with her in the development of the screenplay. That agent together with the writer developed a strategy for going out in the town with it and in a three day period got serious interest by a number of major producers and a studio snapped it up for a huge price on the third day. There's nothing as exciting as doing a significant piece of business for either a newcomer or someone who has struggled to get to a new place in their career.

Jim Preminger
Jim Preminger Agency
Los Angeles

• *A good agent can plan a career for a writer. I can plan out five years of a career for a writer. The show is clearly a stepping stone from staff to story to exec story position on the next show. A good agent thinks* What can I get for my client from this show?

Elliot Stahler
Kaplan Stahler Agency
Los Angeles

• *I insist (though I am not always listened to) that everybody give me an original screenplay at least every two years because there's a real danger of going from assignment to assignment. The development business has never been great, but right now it is pretty bad. You can price yourself out of the market. We all have clinkers. Everybody has good work and bad work. On occasion, you'll get paid a lot of money to write a script for hire and it won't be what you want. I think being a writer for hire is a very difficult business to stay in because writers are very badly abused in the business in the sense that the motion picture business is very much a movie star driven business and the next most important person is the director. Writers seem to be viewed as interchangeable. If a big star comes onto your project and the star has worked with some other writer or script doctor, the star might want that writer to come in and do a polish on your script and perhaps this person is a fine writer and will do a good job, but that becomes the movie star's project. Writers are generally not as well respected as other pieces of talent. I encourage people to get out of that low-man-on-the-totem-pole position by becoming writer-producers.*

Bob Hohman
Richland/Wunsch/Hohman
Los Angeles

• *I think that there is variation between agencies and the amount of the editorial or creative work that writers are given. Also within our agency, there's some variation. Some writers don't want a great deal of input from us. But I do find that most writers that write speculatively are quite interested in our notes and welcome any constructive suggestions or criticism that we might make.*

Jim Preminger
Jim Preminger Agency
Los Angeles

• *We do a lot of in-house development here. We take pride in the fact that we actually read the stuff and can analyze it and do a good job. We do read and we do give notes. Each client is different in how much they want to hear. From the three of us, Martin (Gage), Kirk (Durham) and I, from our different background and different age groups, we have a pretty amazing collective eye here.*

Jonathan Westover
The Gage Group
Los Angeles

• *We have been known to go through three or four drafts with a writer before we go out with a script; in other words, a writer will write a first draft screenplay, give it to us for our comments and we make suggestions and they'll go back and rewrite it based upon those comments. Sometimes that takes two, three, four passes before the writer and we are mutually satisfied that it is in shape to go out.*

> Jim Preminger
> Jim Preminger Agency
> Los Angeles

• *I got into business once with someone that I knew was talented. I had seen some of their work earlier on and that work had not been followed up with work of the same or better caliber. I sat down with them and said,* you're leaving a big agency now. Let me ask you, have people at the agency been talking to you about your work? *The writer said,* No. *I said,* Well, you know, it's not very good. I know a lot about you and you are a lot better than that and you need to write about things that you really care about. *Well, the writer heard me and has blossomed into an incredibly successful writer.*

> Bob Hohman
> Richland/Wunsch/Hohman
> Los Angeles

• *Part of our job is to give writers a little bit of an edge or a different way of thinking. I'll suggest a show.* Why do you hate it? Do you think you can make it better? Write me an Emmy Award winning episode of a show.

> Elliot Stahler
> Kaplan Stahler Agency
> Los Angeles

Above and beyond forging a successful relationship with your agent and continually writing and networking with your fellow writers, there are other things you can and should do to help yourself. You have to be serious about your career as well as the craft. Agents tell me you do this by going to parties, taking classes, having lunches and generally trying to make yourself visible. It's important to just get out there and meet people.

• *One of the biggest mistakes writers make is thinking they have finished their job when they give their script to their agent. Then, they just sit back and expect the phone to ring. This is a business of contacts and relationships. Writers have to be in the sales process as well.*

> Fredda Rose
> Monteiro Rose
> Los Angeles

• *Reinvent yourself. The easiest way to reinvent yourself is to have a script of your own that you have the control over and you can decide what happens with it. I think it's important for artists to reinvent themselves every 3 to 5 years anyway.*
> *Dean Pitchford is someone who has reinvented himself. Dean is an Academy Award winning lyricist for "Fame". In 1984 he wrote a hugely successful screenplay, "Footloose," followed by other successful screenplays, and in 1990, he decided that he was going to become a director. He entered the Discovery Program and out of 600 people, he was one of 5 people who were picked. He did a movie that turned out terrifically. Then he got another film at HBO called "Blood Brothers".*

> Bob Hohman
> Richland/Wunsch/Hohman
> Los Angeles

• *Work on ideas, write spec scripts. We're in a community where everybody knows everybody, so when a writer is playing tennis with somebody and tells him about an idea, he may call and say,* So and so said to send my script over. *That's very helpful. The squeaky wheel sometimes gets more attention. It's an industry town. You need to do anything you can to make things happen.*

> Lynn Pleshette
> Pleshette & Green
> Los Angeles

Jonathan Westover at The Gage Group quoted his mentor, Dan Richland, *Why would you leave 100% of your career to someone who only gets 10% of your money?*

Wrap Up

Writer expects
- ✓ communication
- ✓ honesty
- ✓ market overview
- ✓ feedback
- ✓ taste/judgement
- ✓ agent to read and show work
- ✓ agent to be able to track material
- ✓ career guidance

Agent expects
- ✓ professional behavior
- ✓ you to continually write
- ✓ that you won't embarrass him at meetings

Synergistic relationship
- ✓ writer networks
- ✓ writer continually reinvents himself
- ✓ agent acts as editor
- ✓ agent helps in developmental process

First Aid

11

Life in the business is a constant challenge. Writers are rejected and think they will either never work or never work again. Everyone in a free lance business experiences this at one time or another. This last chapter is filled with ideas, institutions and information that seemed to me to offer help and inspiration.

•   *I think the people who sustain success are good listeners that really know what they want. People who let me know what they want and I help them do it. X% is genes.*

> Bob Hohman
> Richland/Wunsch/Hohman
> Los Angeles

•   *Art comes from art. Art is a reaction to art. Rembrandt didn't start in a vacuum. He just was better than everybody else. A novelist reads novels. You have to drown yourself in this information, reading screenplays: why a scene worked, how these people are interesting, how the writer chose to describe the scene. Watch movies.*

> Lynn Pleshette
> Pleshette & Green
> Los Angeles

•   *A writer has it easier than anybody else because all he or she has do is write* fade in *and use his or her imagination. That's one of the reasons that we are in the writer business because we believe*

that no actor or director can do anything until a writer writes. *So*
if you are a writer, keep writing. Somebody will see it.

Elliot Webb
Broder.Kurland.Webb.Uffner
Los Angeles

• *A really talented screenwriter has just as much chance in this*
town to succeed because the buyers always need good scripts.
Producers may treat them badly, they may rewrite them, but I still
think there's a real dearth. There's room for someone to have a
career if they have the talent and the energy to work at it.

Lynn Pleshette
Pleshette & Green
Los Angeles

• *There are an awful lot of creative and talented people out*
there. Unfortunately, it's not just talent that brings success.
There's luck. There's timing. There's persistence. There's a
whole variety of things that enter into it. You can't get
discouraged, you have to have patience and you can't expect it to
happen overnight. If one, ten, or even twenty agents don't respond
to your work, keep trying. Somebody eventually will, if you keep at
it long enough and if you believe in yourself.

Barbara Alexander
Media Artists Group
Los Angeles

• *Successful writers have all had lives. They've done things.*
They didn't grow up watching movies. They've exposed themselves
to different types of people so they have experiences from which to
write about. They are able to create a three dimensional world on
paper.

Richard Green
Pleshette & Green
Los Angeles

• *I like supporting writers. I believe that writers need to be*
respected and they need to be supported. Their work is very lonely

*and it's very difficult. It's more difficult than people understand.
Anything that can make their lives easier, I am all for.*

Robin Moran Miller
New York

• *Don't get down when an agent rejects you. It's only his
opinion. Opinions are like assholes; everybody has one.*

Raphael Berko
Media Artist Group
Los Angeles

• *I think the '90s for writers is all about figuring out a way to
survive.*

Bob Hohman
Richland/Wunsch/Hohman
Los Angeles

• *An example of what separates good from great is my brother,
Joel Oliansky. He wrote "The Law", "Bird", "Masada", "The
Competition." When he starts to write a scene: he knows his
characters, he knows their whole world and he wants to figure out
what would make the scene work, what would make it interesting,
what would make it novel, not newness for its own sake. He
doesn't cheat on his characters. He figures out how people deal
with each other that makes it interesting and gives insights into
someone's character. What would make them act? I've been
appalled that a writer says,* I want to do a scene like in "Lethal
Weapon." *So much of the writing is so derivative. The spec
market is so devoid of energy because people are not writing from
care. They don't think* what would make an interesting story.
What would make it new? *Inexperienced writers react to what
they've seen that sort of works and begin writing with second hand
information. They don't know their characters and they don't know
how to make a story interesting, so these writers tend to write in
cliche and that's bad writing.*

Lynn Pleshette
Pleshette & Green
Los Angeles

• *My perspective of what the business is about is perception. What you want is to build a perception around a client (hopefully they'll have the talent to back it up) that will give that client some heat. Most agents look to do that very quickly. I think it should be done over the period of time it takes to establish a strong foundation. Some people are in it for immediate money gratification and they tend to burn out because they haven't really learned their craft.*

Elliot Webb
Broder.Kurland.Webb.Uffner
Los Angeles

• *Agents don't bill by the hour. They only get commissions when people work and earn money, therefore the fundamental relationship is economic. Because it's economic and because it's so clear cut and it's so pure and uncontaminated by distractions like* Do I like him? Who cares? It's irrelevant. Who cares if I get Christmas cards or not? *The only thing the agent is entitled to is his 10%. The uncontaminated relationship is economic and therefore it is about as honest a relationship as you're ever going to get because nothing is served by the agent prevaricating with his client. If I was looking at a really good piece of writing, why would I pretend it is not?*

Gary Salt
Paul Kohner Agency
Los Angeles

• *Our clients stay here for two reasons. The first reason is that we do a pretty good job. The second reason is that we need them to stay here. We derive our living from these people and we're trying to do a good job with the people we have. We feel the most effective way to get new clients is to do a good job for the people you already have. We only see people by referral. I am not in the volume business. I don't have 12 sub agents.*

Bob Hohman
Richland/Wunsch/Hohman
Los Angeles

• *Never pitch or show something that is not registered. Especially to an agent. Six months down the line, when the agent is helping improve one of his writer's scripts, he'll use your idea. By this time, he'll think it's his, it's not deliberate stealing.*

> Raphael Berko
> Media Artist Group
> Los Angeles

• *Talented people are always found.*

> Elliot Webb
> Broder.Kurland.Webb.Uffner
> Los Angeles

• *A trait in common with a lot of people who don't make it is that they are self-destructive. There's not a real defining trait among people who do make it other than a real determination to make it.*

> Marty Shapiro
> Shapiro Lichtman
> Los Angeles

No one gets to be a star writer or president of IBM without intense determination to make it. Not everyone needs to be a star and it is a trap to trivialize your accomplishments just because you are not yet visible and/or powerful. Just being one of the 5-10% in the Writers Guild who works regularly is a very large accomplishment.

Although famous names like Diane English or William Goldman or Joe Eszterhas appear to be role models representing the success that we would all like to have, they're only more famous than many other writers with power, prestige and money whose names are unknown except to inveterate credit readers. These writers have achieved their goals and are making a living doing what they want to do. Not many people in the world get to do that.

It's enlightening to consider some of the synonyms the thesaurus lists for success: consummation, prosperity, victory, triumph, fulfillment, achievement, attainment, mastery. Just because you haven't attained your ultimate fantasy, don't wait until they are engraving your headstone to congratulate yourself on how far you have come.

The Writers Guild of America

I can't say enough good things about The Writers Guild. The Writers Guild not only has an extraordinary library with essential reference material and film and television scripts of the past and present, but maintains a very effective registration service in order to assist members and non-members in establishing the completion date and the identity of their literary property written for theatrical motion pictures, television and radio.

This is not as much protection as registering the copyright with the US Copyright Office, but it does cover a multitude of sins quickly and inexpensively. A copy of the material (no brads, staples, fanfold, covers, etc.) must accompany the fee of $10 for members of WGA/West and WGA/East. The fee is $20 for non-members. The Writers Guild will send you more detailed information regarding this service if you write, call or fax them. The registration program is available only through the WGA/West office. Their mailing address is:

The Writers Guild of America/West
8955 Beverly Boulevard
West Hollywood, CA 90048-24566

If you go in person, the registration office is located at:

9009 Beverly Boulevard
(between Robertson & Doheny)
West Hollywood, CA 90048-2456
310-550-1000/fax 310-550-0322

For programs other than the registration program, the address for WGA/East is:

Writers Guild of America/East
555 West 57th Street
New York, NY 10019
212-767-7800.

Through the Human Resources Department at WGA, there are
various programs available to writers in the following categories:
female, ethnic minority, physically disabled, 40 years of age or
older. For this purpose, a voluntary training program has been
established on a company-by-company basis under which novice
writers may train with professional writers on episodic TV series.
Each series must be in its second or subsequent year of production
and under certain terms and qualifications. Write to Georgia J.
Mau at WGA/West for further information.

Requirements for Admission to WGA

In order to become a member of WGA, an aggregate number of
twenty-four (24) units of Credit, which are based upon work
completed under contract of employment or upon the sale or
licensing of previously unpublished and unproduced literary or
dramatic material is required. Said employment, sale or licensing
must be with a company or other entity that is signatory to the
applicable WGA Collective Bargaining Agreement and must be
within the jurisdiction of the Guild as provided in its collective
bargaining contracts. The twenty-four (24) units must be
accumulated within the preceding three (3) years of application.
Upon final qualification for membership, a cashier's check or
money order, payable to the Writers Guild of America/West, Inc.
in the amount of Two Thousand Five Hundred Dollars ($2,500) is
due. Writers Guild/West, 8955 Beverly Blvd., West Hollywood,
CA 90048.

Writers residing west of the Mississippi River may apply for
membership in the WGA/West, Inc. Writers residing east of the
Mississippi River are advised to contact: Writers Guild of
America/East, 555 West 57th Street, New York, NY 10019.

Earning and counting units of credit:

Two Units - For each complete week of employment within the Guild's jurisdiction on a week-to-week basis.

Three Units - Story for radio play or television program less than thirty (30) minutes shall be prorated in terms of ten (10) minutes or less.

Four Units - Story for a short subject theatrical motion picture or any length for a radio play or television program or breakdown for a non-prime time serial thirty (30) minutes through sixty (60) minutes.

Six Units - Teleplay or radio play less than thirty (30) minutes shall be prorated in five (5) minute increments; Television format for a new serial or series; *Created By* credit given pursuant to the separation of rights provisions of the WGA Theatrical and Television Basic Agreement in addition to other units accrued for the literary material on which the *Created By* credit is based.

Eight Units - Story for radio play or television program or breakdown for a non-prime time serial more than sixty (60) minutes and less than ninety (90) minutes.
    Screenplay for a short subject theatrical motion picture or for a radio play or teleplay thirty (30) minutes through sixty (60) minutes.

Twelve units - Story for a radio or television program ninety (90) minutes or longer or story for a feature length theatrical motion picture; or breakdown for a non-prime time serial ninety (90) minutes or longer.
    Radio play or teleplay more than sixty (60) minutes and less than ninety (90) minutes.

Twenty-four Units - Screenplay for a feature length theatrical motion picture, radio play or teleplay ninety (90) minutes or longer.
    Bible for any television serial or prime-time mini-series of at

least four (4) hours.

Long-term story projection which is defined for this purpose as a bible, for a specified term, on an existing, five (5) times per week non-prime time serial as used herein shall be defined as a bible.

A rewrite is entitled to one-half the number of units allotted to its particular category as set forth in the schedule of units.

A polish is entitled to one-quarter the number of units allotted to its particular category as set forth in the schedule of units.

Sale of an option earns one-half the number of units allotted to its particular category as set forth in the schedule of units, subject to a maximum entitlement of four such units per project in any one year.

Where writers collaborate on the same project each shall be accorded the appropriate number of units designated in the schedule of units.

In all cases, to qualify for membership, if the writer's employment agreement or purchase agreement is with a company owned in whole or in part by the writer or writer's family, there must be an agreement for financing, production, and/or distribution with a third party signatory producing company or, failing such agreement, the script must be produced and the writer must receive writing credit on screen in the form of *Written By, Teleplay By, Screenplay By* or *Radio Play By.*

The applicant writer is required to apply for membership no later than the 31st day of employment.

In exceptional cases, the Board of Directors, acting upon a recommendation from the Membership and Finance Committee shall have the power and authority to grant membership based upon work done prior to two years before the applicant has filed an application for membership.

All membership applications are to be supported by a copy of executed employment or sales contracts or other acceptable evidence of employment or sales. Dues are based on a percentage of members' earnings.

The schedule of minimum fees is available free from the Guild and is quite lengthy. Fees for an original screenplay (including treatment) range from $35,076 to $65,793. These fees are paid in a system of WGA guideline installments. Rewrites of Screenplay range from $11,510 to $17,546.

The range exists from low end (budgets of $2,500,000 and under) to high end (budgets of over $2,500,000).

Television minimum fees for week-to-week and term employment minimum (14 out of 14 weeks) is $2,855.

Minimums for television for a teleplay 15 minutes or less are $2,527 and vary by length of script and whether the work includes teleplay or story and teleplay, etc.

These numbers are just to give you a very sketchy idea of compensation. Get a copy of the full schedule from the WGA so you will know what you are aiming for.

Writing Format Guides

The Writers Guild of America/East publishes an indispensable guide for the written form. This guide is available for $4.55 (which includes postage). It is called "Professional Writer's Teleplay/Screenplay Format Guide". WGA/East does not accept personal checks from non-members, so send a money order if you're not a member.

The Writers Guild of America/East
555 West 57th Street
New York, NY 10019

Another highly regarded format guide is <u>Correct Format for Screenplays & Teleplays</u> by David Trottier available from theater bookstores or from,

Dave Trottier
2034 East Lincoln Avenue # 300
Anaheim CA 92806
$9.95 plus $1.50 shipping.

The Dramatists Guild, Inc.

Playwrights are covered by a far different collective. Not a union in the strict sense of the word, the DG, Inc. still manages to protect its members by offering collective bargaining agreements and contracts covering those producers and theater owners as well as guidelines relative to agency agreements and agents. The guild will send you a list of agents handling playwrights for the price of a sase envelope.

There are four categories of membership in The Dramatists Guild:

1. Active Members - to qualify as an Active member, you must have had a *first class* production, an Off-Broadway production with an unlimited run after May 13, 1969 or a mainstage regional theater (LORT) production since May 29, 1980.

2. Associate Members - all writers, whether produced, or unproduced may join in this category. As an Associate Member, you automatically become an Active Member when a work of yours is presented in a *first class*, Off-Broadway or mainstage regional theater production.

3. Student Members - This membership is available to those students enrolled in degree programs at colleges or universities for as long as they remain students. Student membership applications should be accompanied by a letter from the senior administrator of the student's

program confirming the applicant's student status and indicating the projected date of graduation. Upon graduation, students are eligible to become Associate Members of the Guild.

4. Subscribing Members - To qualify as a Subscribing Member, the only requirement is that you be engaged in a drama-related field. Students, producers and patrons may all become Subscribing Members. (Playwrights are not eligible for membership in this category.)

Active members pay annual dues of $100 and are assessed 2% of their *first class* royalties. When motion picture rights are sold, members pay 2% of the proceeds. Associate Members pay annual dues of $65.00, Student Members pay annual dues of $25.00, Subscribing Members pay annual dues of $65.00.

The dues entitle you to use of the Dramatists Guild's Production Contracts, royalty collection, business advice, members' hotline, committee for women, free and/or discounted theater tickets, Health Insurance, The Dramatists Guild Quarterly and the Guild's Newsletter Marketing Information and Symposia (held in major cities across the country) featuring speakers like Comden & Green, Kander & Ebb, John Guare and Marsha Norman. Use of the Guild's headquarters (for readings and auditions), the Newsroom (files on regional New York theaters, awards, contests, grants, etc.) are also benefits of membership.

The Dramatists Guild Quarterly alone is worth the price of membership. Information in the Summer 1992 issue includes:
    Lists of Agents, Conferences and Festivals, Artists Colonies, Fellowships and Grants, Membership and Service Organizations, Residencies, Workshops plus an index of Honors (Pulitzers, Obies, Oscars, etc.)
    A record of plays produced on Broadway and off during the preceding quarter as well as a catalogue of Broadway and off-Broadway producers that lists names, addresses and their latest productions plus the best way to contact them and what they are

each looking for.

Members in New York and Los Angeles enjoy discount theater tickets to certain productions.

The Dramatists Guild maintains a fund to help members in financial need and also sponsors the prestigious Young Playwrights Festival at Playwrights Horizons in New York. The main office of the Guild is in New York with a satellite office in Los Angeles.

Jason Miligin The Dramatists Guild 224 W 44th Street 11th Floor New York, NY 10036 1-800-289-9366	Bill Shick The Dramatist Guild P. O. Box 856 North Hollywood, CA 91603 818-753-5343

Wrap Up

Successful writers
✓ have drive
✓ don't give up
✓ have real lives

Success
✓ being one of the 5%-10%

Guilds
✓ Writers Guild of America/East
✓ Writers Guild of America/West
✓ Dramatists Guild

Rating the Agents

12

When I first started writing about agents, I guess I thought I would rate them as in a restaurant guide, with five ★ agents, four ★, etc., but it turns out that agents and agencies are not at all like chefs and restaurants. You can't rate them with ★'s or even with $'s (though that might be more accurate).

A more reliable way to group agents considers size and experience: star agency conglomerates, boutique star agencies, prestigious agencies representing respected writers who are not as visible, as well as evolving agents building their business who will clearly have status as their client list matures. The rankings involve access, stature and size; there are about six levels.

Use all the resources of this book in making your decision: the client list, the agents' own words and the listing of each agency. I have provided statistics and tried to characterize each agency. If I don't mention client names at the end of a listing, that was the agent's request either because he felt it was an invasion of client privacy, was afraid of another agent stealing the clients or had no one to point to. When you check the list at the WGA, you'll be able to make your own determination.

Names following an agent's name and listed in parentheses indicate an agency where the agent worked previously. When I have known credits of clients, I have included them in the body of the write-up of an agency just as a point of identification. For quick reference, clients are also included at the end of the write-up.

When querying agents, be discriminating. Target the agent that seems right for you and ration yourself. Composer Albert Hague taught a class in New York that was basically about how to get the buyer's attention. His caveat was, *You'd better be terrific when you get it because you're only new once; the impression they get is the one they will keep.*

Literary agents are already inundated with scripts and while they are all looking for the big hit, there are only so many hours in a day. Don't waste their time or yours. If you are just starting, don't expect CAA to come knocking at your door. Choose someone who is at the same level as you are and grow together.

If you have just sold your own script yourself, you will probably have some referrals already. Check them out and see who appeals to you. A sale is not an automatic entree. As you have noted throughout the book, most agents are not interested in a one-shot-deal. They want writers. Writers are people who write. Agents will expect to see your other work once you have their attention.

Since the business is so volatile, agents and agencies come, go, mutate and fracture. For this reason, always confirm addresses before you send a query letter. Either check with The Writers Guild or try the phone number I have listed.

Keep writing.

Agency Listings

Abrams Artists & Associates

9200 Sunset Blvd. #625
W of Doheny
Los Angeles, CA 90069
310-859-0625

Harry Abrams has headed or partnered a string of different agencies over the years, from Abrams-Rubaloff, a commercial force in New York in the late 1960s and 1970s, to Abrams/Harris & Goldberg, forerunner of Abrams Artists and Associates. A tough negotiator and a shrewd businessman, Harry started in the business at MCA. Reluctant to be interviewed for the book because he doesn't like to call attention to himself, I will limit my comments to the agency.

Abrams Artists is well respected and has access. The literary office of this agency is run by ex-producer Ross Fineman. Ross represents writers, directors and producers. Michael Jaffee (Broder.Kurland.Webb.Uffner) is his colleague.

I have no information regarding the size of their list or clientele, so check WGA for that information.

Agents
Ross Fineman and Michael Jaffee.
Client List
Confidential.
Clients
Check WGA listing.
Notes

Bret Adams

448 W 44th Street
btwn 9th & 10th Avenues
New York, NY 10036
212-765-5630

If it's a job in the theater, Bret Adams probably did it. He has been an actor, a publicist, a producer, a manager of ACT, and a binoculars renter at the theater. The number of things that Bret has managed to figure out a way to make money from in the business is a testimony to his creativity.

He started his own agency in 1971 and Mary Harden has been his partner since 1982. Mary's credentials came courtesy of being a dutiful wife to husband, director Richard Harden. The gypsy life of a regional theater director requires moving every six months and Mary went with Richard doing whatever theater jobs were available. As Richard's resume grew, so did Mary's contacts. She has made great use of them as an agent, furthering the careers of writers, actors and directors. Bret Adams and Mary Harden are two of the most respected agents in the business.

Agents
Bret Adams and Mary Harden.
Client List
20
Clients
Mary Gallagher, Bruce Graham and others.
Notes

The Agency

10351 Santa Monica Blvd. #211
at Beverly Glen
Los Angeles, CA 90025
310-551-3000

The Agency has been strengthening its position for years as a mini-conglomerate. In 1992, when InterTalent disbanded and Triad merged with William Morris, The Agency became an even stronger contender as one of the lucky beneficiaries of talent and agents.

Partners Larry Becsey and Richard Berman established The Agency when they bought The William Schuller Agency. Schuller was a successful children's agency and represented client, Ron Howard as a child-actor on through his transition to becoming a successful director, which put The Agency on the map in 1984. Ron was not the force that he is today, but he was important none the less. Jerome Zeitman merged with Becsey and Berman at that time. Zeitman, one of the pioneers of the packaging concept at both William Morris and MCA, was also in production at Wolper Productions and Columbia Pictures. The strength of this agency (which represents actors and most other industry personnel) is in its writers and directors. Writer's representatives are Neil Bagg, Sharon Mitchell, Michael Van Dyke, Larry Roth.

Agents
Jerome Zeitman, Nav Sandu, Larry Roth, Laura Sutton, Caron Champoux, Sharon Mitchell and Michael Van Dyke.
Client List
150
Clients
William R. Applebaum
Notes

Agency for the Performing Arts (APA)

9000 Sunset Blvd. #900
btwn San Vicente & Doheny
Los Angeles, CA 90069
310-273-0744

APA has taken some hits lately. Roger Vorce took over as
president in 1992 after beloved president Marty Klein and powerful
John Gaines died. Further change occurred when Tom Korman and
Larry Masser joined The Artists Group. The agency, at this point,
is describing itself as a mid-level agency and is struggling to focus
itself.

Selling itself as an alternate to corporate representation, this agency,
originally formed to represent artists for personal appearances, will
continue to thrive.

The Los Angeles literary department led by Stuart Miller, was
recently strengthened by the addition of Justen Dardis (Susan Smith
& Associates and The Agency) who now heads the feature film
literary department. Michael Bennahum is head of the literary
department in New York and is joined by colleague Anna Maria
Alessi.

Representative of APA's combined list of writers include: David
Newman ("Bonnie and Clyde," "Superman"), Edwin Baker
("Combination Platter"), Mike France ("Cliffhanger"), writer-
director Nick Cassavetes ("Unhook the Stars"), Diane Drake
("Him") and Elisa Bell ("Thirty Wishes"), Michael Barrie ("The
Tonight Show"), Marc Wilmore ("In Living Color") Douglas
Berstein ("Silver Spoons," "The Charmings"), Cory Tynan and
John Ries ("Ghost Hunter") and Chris Miller and Mary Hale
("Multiplicity").

Agency for the Performing Arts (APA)

888 Seventh Avenue
at 59th Street
New York, NY 10016
212-582-1500

Agents
Los Angeles: Stu Miller, Justen Dardis, David Saunders and Cory
Concoff.
New York: Michael Bennahum and Anna Maria Alessi.
Client List
Very large.
Clients
Stephanie Liss, Randal Patrick, Stephen Banks, David Brenner,
Richard Alfieri, Mike France, Nick Cassavetes, Diane Drake, Elisa
Bell, Michael Barrie, Marc Wilmore, Douglas Berstein, Cory
Tynan, John Ries, Chris Miller, Mary Hale and others.
Notes

Marcia Amsterdam Agency

41 W 82nd Street, 9A
just off Central Park West
New York, NY 10024
212-873-4945

Marcia Amsterdam started in the business as a book editor. When her authors ended up with film deals, she represented them and started her own agency. This was back in 1969. Today, her list of clients numbers about 30 and she rarely adds to that list. She does read brief query letters.

Query letters should include a brief paragraph with the main concept, not all the details. What she and other agents are always looking for is *a slightly offbeat voice that says something in an interesting way.* Ms. Amsterdam handles scripts for film and television, no playwrights. She is not interested in pilots. One of her clients is Robert Leininger ("The Lemonmobile").

Agents
Marcia Amsterdam.
Client List
30
Clients
Robert Leininger and others.
Notes

The Artists Agency

10000 Santa Monica Blvd. #305
at Century Park East
Los Angeles, CA 90067
310-277-7779

This elegant agency was originally known as The Sandy Bresler Agency in 1971 when Sandy left ICM to start a smaller more personal agency. ICM expatriates Jim Cota, Mike Livingston and Don Wolff joined him, and Bresler, Wolff, Cota, and Livingston was the agency name until it was changed to The Artists Agency in 1980. Because Sandy still really wanted a smaller operation, he left to start The Sandy Bresler Agency again.

The current partners are the above-mentioned founders plus Mickey Freiberg and Dick Shepherd. Jimmy Cota was gracious enough to still speak to me even though he said the onslaught of mail he received from The LA Agent Book was somewhat more than he might have wanted to handle. With this in mind, please do not send material to this agency or any other without sending a query letter first. The material won't be read and may or may not be returned.

Agents
Mickey Freiberg, Dick Shepherd, Andy Patman and Merrily Kane.
Client List
100
Clients
Check WGA listing.
Notes

The Artists Group

1930 Century Park W #403
S of Santa Monica Blvd.
Los Angeles, CA 90067
310-552-1100

Founding partner Arnold Soloway has been on the agency scene for a long time. He opened the first Los Angeles offices of Susan Smith before joining the prestigious old-line Kumen-Olenick Agency (now Progressive Artists) before finally deciding to open his own one-man office in 1975. Today that office includes partners Hal Stalmaster and Robert Malcolm, plus associate agents Barry Salomon, Art Rutter, Nancy Moon, Ed Goldstone, Tom Korman and Larry Masser.

The head of The Artists Group literary department, Art Rutter has a diverse background: he started his career working as a production administrator on ABC Television's now defunct soap opera, "Ryan's Hope," became a network executive at ABC Entertainment, an agent trainee at William Morris, a talent agent at The Agency, and helped form the literary department at Harry Gold and Associates. He was brought to The Artists Group in 1991 to reorganize the literary department. Art represents 18 writers and 2 directors personally and is on call for the handful of other literary clients handled by the other agents at The Artists Group. Some of his clients include Emmy nominees Harry Dunn ("In Living Color"), Michelle Jones ("In Living Color"), Evan Sayit ("Arsenio Hall"), Adam Lapidus ("The Simpsons," "Who's the Boss") and Lew Green who has written features ("The Wire" and "Premonition"). Director clients are Ted Lange ("Fall Guy," "Fantasy Island," "Love Boat," "Gidget," etc.), Mario Azzopardi ("Wise Guy," "In the Heat of the Night," etc.) and a woman director, Deryn Warren, whose first feature is "Black Magic Woman."

Art does not look at unsolicited material although a letter of inquiry would not get thrown in the wastebasket. Barry Saloman also represents literary clients. The Artists Group also handles below the line talent.

Agents
Art Rutter and Barry Salomon.
Client List
18
Clients
Harry Dunn, Michelle Jones, Evan Sayit, Gary Goodrich, Lew Green, Linda Saltzman and others.
Notes

The Brandt Company

12700 Ventura Blvd. #340
across from Jerry's Deli
Studio City, CA 91604
818-506-7747

Geoffrey Brandt manages as a sole proprietor with the power client list of a large conglomerate. With names like William Wisherthe ("Terminator 2") and one of my favorite directors, multiple Emmy winner, Lamont Johnson ("Last Great American Hero," "My Sweet Charlie," "The Execution of Private Slovak," etc.), one gets the idea that this guy knows what he is doing. From a show biz family (relatives founded The American Film Institute, the National Association of Theater Owners, the Brandt Theaters, etc.), Geoffrey must have found it just a hop, skip and a jump from working as the Associate Artistic Director of the New Jersey Shakespeare Festival to being a talent agent at William Morris and creating the directors division at APA. In 1989, Brandt formed this company with a very small list of important writers, directors, editors, costume designers and producers. A charming and articulate man, Geoffrey displays humanity, taste, class and clout.

Other writers on his list include Michael Backes ("Rising Son"), Stuart Birnbaum ("Summer School"), Doug Borghi (created "Jake and the Fat Man"), Dennis Lynton Clark ("Comes a Horseman"), Duncan Gibbins ("Crossbow: The Legend of William Tell") and Fred Walton ("When a Stranger Calls").

Agents
Geoffrey Brandt.
Client List
22
Clients
Michael Backes, Stuart Birnbaum, Doug Borghi, Sue Browdy, Sandy Dvore, Shelley Komarov, Dennis Lynton Clark, Duncan Gibbins, Jim Goldstone, Larry Peerce, Eric Sears, Fred Walton and others.
Notes

The Broder•Kurland•Webb•Uffner Agency

9242 Beverly Blvd. # 200
at Maple Drive
Beverly Hills, CA 90210
310-281-3400

At Broder•Kurland•Webb•Uffner, gazing at the waiting room walls covered with Writers and Directors Guild Awards and Emmy Citations for people like Donald Bellisario ("Quantum Leap) James Burrows ("Cheers") and Les and Glen Charles (creators of "Cheers"), I'm hard put to think of anyone with more impressive clients. Who could possibly be left for CAA? BKWU's list also includes directors, cinematographers, editors, costume designers and more.

Bob Broder was an agent at IFA and Norman Kurland worked for Leonard Hanzer (Major Talent) before they decided to join forces to represent writers and directors in 1978 (Broder•Kurland). I interviewed the third partner to join the operation, Elliot Webb, whose degrees in marketing and finance are a perfect background for an agent. Although his first job was finding employment for high priced accounting and financial personnel, it was a side-line venture selling sweat shirts to Madison Square Garden and negotiating with The William Morris Agency that led Webb to the WMA mailroom in 1972.

Creative enough to circumvent actually delivering mail by driving executives to the airport and any other excuse, Elliot became secretary to various agents and as Elliot describes it, *I was the secretary to the agent who handled the horse, Secretariat. My career was nowhere when I left for California with an entree to IFA.* IFA soon merged with CMA to form ICM, where Elliot spent 10 years, eventually running the television literary department.

Webb's partners, Kurland and Broder, urged Webb to join their partnership for years before he finally succumbed in 1983. Former ICM colleague, Beth Uffner, was not only head of development at MTM, but ran her own successful agency before becoming the fourth partner in 1989.

Elliot is happy to point out that although most of their clients have been with them for many years, the life blood of the agency is acquiring new young talent. Although they look at query letters, the main avenue for new people is referrals from someone already in the business, so be creative and find someone connected to this agency before querying.

Agents
Bob Broder, Norman Kurland, Elliot Webb, Beth Uffner, Joel Milner, Rhonda Gomez, Bruce Kaufman, Ian Greenstein, Tammy Stockfish and Gayla Nethercott.
Client List
Check WGA listing.
Clients
Check WGA listing.
Notes

CNA & Associates

1801 Avenue of the Stars #1250
at Little Santa Monica
Los Angeles, CA 90067
310-556-4343

CNA opened its doors in 1981 with its business pretty much theatrically based. Although owner Christopher Nassif handled a few writers, producers and below the line personnel, the strength was in the actors. Things are different today. In 1991, Stuart Jacobs left The Irv Schechter Company and organized these clients into a thriving respected literary department. Originally an actor, Stuart assisted Don Buchwald in New York before leaving snow and sleet for sun and sand. A few months after his arrival, he invited Glen Brunswick (another Schechter alumnus) to join him. Brunswick picked up other important agency experience at both ICM and APA before meeting Stuart. Together these two men, clearly hard working, caring, knowledgeable people, have built a rather daunting list. They have several clients on staff on network television, Peter Gallay ("Empty Nest"), Jamie & Chuck Tatham ("Full House"), as well as film scriptwriters like E. Paul Edwards ("My Cuba"), Brendan Burnes ("VTV"), Charles Holland ("Black Panther") and Michael Kane ("All the Right Moves," "Southern Comfort"). CNA reps playwright Bobby Moresco who has a screenplay beginning production soon ("Barlow Stuart"), and another playwright, Bill C. Jones ("Mass Appeal" and "Dancing in the End Zone"), as well as double threat Kevin Bernhardt who has not only written, but will star in his new screenplay, "Veronica."

Stuart and Glen both impressed me as the kind of guys I would like to have in my corner. They care, they are motivated, they obviously have entree and they're just folks. An agency that believes in a full partnership, you'll find out more from Glen and

Stuart elsewhere in the book.

Agents
Christopher Nassif, Stuart Jacobs and Glen Brunswick.
Client List
25-30
Clients
Peter Gallay, Jamie & Chuck Tatham, E. Paul Edwards,
Brendan Burnes, Bill C. Davis, Charles Holland, Michael Kane,
Bobby Moresco, Steve Kluger and others.
Notes

The Cooper Agency

10100 Santa Monica Blvd. #310
at Century Park East
Los Angeles, CA 90067
310-277-8422

Frank Cooper was secretary to the *real* William Morris in New
York during the early years of the Depression. Morris asked Frank
why he was studying accounting when he could focus his sights on
what was going to become *an interesting business.* When Morris
died, Frank took Morris' advice and started his own agency
representing talent. Whether he was working for ICM or back at
one of the many incarnations of his own agency, Mr. Cooper
pioneered what is now known as packaging: marrying writers,
talent and producers. He was Frank Sinatra's first agent, as well as
Dinah Shore's. By 1964, Cooper had an agency that represented
over 500 writers, producers, directors, entertainers and actors.
With so many important clients all over the world, Cooper spent
two weeks out of four on an airplane and it all became too much.
He sold his agency to Ashley-Famous and though he stayed on with
his clients, he wasn't happy.

Finally, he quit show business. For one day. After a week, old
clients were on his phone night and day for guidance. Finally, his
wife said, *You need an office if you are going to do this.*

Still going strong, The Cooper Agency has three generations of
Coopers representing the 50 or so high profile clients on the list.
Frank's son, Jeff, has been associated with his dad for 27 years and
now Frank's grandson, Bryan Cooper continues the dynasty.

The Cooper Agency represents writers, producers, directors,
composers, lyricists and authors. Some of Cooper's clients include

Clifford Irving ("Trial"), Jimmy Webb and Peter Stone ("Sidney and the Werewolf") and Bruce Henderson and Vince Bugliosi ("And the Sea Will Tell")

Agents
Frank Cooper, Jeff Cooper and Bryan Cooper.
Client List
55
Clients
Clifford Irving, Jimmy Webb, Peter Stone, Bruce Henderson, Vince Bugliosi and others.
Notes

The Coppage Company

11507 Chandler Blvd.
at Tujunga
North Hollywood, CA 91601
818-980-1106

Tired and discouraged after driving around in the rain for the second night looking for her office, I almost skipped my interview with Judy Coppage. I'm happy I persevered because sixty seconds after meeting Judy, her energy had infected me and I was ready for another day's work.

It's easy to see how Judy Coppage, the personification of charisma, became a vice-president of production and development at Hanna Barbera Studios before anyone even knew what that meant. And it's easy to see how she was one of the first women to break through into the executive area in show business.

One of those fortunate people who knew from the get-go that she was destined for Hollywood, she left home in Seattle for UCLA as quickly as possible, earned two degrees and hit the ground running. An executive at Paramount as well as HB, it didn't take long for Judy to see that as a woman in corporate show biz, there were plenty of limitations and that she could parlay her entrepreneurial skills and her love of writers into a much more satisfying life on her own. Judy started her own business in 1984 and loves what she does. Because she truly believes that the script is what it is all about, she is fearless in helping and selling her writers. Although she is famous for jump-starting careers, it's clear to me that anything this woman set her mind to, she would be famous for.

Besides being a successful representative for film and television writers like Scott Davis Jones ("Mavis Keates") and Harry & Renee

Longstreet ("With a Vengeance"), Judy is successful selling books as well. Two of her most visible success stories are Roderick Thorp ("Die Hard") and Brian Garfield ("Death Wish" and "Hopscotch").

Fiercely committed to the clients she already has, Judy only accepts industry referrals. She is assisted by Tim Reilly and Danny Ostrov.

Agents
Judy Coppage.
Client List
24
Clients
Scott Davis Jones, Harry and Renee Longstreet, Roderick Thorpe, Brian Garfield, Larry Bishop and others.
Notes

Creative Artists Agency (CAA)

9830 Wilshire Blvd.
at Little Santa Monica
Beverly Hills, CA 90212-1825
310-288-4545

Much has been written about the power, prestige and inscrutability of Creative Artists Agency. Many people are heard to say that instead of the big three which used to mean CAA, ICM and WMA, there is now really the big *one* and that the one is CAA. With the inroads ICM has made this year, the distance has narrowed considerably, but Mike Ovitz is still the number one power broker in town. Instrumental in the buyout of Universal Studios by Matsushita, Ovitz incurred the wrath of rival agencies by his role as consultant to France's Credit Lyonnais bank. Thought to be a conflict of interest, Ovitz drew fire on all fronts. Whatever the outcome, Ovitz and company continue to be the dominant force in the entertainment business.

The agency was founded in 1975 by Michael Ovitz, Will Haber, Rowland Perkins, Ron Meyer and Michael Rosenfield. When these dynamic men left William Morris, they

• *...didn't have any clients. They didn't have any financing. They didn't have any offices. In fact, between the five of them, they only had one car....They couldn't afford to hire a receptionist. So each of their wives filled in one day a week.*
                    "CAA: Packaging of an Agency"
                    Charles Schreger
                    Los Angeles Times
                    April 23, 1979

In 1990, the carless wonders moved into a magnificent building designed by I.M. Pei. As students of Japanese management techniques, they teach fellow agents to suppress individual ego. This method of doing business has been credited with their success, but as Ovitz sees it, *CAA grew simply because it was better than others at helping the talent realize its ends.*

> "Inside the Agency"
> Michael Cieply
> Los Angeles Times
> July 2, 1989

According to The New York Times July 9, 1989 article by L.J. Davis entitled "Hollywood's Most Secret Agent"), *CAA not only has 134 actor clients but also 288 writers, 146 directors, and Magic Johnson.* Clients include the cream of theater, film and television talent: Ruth Prawer Jhabvala ("Howard's End"), Bo Goldman ("Scent of a Woman"), Neil Simon (everything), Joshua Brand and John Falsey ("Northern Exposure"), Dick Wolf ("Law and Order") David Jacobs ("Knots Landing"), John Pasquin ("Home Improvement"), Jerry Seinfeld, David Letterman and many others.

There is more information on CAA in Chapter 8.

Agents
Mike Ovitz, Bill Haber, Ron Meyer, Rowland Perkins, Todd Smith, David O'Connor, David Tenzer, Tina Nides, Adam Krentzman, Glenn Bickel, Sonya Rosenfield, Jack Rapke, Rosalie Swedlin, David Lonner, Justin Connolly and many more.
Client List
Very large.
Clients
Marshall Brickman, William Goldman, Barry Levinson, Melissa Mathison, Rob Reiner, Ruth Prawer Jhabvala, Bo Goldman, Tracy Keenan Wynn, Neil Simon, George Stevens, Jr., David Jacobs, Joshua Brand, John Falsey, Dick Wolf, Jerry Seinfeld, David Letterman, John Pasquin and many others.
Notes

Douglas, Gorman, Rothacker & Wilhelm, Inc. (DGRW)

1501 Broadway, #703
btwn 43rd & 44th Streets
New York, NY 10036
212-382-2000

DGRW (known primarily as an effective and distinguished agency for actors) has recently added a small literary department. Guided by partner Fred Gorman, DGRW currently represents scriptwriters for theater, film and television. Client R.T. Robinson ("Cover of Life") is one name from their list of about ten. DGRW was established in 1988 when Fred Gorman (Bret Adams) joined Flo Rothaker (Ann Wright), Jim Wilhelm (Lionel Larner, Eric Ross, The Barry Douglas Agency) and Barry Douglas (ICM) to form a New York mini-conglomerate that is congenial and well connected.

Gorman is more interested in finding clients through his own means than reading query letters. He's constantly checking out new playwrights within the New York theater scene and gets referrals within the industry. DGRW also represents directors, choreographers, and musical directors. Their Los Angeles liaison is Badgeley and Connor.

Agents
Fred Gorman.
Client List
10
Clients
R.T. Robinson and others.
Notes

Epstein/Wyckoff & Associates

280 S Beverly Dr. #400
S of Wilshire Blvd.
Beverly Hills, CA 90212
310-278-7222

Craig Wyckoff and Gary Epstein each left careers as actors to become agents. Craig, because he felt agenting would be more of a challenge and Gary because he wanted to pay his rent on a regular basis. Craig joined The William Felber Agency developing the television and film department and Gary answered phones for his own agent, Mort Schwartz before moving forward to New York's prestigious Hesseltine/Baker. Soon each man owned his agency. Wyckoff's west coast agency merged with Epstein's east coast agency in 1991.

The literary department at this agency is headed by Karen Wakefield. Karen's background includes a stint working with Dan Curtis in development as well as a career as an independent producer. Since Karen joined E/W in 1988 the literary department has grown steadily. Clients from her list of 20 include Hanna Louise Shearer ("Star Trek: Deep Space Nine") and Stephen Beck ("Murder, She Wrote"). Epstein/Wykoff also represents directors and producers.

Agents
Karen Wakefield, Craig Wyckoff and Gary Epstein.
Client List
20
Clients
Hanna Louise Shearer, Stephen Beck and others.
Notes

Favored Artists Agency

8150 Beverly Blvd. #201
1 block W of Crescent Heights
Los Angeles, CA 90048
213-653-3191

A press agent with Rogers and Cowan before he entered the business as an assistant at Writers & Artists, George Goldey became a full fledged agent while working with Yvette Bickoff. Bickoff's liaison with the prestigious New York literary agency, The Artists Agency, Inc. introduced Goldey to AA owners, Barry Weiner and Jonathan Russo who joined with George to form this agency after the writers' strike in 1989.

Strongest as an agency for writers, producers and directors, the New York office divides duties with Russo representing writers of daytime while Weiner covers the reality bases with Robin Leach and writers on "Hard Copy" and "Inside Edition." In Los Angeles, Scott Henderson (Writers & Artists) covers film and television writers with clients like Phil Rosenberg ("The Terry Anderson Story," "Murder Between Friends").

Agents
George Goldey, Scott Henderson, Jonathan Russo and Barry Weiner.
Client List
25-30
Clients
Robin Leach, Phil Rosenberg and others.
Notes

Maggie Field Agency

12725 Ventura Blvd. # D
Calico Corners shopping area
Studio City, CA 91604
818-980-2001

Although Maggie Field says she became an agent by mistake, I prefer to call it fate. From her first job typing "Ironside" scripts in the steno pool at Universal, she advanced to secretary/assistant to a perfect group of trainers: a literary agent at William Morris, a publishing company, and another literary agent before finally becoming an agent at Zeigler Ross. She worked at Writers & Artists and Robinson Weintraub before suffering burnout and leaving the business altogether in 1984.

Burnout didn't last too long and Maggie decided to try the other side of the desk by joining Disney as a buyer. That experience focused her intentions to open her own office to protect and represent writers.

Fiercely vigilant for her clients, Maggie's list of lucky clients includes Deborah Joy LeVine ("Lois and Clark," "Equal Justice"), Nancy Ann Miller ("The Roundtable"), Linda Voorhees ("Crazy from the Heart"), Jenny Wingfield ("Man in the Moon"), and Sharon Elizabeth Doyle ("Stolen Babies"). Maggie represents 35 writers and producers and one director.

Maggie only reads material recommended by someone she already does business with: a client, producer, director, network or studio executive, so don't waste stamps, just get to know someone.

Agents
Maggie Field, Deborah Bayer and Larry Kennar.
Client List
35
Clients
Deborah Joy LeVine, Sharon Elizabeth Doyle, Beverly Sawyer,
Linda Voorhees, Jenny Wingfield, Bob Rodat and others.
Notes

Marje Fields/Rita Scott

165 W 46th St. #909
E of Broadway
New York, NY 10036
212-764-5740

Marje Fields is one of the most creative and aggressive agents in
the business. She started in radio soap operas years ago and is still
going strong. Originally an agency that represented actors only for
commercials, today her agency represents actors in all fields and
has joined with the prestigious literary agent, Rita Scott (Rita Scott
Agency), to produce a separate business run by Ray Powers. Ray
has worked in all parts of the business from acting to writing, but
his greatest accomplishments have come from being a personal
manager and agent. He not only managed Gena Rowlands and
Thelma Ritter among others, but is credited with starting Jane
Fonda when he was at Famous Artists. His command of the
literary side of the business includes writers of novels, non-fiction
and plays. He represents the estate of Patrick Dennis ("Auntie
Mame"), and has considerable success starting out first writers
(now established) such as novelists John Westermann ("Exit
Wounds"), Nicole Jeffords ("Hearts of Gold") and Timothy Watts
("Cons"). Ray also represents playwright Randall Buck ("Swamp
Gas" and "Trances"). Some of the non-fiction books repped by this
agency include "Encyclopedia of the Aging and the Elderly" and
"The Wheat and Oat Bran Cookbook."

Query letters to this agency should include a brief background of
the writer as well as a general idea of what he/she plans to write
about. Ray says one or two lines are sometimes more compelling
than three pages, so choose your words carefully. The office is
represented in Hollywood by Robert Goldfarb.

Agents
Ray Powers.
Client List
30
Clients
Patrick Dennis, John Westermann, Nicole Jeffords, Timothy Watts, Randall Buck and others.
Notes

The Gage Group

9255 Sunset Blvd. #515
just W of Doheny
Los Angeles, CA 90069
310-859-8777

A brilliant agent and a crazy human being, Martin Gage is someone you can't help but like. This affable/irascible man helms a homey successful agency that represents writers, directors and actors.

President of the literary department, Jonathan Westover was an assistant who helped cast commercials at JHR (Joseph Heldfond and Rix) and interned at Richland/Wunsch/Hohman Agency before coming to the GG and assisting previous literary department head, Karen Bohrman. When Karen left to pursue other interests, Martin offered Jonathan the chance to make the department his own. Agent-in-training/assistant, Kirk Durham has used his degree in screenwriting to become an invaluable part of the team.

Gage Group clients write for theater, film and television. A few from the list include Jane Anderson ("Baby Dance," "The Positively True Adventures of the Alleged Cheerleader-Murdering Mom"), Al Martinez ("Betrayal of Trust," Dancing Under the Moon) and Bryan Nelson. There are insightful comments by Jonathan elsewhere in the book.

Agents
Martin Gage and Jonathan Westover.
Client List
17
Clients
Jane Anderson, Bryan Nelson, Al Martinez and others.
Notes

Laya Gelff Associates

16122 Ventura Blvd., #700
just W of Sepulveda
Sherman Oaks, CA 91436
818-342-7247

Executive director of the Emmys for ten years as well as associate producer of news for NBC, Laya Gelff became an agent because of her husband, who is an actor. Unhappy with his representation, Laya's background enabled her to function as his agent, making phone calls and handling details of his career. It didn't take long for both Laya and her husband to decide that she should get an agency franchise and get paid for her expertise.

Since that time (1985), she has expanded her list to add 8 writers and 2 directors who function in both film and television. Client Malvin Wald conceived and wrote the original "Naked City" and will forever be famous for his line: *There are 6 million stories in the naked city and this is one of them.* He also won an Oscar for "Al Capone." Ed Metzger is another writer/director client.

Laya does not read unsolicited scripts and like most agents, prefers referrals. She will read a letter with a brief (two sentence) description of the piece along with a sase and will let you know if it is something she would like to pursue further. She only responds with a request if she feels the material is viable, so only a small percentage receive a request note.

Agent
Laya Gelff.
Client List
10
Clients
Barbara T. Azrialy, Malvin Wald, Ed Metzger and others.
Notes

The Gersh Agency

232 N Canon Drive
S of Little Santa Monica
Beverly Hills, CA 90210
310-274-6611

Phil Gersh has been part of the Hollywood scene since the days
when agents were not allowed past the studio gates. A legend in
the business well before he opened The Gersh Agency in the late
70s, his agency has become one of the most prominent and
prestigious independent agencies in town. The Gersh Agency has a
glittering list of writers, directors, actors and below the line
personnel that quickly command attention and respect.

Clients shared by both coasts include Bill Gerber ("Roseanne"),
Marlane Meyer Jeanne Betancourt ("Tattle: When to Tell on a
Friend," "Supermom's Daughter"), Ntozake Shange and others.

Gersh sons, David and Phil, head the literary department.

Agents
David Gersh, Phil Gersh, Richard Arlook, Dan Aloni, Ron
Bernstein, Ken Neisser, Nancy Nigrosh and Matt Solo.
Client List
220 (NY/LA)
Clients
Check WGA listing.
Notes

The Gersh Agency New York

130 W 42nd Street #2400
btwn 5th & 6th Avenues
New York, NY 10036
212-997-1818

The Gersh Agency New York was formed when David Guc
(pronounce Gus), Scott Yoselow, Ellen Curren and Mary Meager
decided to leave Don Buchwald & Associates to form a New York
office for the prestigious Los Angeles firm Phil Gersh started long
ago. The Gersh Agency New York has continued to add stature to
the Gersh legend. A significant agency for writers, directors,
actors and below the line personnel, the bulk of the literary
department is handled through the Los Angeles office, but the New
York office manages to be busy enough to enlist the efforts of four
agents, so Los Angeles is obviously not doing all the business.

Partner Scott Yoselow represents writers and directors, Susan
Morris is the book agent and Jennifer Lyne handles below the line
clients. New clients in this agency are mostly seen by industry
referral.

Agents
Ellen Curren, David Guc, Scott Yoselow, Susan Morris and
Jennifer Lyne.
Client List
220 (NY/LA)
Clients
Check WGA listing.
Notes

Gold Marshak and Associates

3500 W Olive #1400
at Riverside Dr.
Burbank, CA 91505
818-972-4300

In 1981 Harry Gold opened this agency and asked Darryl Marshak to be his partner and in 1992, Darryl accepted. If Harry is as persistent getting his clients jobs, it's easy to see how this agency continues to thrive. The literary department at Gold Marshak is headed by Jeff Melnick. After years as a studio executive at Universal, Columbia and Metromedia, Jeff opened his first agency in 1989 repping such talent as John Patrick Shanley ("Moonstruck") and Rob Epstein and Jeff Friedman ("Common Threads"). He worked for the noted literary office of Curtis Brown before joining GMA where his clients include Charles Busch ("Vampire Lesbians of Sodom") and playwright/screenwriter Lee Blessing ("A Walk in the Woods," "Cooperstown"), Lee Thuna ("Torch Song"), Bob Randall ("Kate & Allie") and James Duff ("Doing Time on Maple Drive"). Jeff proudly points out that every year at least one of his clients receives some industry accolade whether it be Oscar, Emmy or DGA award. Evan Corday, whose background includes Triad and Lorimar, is Jeff's colleague. She represents episodic series writers.

Agent
Jeff Melnick and Evan Corday.
Client List
25
Clients
James Duff, Bob Tandall, Charles Busch, Lee Blessing, Lee Thuna and others.
Notes

Gray/Goodman, Inc.

211 S Beverly Dr. #100
S of Wilshire
Beverly Hills, CA 90212
310-276-7070

The crippling writers' strike in 1987 produced several agencies who merged in order to withstand the bad times and although Mark Goodman and Stephen Gray started their business just prior to the strike, the shared misery only deepened their bond. Stephen (pronounce it Stef-an) Gray was a successful agent in Chicago for ten years before he started his Los Angeles office in 1984 and Mark's previous experience as a personal manager complemented his efforts.

Stephen and Mark have recently changed the shape of their agency, shifting attention from theatrical clients to below the line representation of line producers for film and television and some cinematographers.

They retain a literary department under the leadership of ex-writer/director, Joe Worsley.

Agents
Joe Worsley.
Client List
20
Clients
Check WGA listing.
Notes

The Charlotte Gusay Literary Agency

10532 Blythe Avenue
near Pico & Overland
Los Angeles, CA 90064
213-559-0831

Charlotte Gusay's love of the literary has such deep roots that she founded and owned the prestigious George Sand Bookstore in Los Angeles. When she burned out of the book business after twelve years, she learned the agent business representing artists. Gusay became franchised and opened her own literary agency in 1988 because she was *too qualified, too old,* you name it, she was *too everything* to be hired by anybody else. It didn't take her long to make a sale (Miriam Marx Allen's book, "Love, Groucho") and her credibility was established.

Other clients include Patsy Hilbert ("Love Addict"), Tom Kara ("Sherman's War") Ann Reiner ("A Visit to the Art Galaxy"), Mark St. Pierre ("Holy Women, Healers, and Pipe Carriers"), Vassilis Boudouris ("The City of the Sun"), David Shields ("Dead Languages") and Ken Grissom ("Big Fish").

Charlotte represents fiction, non-fiction, children's books, children's book illustrators, entertainment rights, books to film, selected screenplays and screenwriters.

The Charlotte Gusay Literary Agency is looking for fiction and non-fiction books, film projects and children's books that are innovative, unusual, eclectic and nonsexist. Send a brief query letter first.

Agents
Charlotte Gusay.
Client List
30+
Clients
Patsy Hilbert, Tom Kara, Vassilis Boudaris, David Shields, Miriam
Marx Allen, Ken Grissom, Annie Reiner, Mark St. Pierre and
others.
Notes

The Graham Agency

311 W 43rd Street
btwn 8th & 9th Avenues
New York, NY 10036
212-489-7730

Earl Graham was a music student when he took a job selling tickets at the McCarter Theater solely to make money. That first exposure to the business proved prophetic and in the '60s, Earl found himself managing Equity Library Theater and running a placement service for actors. Equity ran out of money for the project and someone suggested that instead of getting civilian work for actors, he should become an agent. Ashley-Famous was the lucky agency that ended up with Earl as their secretary. Bored with other duties, Earl created a job for himself that consisted of viewing every play off and off-off-Broadway and writing reviews of the talent and material for the agency. One day, literary giant Audrey Wood stopped by his desk to inquire just why he was doing what he was doing. She pointed out that his analytical skills spotting good material would be better served if he were, in fact, a literary agent. With Wood as a mentor, Earl soon made that transition.

In 1971, when A-F reorganized and became IFA (forerunner to ICM), Earl was one of the casualties. Not to worry, IFA was good to him and allowed Earl to take all 50 of his clients with him. One of his first big finds was actor-turned-writer Jason Miller and his prize winning play "That Championship Season." To prove it wasn't just a fluke, he also discovered actor-turned-writer Ernest Thompson who wrote "On Golden Pond."

Earl reps about 35 writers. He says the business has changed so much and it is so difficult to start new writers, that plays need to be through the developmental period before he is interested. He won't take on screenwriters as such, or writers of musicals. Clients include Leslie Steele ("Hide & Seek"), John MacNicholas ("Dumas") and George Sibbald ("Brothers") and Richard Browner ("Morning Dew with Trellis").

Agents
Earl Graham.
Client List
35
Clients
Leslie Steele, John MacNicholas, George Sibbald, Richard Browner and others.
Notes

Innovative Artists

1999 Avenue of the Stars #2850
S of Little Santa Monica
Los Angeles, CA 90067
310-553-5200

The prestigious talent agency that Scott Harris and Howard Goldberg created has transformed significantly since its 1982 inception as Harris & Goldberg. A glittering client list coupled with major agency additions like status literary agent Frank Wuliger have resulted in even more dimension and credibility. In 1991 when Wuliger arrived and Ken Kaplan opened the east coast office, the new incarnation, Innovative Artists Talent and Literary Agency, was born.

Frank Wuliger, who heads the literary department, traveled the route of many big-time-agents from the mailroom at The William Morris Agency on to assisting at a prestigious office before creating the literary department at APA in 1980. He was the senior executive in the motion picture department at ICM before producing for two years with Walter Mirisch. He was also an executive at DEG. Frank returned to agenting at The Agency in 1986.

Colleagues at Innovative who represent writers and directors also have brilliant pedigrees. Sandy Weinberg was Bill Block's assistant at ITA before moving over to the prestigious old-line office, H.N. Swanson. Judith Everett was at Robinson/Weintraub & Gross.

Writer clients include Jeanne Rosenberg ("Black Stallion," "White Fang," "The Journey of Natty Gunn"), Gary Devore ("Dogs of War," "Back Road," "Running Scared"), Bob Comfort ("Dogfight") and Linda Woolverton ("Beauty and the Beast").

Innovative Artists

1776 Broadway #1810
at 57th Street
New York, NY 10019
212-315-4455

Innovative represents writers, directors, producers and below the line personnel. New clients usually come through industry referral. Query letters are discouraged...but are always read. Do not query this agency unless you have entree.

Agents
Frank Wuliger, Sandy Weinberg and Judith Everett.
Client List
65 NY/LA
Clients
Jeanne Rosenberg, Gary Devore, Bob Comfort, Linda Woolverton, Tommy Lee Wallace, Robert Resnikoff and others.
Notes

ICM/International Creative Management

8942 Wilshire Blvd.
just W of Robertson
Beverly Hills, CA 90211
310-550-4000

CAA (Creative Artists Agency) may be the most powerful agency in the world, but ICM is making inroads. In 1991, power shifted appreciatively. ICM made big advances when important WMA agents defected to ICM and brought significant clients (Julia Roberts, Tim Robbins, Angelica Huston, etc.) with them to join big guns Eddie Murphy and Arnold Schwarzenegger who were already in residence. Then, in the great agency shakeup of 1992, Bill Block (head of prestigious boutique, InterTalent) disbanded his agency and returned to ICM as head of the west coast office.

Known to be less corporate than WMA and CAA (that means everyone in the corporation doesn't have to be called in to review your latest contract), ICM is described by insiders as a stylish, forward-thinking operation. Headed by president Jim Wiatts, powerful ICM is intent on replacing powerful CAA as the number one talent agency in the world.

Number two in the current agent-hierarchy, ICM is poised for combat. Formed when Ashley-Famous and CMA merged in 1971, this agency has many, many clients and many, many agents. The most famous are powerful Sam Cohn who heads the New York office and charismatic Ed Limato who was the first defection from WMA a year earlier. Ed was profiled in a <u>Vanity Fair</u> article, "The Famous Eddie L." in January 1990. If you have the credits to consider this agency, a trip to the library to read this article is a must. Among many other distinguished writers, ICM represents Neil Jordan ("The Crying Game"), Nick Enright ("Lorenzo's Oil")

ICM/International Creative Management

40 W 57th Street
just W of 5th Avenue
New York, NY 10019
212-556-5600

and Julie Brown ("Medusa: Dare to be Truthful").

The conglomerates frown on publication of their agents names, so
these are heresay. If you plan to send something, check.

Agents
Los Angeles: Scott Arnovitz, Ben Benjamin, Jeff Berg, Alan
Berger, Diane Cairns, Tricia Davey, Patty Detroit, Barbara
Dreyfus, Ariel Emannuel, Richard Feldman, Amy Ferris, Lee
Gabler, David Greenblatt, Alan Greenspan, Bob Gumer, Paul Haas,
Bill Haber, Nancy Josephson, Ken Kamins, David Lonner, Tom
McNeal, Chris Moore, Lou Pitt, Joe Rosenberg, Mark Rossen,
Richard Saperstein, Steve Sanford, Scott Schwartz, Tom Strickler,
Irene Webb, Jim Wiatt, Jeanne Williams, David Wirstchafter and
others.

New York: Lisa Loosemore, Boaty Boatwright, Lisa Bankoff,
Mitch Douglas, Paul Martino, Andrea Eastman, Sue Leibman,
Kristine Dahl, Suzanne Gluck, Gordon Kato and Esther Newberg
and others.
Client List
Very large.
Clients
Neil Jordan, Nick Enright, Ralph Bakshi, Rene Balcer, Peter P.
Benchley, Woody Allen, Garry Marshall, Mike Nichols, Julie
Brown, Cynthia Whitcomb, Greg Daniels and others.
Notes

Leslie B. Kallen Agency

15303 Ventura Blvd. #900
near Sepulveda Blvd.
Sherman Oaks, CA 91403
818-906-2785

Leslie Kallen says she is a cheerleader for new writing talent and that this is why she became an agent. Starting in the business as a reader, she also led script writing seminars from a reader's perspective. Finding herself with a client base of new screenwriters from this experience, it was a short move to starting her own agency in 1986. Leslie is known in the business as an alternative source for quality new scriptwriters. Her stable of 20 plus writers includes international stars like professor/playwright/screenwriter Andy Wolfendon, writing team Ethlie Ann Vare & Marshall New, award-winning Allan Hollingsworth and Paul Dreskin.

Agents
Leslie B. Kallen.
Client List
20+
Clients
Paul Dreskin, Allan Hollingsworth, Ethlie Ann Vare & Marshall New, Andy Wolfendon and others.
Notes

Kaplan Stahler Agency

8383 Wilshire Blvd. #923
at San Vicente Blvd.
Beverly Hills, CA 90211
213-653-4483

Mitch Kaplan and Elliot Stahler graduated from the WMA mailroom, class of '74. After graduation, Mitch went into production and Elliot went to law school by night and worked as a literary agent at WMA by day. When Mitch decided that production was not his forte, he joined Progressive Artists Agency as a theatrical agent. Soon Elliot left WMA and, as he describes it, they *naively and successfully* started the literary department at PAA. In 1981, they opened their own offices and are now recognized as one of the most prestigious, tasteful and successful agencies in town.

KS believes in 30-year-careers for their clients and they invest the time to nurture beginners whether they are writers or directors. For all their success (and they have a lot of it), Elliot and Mitch still take time to read material and value new talent. New associate Todd Koerner, came to KS via United Talent where he traveled from mailroom to assistant for partner Gary Cosay.

Clients include David Angell ("Wings") and Ross Brown ("Step by Step"). Their list of 40 clients includes 22 writers and writing teams, line producers and Emmy award winning directors.

Agents
Mitch Kaplan, Elliot Stahler and Todd Koerner.
Client List
22
Clients
David Angell, Ross Brown and others.
Notes

Patricia Karlan Agency

4425 Riverside Drive #102
near Pass Avenue
Burbank, CA 91505
818-752-4800

Since the network and studio business affairs folk are those that
negotiate all the contracts, it seems as though a background in this
field must be second only to the conglomerate mailrooms as an
educational prerequisite for agents. It surely takes a lot of the
praying and guess work out of how far to push. This is exactly
what Patricia Karlan's pre-agent duties entailed.

Armed with this experience, Karlan runs a successful business
representing screenwriters and film rights for published authors.
She is not interested in episodic. Some of her writing clients
include Dean R. Koontz ("Whispers," "Face of Fear") and Judith
Guest.

Agents
Patricia Karlan.
Client List
20
Clients
Dean R. Koontz, Judith Guest and others.
Notes

Joyce Ketay

334 W 89th Street
just E of WEA
New York, NY 10024
212-779-2398

Cancer Research Diagnosis and non-profit theater have produced an unusually synergistic partnership. Joyce Ketay left the scientific community in search of a less depressing life. To sustain her during the search, a friend suggested work as an assistant to literary agent Ellen Neuwald. Dealing with Neuwald clients like David Rabe and John Guare helped clinch Joyce's decision to embark on a new life as a literary agent. When Ellen died in 1980, Joyce started Joyce Ketay Agency and ran it alone for 10 years.

Carl Mulert was a production and theater manager for Arena Stage and Playwrights Horizons. Also burned out and seeking a new life, he confided to old friend Joyce that he was going to find a job as a secretary in a law firm someplace while exploring new options. Knowing how these things work, Joyce persuaded him to be her assistant and, of course, now he is her partner.

Carl joins a growing list of ex-production stage managers who find their stage manager skills more valuable than they imagined. Stage manager skills include a whole raft of valuable assets from resourcefulness to contacts from the other side of the desk that are great boons to any theatrically related business.

Joyce's and Carl's clients include Pulitzer Prize winner Tony Kushner, Tony winner Michael Cristofer and writer/director Stuart Ross ("Forever Plaid"). They handle writers, directors and designers.

Agents
Joyce Ketay and Carl Mulert.
Client List
50
Clients
Tony Kushner, Michael Cristofer, Stuart Ross, Eric Simonson and others.
Notes

Paul Kohner, Inc.

9169 Sunset Blvd.
just W of Doheny
Los Angeles, CA 90069
310-550-1060

The late Paul Kohner built this prestigious agency into one of the most successful and famous boutique agencies in town. His list of writers, directors and actors is filled with famous names from Europe and America. In 1987, a year before Paul died, colleagues Gary Salt and Pearl Wexler bought the agency and they continue to deal in the old-world manner with which clients Billy Wilder and Ivan Passer are familiar.

While finishing a graduate degree at Stanford in the Drama Department in 1972, The Contemporary Korman agency presented Gary with an opportunity to enter the agency business. He was trained by ex-MCA agent, Ron Leif, at C-K (now Contemporary Artists). From there, he moved on to Smith Stevens Associates (now Smith and Associates) where he inaugurated their literary department.

Since joining PK in 1977, his focus in the literary marketplace has become more diverse as he carves out his own niche in a variety of endeavors. He reps publishers, authors, book material, composers, directors and producers as well as screen writers and television writers.

The list of 35 writers and 12 directors also contains names like Istvan Szabo ("Meeting Venus," "Mephisto"), Donald Westlake ("The Grifters"), John Toles-Bey ("Rage in Harlem"), Tom Clancy ("The Hunt for Red October"), etc. Gary not only heads the literary department repping writers, directors and producers, but also handles a few theatrical clients as well.

For legal reasons, PKI accepts no unsolicited material, but does answer every query letter that is accompanied by sase.

Agents
Gary Salt.
Client List
65
Clients
Istvan Szabo, Alan Sharp, Donald Westlake, Ed McBain, Chris Beaumont, Tony Huston, John Toles-Bey, Denise Nicolos, Charles Marowitz and others.
Notes

The Kopaloff Company

1930 Century Park W #403
S of Little Santa Monica
Los Angeles, CA 90067
310-203-8430

Don Kopaloff's job as a messenger for Twentieth Century Fox in New York launched him into show business. Helen Straus, head of the literary department at WMA, noticed Don and urged him to become involved in the training program there. After graduating from the mailroom, with time out for the Korean war, Don returned to his alma mater and worked in almost every department. Freddy Fields and David Begelman invited Don to join them when they formed CMA (forerunner of ICM) with the understanding that they would send him to Los Angeles.

Don's versatile background served him well in his next job as head of production for Avco Embassy. There, Don created projects, found new writers and directors and started many now famous names on their way. After the Avco experience, he started Donburry Management, Ltd., a small boutique agency. This was folded into IFA, where Don remained until the IFA/CMA merger begot ICM. At that point, he left and once again started his own agency.

Agents
Don Kopaloff.
Client List
Confidential.
Clients
Check WGA listing.
Notes

Lucy Kroll Agency

2211 Broadway
at 79th Street
New York, NY 10024
212-877-0556

Located in the historic Apthorp Apartments on Broadway and 79th, Lucy Kroll and her agency live up to their residence. Distinguished and respected, Lucy was educated as an actress at Hunter College, The School for Stage and by teachers who were performers at the Moscow Art Theater under the aegis of Stanislavski and Meyerhold. She also had classical ballet training. She was the co-founder of the American Actors Company in 1935 with Horton Foote, Agnes De Mille and others. In 1940 she became a story analyst at Warner Brothers and co-founded the Hollywood Music Alliance. In 1945, Sam Jaffee asked her to open his office. That office was the forerunner of LKA. For most of the almost 50 year history of this agency, Lucy ran it as a one-woman show, but times change and so did she. Realizing that she had an important legacy to bestow (both for actors and for writers), Lucy began to expand her agency in 1986.

At that time, Barbara Hogenson (who is now Lucy's partner) was leaving a position as Director of Creative Research at Foote, Cone and Belding. Barbara's background in research extended to an interdisciplinary graduate degree in Film, Photography and Art Library plus a job at the Museum of Modern Art. Lucy realized that these same qualities would make Barbara a first rate agent. Barbara oversees the office which has now grown to include a total of four agents. Beth Gardiner joined LKA after a career with theatrical advertising agency Russek Advertising.

LKA represents several journalists from <u>The New York Times</u> as well as playwrights and composers of Broadway musicals. There is not much that Lucy Kroll has not done. A legend whose papers reside in the Library of Congress, there is no more prestigious name in literary circles.

Agents
Lucy Kroll, Barbara Hogenson and Beth Gardiner.
Client List
60
Clients
Horton Foote, Nan Robertson, Carol Brightmerr, Penelope Niven and others.
Notes

The Lantz Office

888 Seventh Ave.
btwn 56th & 57th Streets
New York, NY 10106
212-586-0200

The Lantz Office is one of the class acts in the annals of show biz. When I quizzed New York agents as to other agents they admired, Robert Lantz was the name most mentioned. He started in the business as a story editor. On a Los Angeles business trip from his London home in 1950, Phil Berg of the famous Berg-Allenbery Agency made him an offer he couldn't refuse, *Don't go home. Come to New York and open our office there.* Mr. Lantz indeed did open the New York office at 3 East 57th Street representing Clark Gable, Madeleine Carroll and other illustrious stars until William Morris bought that company a year later.

Lantz worked for smaller agencies for a few years before opening Robert Lantz, Ltd. in 1954. In 1955, he succumbed to Joe Mankiewicz's pleas and joined him to produce films. It only took three years to figure out that he found agenting a much more interesting profession. In 1958, Lantz reentered the field as a literary agent. Feeling a mix of actors and directors and writers gave each segment more power, his list soon reflected that.

Colleague Dennis Aspland worked for the legendary Sam Cohn before joining Lantz representing screenwriters and directors. The list of writers numbers about 20 and includes Jules Feiffer, Peter Shaffer, Anthony Shaffer, Bruce Wolf, Peter Feibleman and the estate of Sean O'Casey.

Agents
Robert Lantz and Dennis Aspland.
Client List
20
Clients
Jules Feiffer, Peter Feibleman, Peter Shaffer, Anthony Shaffer, the estate of Sean O'Casey, Bruce Wolf and others.
Notes

The Literarium

406-A Hudson Street, # E-16
below 14th St.
New York, NY 10014
212-741-0125

Jim Bormann is an interesting fellow. In 1964, he left Gordon, Nebraska to become a great actor. While he was waiting to be discovered (and needing to pay his rent), he got a temporary job assisting a writer of self-help books. He typed manuscripts and edited. After three years, Jim decided that perhaps his niche might be Los Angeles, so he journeyed there. By kismet, he ended up in yet another literary endeavor, The Mitchell J. Hamilburg Agency. At Hamilburg, Jim became their reader and prepared packages when the agency was pitching for clients. In 1970, he returned to NY and while again pursuing acting, worked on staff for The Blackfriars Theater, the oldest continuously run off-Broadway theater in New York (until its incendiary demise in 1972). Again, Bormann was cast not as an actor, but as a developer of writers, organizing and directing readings and focusing authors.

While he managed to get away from show business from time to time working for such disparate people as Merrill Lynch and McGraw-Hill, he always ended up either writing or editing any publications produced by his employers. Finally, after only 20 years in New York, he managed to notice that fate was trying to tell him something, so he gave up and opened his own agency. He has made many writers very happy.

Because The Literarium responds to all correspondence, this agency feels justified in setting a few guidelines, i.e., in your letter, don't just include information regarding whether or not you have been published or produced, but whether you are or have been involved in a writer's workshop and where.

Bormann is not interested in material for television series, but will look at films for television. He wants a sample of the first 10-15 *consecutive* pages of whatever you are writing. If it is a novel, the first 35 *consecutive* pages. Bormann says, *It's a waste of money to send it Fed Ex or return receipt requested* and that you should be patient, he will get to you, although it may be months.

If you feel the need to call to know if the material arrived or where you are on the list, be brief. If he's talking to you, he's not reading your work.

Jim says, *dancers dance, singers take singing lessons, actors act and writers write. If you are talking to me, you're not writing.* Beau Ruland is Bormann's assistant.

Agents
Jim Bormann.
Client List
20
Clients
Check WGA listing.
Notes

Major Clients Agency

2121 Avenue of the Stars #2450
at Olympic Blvd.
Los Angeles, CA 90067
310-284-6400

Major Clients Agency has gone through a taxing period during
which principals Jeffrey Benson and Richard Weston merged their
celebrated literary agency with an equally prestigious talent agency,
McCartt, Oreck and Barrettt (MOB) to form the mini-conglomerate,
Metropolitan Talent Agency.

Irreconcilable business ideas caused the promising merger to fall
apart just three years after the wedding and now Benson and
Weston are back under their own banner as one of the prime
literary offices in Los Angeles.

Colleagues Mark R. Harris (The Harris Company), Stephen Marks
(ICM) and David McIlvain (Innovative Artists Agency) followed
from Metropolitan bringing along their own 93 writers, producers
and directors. Harris, Marks and McIlvain also brought their
clients giving the agency added cachet.

Richard Weston was head of television production at Paramount and
Jeffrey Benson was an executive vice-president at Lorimar before
they entered the agency business. Their clients include Paul Haggis
("thirtysomething") and Mark Ganzel ("Coach").

Agents
Jeffrey Benson, Richard Weston, Diane Fraser, Stephen Rose,
Mark R. Harris, Stephen Marks and David McIlvain.
Client List
100+

Clients
John Conboy, Bob Jaffe, Buddy Sheffield, Gary Pudney, Paul
Flattery, Jim Yukich, Dean Cain, Paul Haggis,
Mark Ganzel and others.
Notes

Media Artists Group/MAG

8383 Wilshire Blvd. #954
at San Vicente
Beverly Hills, CA 90011
213-658-5050

If Raphael Berko can't get you through the door, I don't know who can. A man brimming with ideas and passion, Raphael Berko became an agent because he was an enterprising and creative actor. Since he couldn't get an agent, Raphael took a job as an agent's assistant in order to submit himself for auditions. When The Hollywood Reporter wrote a story about his double life, the jig was up.

Screen Actors Guild told him he could be an actor or an agent, but not both. His choice has made his clients eternally grateful. When Raph was 29, he bought The Caroline Leonetti Agency and his fortunes have steadily risen.

Barbara Alexander heads the literary department and she's no slouch, either. Alexander has been a writer/director/producer of short films, a VP of development at Odyssey Films, an independent producer and a production assistant. An agent for over 10 years, she's an empathetic writer's advocate. Colleague Ken Greenblatt was a consultant on Wall Street and a few years ago, he was the general manager for "A Chorus Line" in Los Angeles. His humanity, business savvy and show biz history perfectly complement the rest of this agency making MAG one of the most appealing offices in town.

Open and down to earth, this full service agency represents writers, directors, director-producers, writer-producers as well as both theatrical and commercial actors.

Barbara, Ken and Raphael are dedicated to developing careers and taking clients on for the long haul. Their clients write for film and all areas of television, including interactive. The list of 25 writers includes playwright/novelist Susan Dworkin ("Queen of the Stardust Ballroom," Stolen Goods), feature and television writer, Madeline Di Maggio ("Stroke of Midnight") and playwright, feature and television writer Shirl Hendryx ("Running Brave", "The Jumping Fool", "Final Jeopardy.")

Media Artists looks at new material only through industry referral. Although they do respond to some query letters, Barbara says the ration is about 1 out of 200.

Agents
Barbara Alexander, Ken Greenblatt and Raphael Berko.
Client List
under 25
Clients
Shirl Hendryx, Bruce Taylor, Ric Weiss, Susan Dworkin, Madeline Di Maggio and others.
Notes

Metropolitan Talent Agency/MTA

9320 Wilshire Blvd. #627
at Doheny
Beverly Hills, CA 90212
310-247-5500

Former actor and writer Chris Barrett is the only founding partner remaining at Metropolitan Talent Agency, following a time of upheaval discussed on page 219.

Although Jeffrey Benson and Richard Weston departed with their writers to regenerate their previous agency, Major Clients, Barrett is aggressively on the build of a new literary department.

He has hired former WMA agent Maryann Kelly to represent writers and says there will be more high profile literary personnel to give support to Ms. Kelly soon.

First literary client under the new regime is Patrick Clifton who wrote "The Son-in-Law."

Since this established agency is rebuilding its literary list, it might be more open to new writers than usual.

Agents
Maryann Kelly and more to come.
Client List
Building.
Clients
Patrick Clifton with more to come.
Notes

The William Morris Agency (Triad)

1350 Avenue of the Americas
at 55th Street
New York, NY 10019
212-586-5100

There really was a man named William Morris who started this
agency in 1898. The IBM of the Big Three, WMA has recently
gone through major restructuring in an attempt to compete with #1
(CAA) and #2 (ICM). In late 1992 in a bid to transform, WMA
merged with prestigious Triad to capture more big names.

The agency represents not only writers, directors, producers and
actors, but athletes, newscasters, political figures and almost any
other being of notoriety. If your career is heating up and you are
so inclined, venerable William Morris is now in the position of
really trying harder, since they are number three.

I'm told by my Los Angeles WMA friends that the word from on
high is *never to take no for an answer* in pursuing clients'
opportunities. The trick is to become the client WMA is looking to
please. My knowledge of the Triad bunch leads me to believe
chances of person-to-person treatment at WMA have greatly
improved. Every day in the trades I read of yet another prestigious
client or agent who has moved to WMA where there seems to be a
concerted effort to raid high-profile film makers. I don't think
William Morris plans to be #3 for very long. More on this agency
in Chapter 8.

Lists of agents are confidential at WMA. Although you are better
off perusing the lists at the Writers Guild, I will list a few names
that I have either picked up in the trades or other news stories.

The William Morris Agency (Triad)

151 El Camino Drive
S of Wilshire
Beverly Hills, CA 90212
310-274-7451

Agents
Todd Harris, Carol Yumkas, Dodie Gold, Ron Mardigian, Mike
Peretzian, Jeff Field, Lee Cohen, Marcy Posner, Phil Liebowitz,
Owen Laster and many many more.
Client List
more and more every day.
Clients
Michael Tolkin, Peter Barnes, Henry Bromwell, Pamela K. Long,
Anna Sandor, Bruce Vilanch, Noah Stern, Roger Wilson, Diane
Wilk, David Wickes and many others.
Notes

Monteiro Rose Agency, Inc.

17514 Ventura Blvd. #205
1½ blocks E of White Oak
Encino, CA 91316
818-501-1177

Candy Monteiro wrote, produced, directed and hosted a rock n' roll radio interview show, and would-be opera singer Fredda Rose was a Wall Street lawyer before each embarked on the journey leading to the establishment of the eclectic Monteiro Rose Agency. Deciding she knew more rock n' roll gossip than was good for her brain, Candy got a job as a literary assistant and reader for New York book agent Henry Morrison.

Fredda moved from Wall Street to ABC television business affairs learning *all those things* buyers do to writers. She got a chance for graduate study when ABC moved her to Los Angeles. Fredda later joined The Sy Fisher Agency and successfully agitated to become a literary agent.

During this time, Candy traveled from New York to Los Angeles becoming assistant to Bettye McCartt at MOB (now Metropolitan) and Sylvia Hirsch at Lew Weitzman (Preferred Artists). As low-woman-on-the-totem pole, she drew those clients less financially viable: the animation writers. When animation gained more respect, her writers were not only animation stars, but also graduated to features.

Candy and Fredda met when Fisher and Weitzman merged. That happy working relationship resulted in Monteiro Rose in 1987. Their list of 50 + includes writers and producers for film, movies for television, series, animation and interactive. They also represent authors and they package. MR preferred not to print clients' names, so check WGA lists for more information.

Monteiro Rose is very selective about new clients and has only taken on a very few new clients from query letters in almost seven years. If you are already in the business in some capacity, your chances are better, but still, you'd better have many scripts and they better be good. Rose and Monteiro stress that any script ever submitted to an agent had better be the fourth or fifth pass, never the first.

Agents
Fredda Rose and Candy Monteiro.
Client List
50+
Clients
Check WGA Listing.
Notes

Helen Merrill

435 W 23rd Street #1A
btwn 8th and 9th Avenues
New York, NY 10011
212-691-5326

One of the most reputable literary agencies in New York and certainly one of the most difficult to penetrate is Helen Merrill, home to some of the most important writers, directors and designers in the business. I was delighted to finally meet Ms. Merrill even if it was only on the telephone.

Originally a photographer, Merrill became an agent out of financial necessity and from the names on her client list (confidential), it's clear that money has not been a problem since she started her business in 1976.

Helen Merrill represents authors, playwrights and screenwriters and only considers query letters accompanied by sase. These letters should contain not only brief descriptions of the project, but information regarding any productions and/or published works with the publishers attached to it. Don't inundate this office with material unless you have the resume to back it up.

Agents
Helen Merrill and others.
Client List
30
Clients
Check WGA listings.
Notes

Fifi Oscard Agency

24 W 40th Street
W of 5th Avenue
New York, NY 10018
212-764-1100

Fifi Oscard was a frustrated housewife and mother in 1949 when she began working gratis for Lee, Harris, Draper. When I asked her in what capacity she was working, she said, *mostly as a jerk*, but added that in nine months she was no longer inept and had worked herself up to $15 a week. Always interested in theater and with the ability to do almost anything, Fifi has prospered.

From LHD, Fifi moved to The Lucille Phillips Agency, working three days a week. That inauspicious beginning led to Fifi's purchase of LPA in 1959 and the birth of Fifi Oscard Associates, Inc. This agency deals with writers, directors, producers, singers, composers, actors - every arm of showbiz except the variety field.

Scriptwriters at this agency are represented by Carmen Le Via and Bruce Ostler. Kevin McShame and Ivy Stone represent authors.

Agents
Carmen La Via, Bruce Ostler, Kevin McShame and Ivy Stone.
Client List
Check WGA listing.
Clients
Check WGA listing.
Notes

The Daniel Ostroff Agency

9200 Sunset Blvd. #402
W of Doheny
Los Angeles, CA 90069
310-278-2020

Daniel Ostroff's advice to young scriptwriters is to *find a hot new agent and grow up with him.* He says that is what happened to him and a look at some of his clients confirms the wisdom of the plan for both writer *and* agent. Prestigious clients like Michael Blake ("Dances with Wolves") and Richard Friedenberg ("A River Runs Through It") are prime examples of clients that were young and scratching at the same time that Daniel was making the journey from the mailroom at ICM to agenting, moving to Writers & Artists, partnering with Robert Wunsch (Wunsch/Ostroff) and then opening his own office in 1987. Other clients include Thom Eberhardt ("Night of the Comet," "Honey I Blew Up the Kid"), Ken Kaufman ("The Air Up There"), Dave Fuller and Rick Natkin ("Necessary Roughness") and Josann McGibbon and Sara Parriott ("Runaway Bride").

He's only got 15 clients and it seems like they are all currently cutting big time deals. Originally from Washington, D. C., Daniel is an excellent illustration of how genuine the old adage *everyone knows somebody some place and that's how to get into show business* really is. His introduction to the mailroom at ICM came about because his brother lived next door to a television producer. In an article in Variety by John Evan Frook (November 5, 1992), Daniel told an inspiring story about success: *Years ago, I read a profile in The New York Times about the world's greatest piano salesman. He worked long hours, played the piano, kept voluminous files...and knew everyone in the music business...I realized the key thing was left out: yes, he did all of those things but he also sold Steinways. Like him. I sell Steinways.*

Even if you feel you are a Steinway, don't get excited and compose a query letter, this man is highly committed to the list of clients he already has. He feels agents are being irresponsible to their clients spending time reading others scripts instead of paying attention to the clients they already have. So instead of wasting your time and postage, check out the ideas he offers throughout the book.

Agents
Daniel Ostroff.
Client List
15
Clients
Michael Blake, Richard Friedenberg, Thom Eberhardt, Ken Kaufman, Jim McBride, Dave Fuller and Rick Natkin, Josann McGibbon and Sara Parriott and others.
Notes

paradigm
a talent and literary agency

10100 Santa Monica Blvd.
at Century Park East
Los Angeles, CA 90067
310-277-4400

In 1969, after 21 collective years interning with various big
agencies, Stu Robinson and Bernie Weintraub opened their own
offices. Tired of endless staff meetings, wasted time and limited to
coverage *west of La Brea*, they wanted to represent the whole town
and do it their way. Ken Gross left his own business in 1985 to
join RW and in 1990 a new name, Robinson, Weintraub and Gross,
reflected his accomplishments.

In 1993 RWG joined the current trend and merged with two
prestigious agencies (STE and Gores/Fields) known primarily for
wonderful actors and with another prominent literary agency,
Shorr, Stille & Associates, to form a new prestigious and powerful
mini-conglomerate.

Partners at paradigm are Sam Gores, Clifford Stevens, Tex Beha,
Stuart Robinson, Bernie Weintraub and Ken Gross. A true merger,
no agent from any of the three agencies lost a job. This talented
and humanistic list of agents expects to continue intimate family
style representation while reaping the informational rewards of their
expanded coverage.

paradigm reps 100-125 writers, directors, producers,
documentaries, properties of all kinds (series, full length
presentations, plays, books, etc.). Stu Robinson says,
they don't represent books until they are books and then they
represent east coast writers for movie rights.

paradigm
a talent and literary agency

200 W 57th Street # 900
btwn 7th & 8th Avenues
New York, NY 10019
212-246-1030

Clients include writer/director John Sayles ("Brother From Another Planet" and "Eight Men Out"), novelist/screenwriter Hubert Selby Jr. ("Last Exit to Brooklyn") and Marty Cohan (Co-creator "Who's the Boss").

paradigm does not accept unsolicited material, so you'll have to find someone who knows someone to gain entree to this important energized addition in the Los Angeles marketplace. Agents who represent writers at paradigm are Ken Gross, Bernard Weintraub, Gary Pearl, Doug Brodex, Lucy Stille and Lucy Stutz.

Agents
Ken Gross, Bernard Weintraub, Gary Pearl, Stu Robinson, Doug Brodex, Kerry Jones, Lucy Stille and Lucy Stutz.
Client List
150+
Clients
John Sayles, Hubert Selby Jr., Marty Cohan and others.
Notes

Paramuse Artists Associates

1414 Avenue of the Americas
at 58th Street
New York, NY 10019
212-758-5055

Shirley Bernstein started in the business as a producer for theater, television and film. Her experiences with agents made her unwilling to even discuss the possibilities of being an agent with the folks from William Morris who courted her in the 1960s. Finally, after her television show was cancelled, it occurred to her there might be a more stable way of making a living than producing.

At that point, the distinguished Ted Ashley (IFA) asked Shirley to join his agency. Because Ted Ashley is such a smart, soft-spoken and terrific man and would allow Shirley to float until she decided in which area she wanted to specialize, she surrendered.

As a result, Shirley has a brilliant overview of all parts of the agency business. In 1972 Shirley opened her own office with partner Doris Vidor (the daughter of Harry Warner) with one client, Stephen Schwartz ("Pippin"). Shirley works alone these days with clients like Joe Stein ("Fiddler on the Roof," "Zorba") and Arthur Laurents ("Gypsy"). Her newest clients wrote the musical version of "Wings".

Ms. Bernstein takes on new clients rarely and usually only by referral. Paramuse represents writers, composers, lyricists and directors.

Agents
Shirley Bernstein.
Client List
10-15
Clients
Joe Stein, Arthur Laurents and others.
Notes

Pleshette & Green

> 2700 N Beachwood Drive
> N of Franklin
> Los Angeles, CA 90068
> 213-465-0428

Pleshette & Green is strictly a writers agency. Respected in the business before she even had one, Lynn Pleshette has been enormously successful parlaying her background in publishing into one of the most respected literary agencies in Los Angeles. When she moved to Los Angeles in 1975 with her husband, actor John Pleshette, her best friend asked her to represent film rights to her novel. She figured she already knew how to *lunch* so why not?

P&G represents clients for New York prestigious book agents Elizabeth Darhansoff and Maxine Grosky. Some of those clients are William Kennedy (Iron Weed), Patty Dann (Mermaids) and Sue Miller (Family Pictures). In addition to her east coast publishing liaisons, representative clients include Emmy winning screenwriter Darlene Craviotto ("Love is Never Silent") and Ann Hamilton ("Sirens", "thirtysomething").

I was particularly impressed that Lynn arranged our interview to include both partner Richard Green (who has been with Lynn for eight years) and colleague Howard Sanders (WMA, Joel Gotler). There are perceptive quotes throughout the book that illustrate this agency's insights into the business and though I have attributed most of the quotes to Lynn, both Richard and Howard made integral contributions to the conversation.

Pleshette & Green sees people only through referral.

Agents
Lynn Pleshette, Richard Green and Howard Sanders.
Client List
30
Clients
Darlene Craviotto, Camille Marshetta, William Kennedy, Patty
Dann, Sue Miller, Ann Hamilton, and others.
Notes

Preferred Artists

16633 Ventura Blvd. #1421
2 blocks W of Havenhurst
Encino, CA 91436
818-990-0305

Lew Weitzman somehow mutated from a UCLA student with a major in Russian into a major literary agent. His first exposure to the business was via the MCA training program in 1962. Already on the rise, Lew was invited to join prestigious Park Citron (which became Chasin-Park-Citron) when government anti-trust laws forced the break up of MCA. He spent 7 years in the motion picture and television literary department of The William Morris Agency before starting Lew Weitzman and Associates.

Taft Broadcasting pursued them for merger. When American Financial bought Taft, Lew was free to start Preferred Artists with partner Roger Strull. The balance of the Preferred team includes Sylvia Hirsch (WMA), Susie Weissman (ICM) and Jerry Adler. Since 1988, Preferred Artists has been representing about 90-100 writers, producers and directors such as Bob Bendetson ("Coach"), Stuart Raffill ("Passenger 57"), Billy Van Zandt and Jane Milmore ("Martin") and Artie Julian.

Agents
Lew Weitzman, Roger Strull, Sylvia Hirsch, Susie Weissman and Jerry Adler.
Client List
90-100
Clients
Artie Julian, Bob Bendetson, Billy Van Zandt, Jane Milmore, Stuart Raffill and others.
Notes

Jim Preminger Agency

1650 Westwood Blvd. #201
S of Wilshire
Los Angeles CA 90024
310-475-9491

One of the most elegant agencies in town is run by Jim Preminger. Jim's original show-biz goal was to become a producer. After spending three years optioning properties, working with writers on screenplay adaptations and generally trying to get into the business, The Artists Agency countered his offer of a project he hoped to package for Jack Nicholson, with an offer to open their literary department. Not only had show business opened its door to Jim, it invited him in, for just two years later in 1977, Jim became a partner.

In 1980 he decided to open his own agency with a dozen clients. Jim and colleagues Monica Riordan and Harvey Harrison represent about 60 clients covering all principal literary areas: motion pictures, long form television, series television, plus animation and interactive media. Of these clients, about 10 are directors and the balance are writers and/or writers/directors. The Jim Preminger Agency is one of Los Angeles' most respected and thriving independent agencies.

Agents
Jim Preminger, Monica Riordan and Harvey Harrison.
Client List
60
Clients
Edward G. Rugoff, Stephen M. Hatman and others.
Notes

Renaissance Literary Talent Agency

152 N La Peer Drive
1 block N of Wilshire
2 blocks E of Doheny
Beverly Hills, CA 90211
310-246-6000

Fallout from the Metropolitan Talent Agency breakup has resulted in a new literary agency headed by ex-MTA-ers Joel Gotler and Irv Schwartz plus long time Irving Lazar associate, Alan Nevins. Joel, who merged his own management company into MTA (Joel Gotler Inc.), is picking up his marbles along with Irv Schwartz, an old buddy from WMA mailroom days, and they are starting their own business with Nevins. Another friend and associate from MTA, Mark Jacobson, is joining them. According to Daily Variety, these guys are starting business with a class list:

• *Among Gotler's clients are Piers Anthony, Lucian Truscott IV, Greg Dinallo, Eric Hughes, Mel Frohman and director/producer John Nicolella, Shep Gordon, Suzanne Finstad and Sidney Kirkpatrick.*

Recent deals include "Indecent Proposal," based on the novel by Jack Englehard; "The Woman Who Loved Elvis," the ABC television film starring Roseanne and Tom Arnold, based on the novel by Laura Kalpakian; Lawrence Sanders' "McNally's Risk" and Michael Connelly's "Black Echo," both sold to Neufeld/Rehme Prods; and John Jakes' "Homeland" to the Wolper Organization-Warner Bros.

"Ex-literary Agents Gotler,
Schwartz Set Up Renaissance"
Kirk Honeycutt
The Hollywood Reporter
April 23, 1993

This new agency bills itself as Renaissance Literary Talent Agency and although the concentration is on writers and directors, RLTA has one performer, Ray Combs, host of "Family Feud" on its list and vows to be flexible.

RLTA was just forming as I was sending this book to press, so I have not interviewed these gentlemen personally. Since they are new, even though they already have a good list, these agents might be open to new talent. However, don't spoil your chances (and everyone else's) by querying Renaissance until you have appropriate material and/or entree.

Agents
Joel Gotler, Irv Schwartz, Alan Nevins and Mark Jacobson.
Client List
Check WGA listing.
Clients
Lawrence Sanders, Michael Connelly, Piers Anthony, Lucian Truscott IV, Greg Dinallo, Eric Hughes, Mel Frohman, Shep Gordon, Suzanne Finstad, Sidney Kirkpatrick and others.
Notes

The Richland/Wunsch/Hohman Agency

9220 Sunset Blvd. #311
W of Doheny
Los Angeles, CA 90069
310-278-1955

Where else can you get an agent like Dan Richland, who not only pilots his own jet, but is profiled in <u>Los Angeles Magazine</u> as ferrying around the likes of Burt Reynolds, Henry Winkler and such diverse Presidents as Ronald Reagan and Bill Clinton? Dan embodies the spirit of this agency which says, in fact, you can have a real life and still be successful.

Though they don't fly airplanes, partners Bob Wunsch and Bob Hohman bring diversity, prestige and experience to RWH. Wunsch started the agency in 1982 after time spent as a VP of production at United Artists, a network executive and an independent film producer ("Slapshot" with Paul Newman). Richland ran his own successful agency before joining Wunsch in 1987.

Partner Bob Hohman first entered the agency business working for The Artists Agency. He moved on to Stanford Beckett and Associates where he became an agent in 1983 and a partner in 1984. In 1985, Bob relocated to Triad and by 1988 was head of their motion picture literary department.

In 1991, Hohman, Wunsch and Richland united to provide a small agency environment with big agency entree. RWH represent Marisa Silver ("Permanent Record," "Vital Signs"), Stephen Tolkin ("Daybreak"), Neal Jimenez ("For the Boys," "Rivers Edge," "The Waterdance"), Dean Pitchford ("Fame," "Footloose"), Randy and Perry Howze ("Mystic Pizza," "Chances Are") and Bob Tzudiker and Noni White ("Roger Rabbit" sequel, "Mrs. Faust"), Dan

Petrie, Jr. ("Beverly Hills Cop"), Mark D. Andrews and others.

Most of the list of 15 directors started with this agency as writers and have made successful transitions to writer/director status.

Agents
Bob Wunsch, Dan Richland, Joe Richland, Bob Hohman and Bayard Mabank.
Client List
50
Clients
Marisa Silver, Stephen Tolkin, Andrew Schneider, Neal Jimenez, Dean Pitchford, Randy and Perry Howze, Bob Tzudiker and Noni White, Dan Petrie, Jr., Mark D. Andrews and others.
Notes

The Rosen Group

13116 Chandler Blvd.
btwn Woodman & Coldwater
Sherman Oaks, CA 91401
818-990-9020

The Rosen Group rises again. Mike Rosen was partnered for years
with Ernie Dade (Dade-Rosen) representing actors, but when Mike
and Ernie decided to end that relationship, Mike embarked on a
successful career as a literary agent. He organized literary
departments at other agencies before he organized The Rosen
Group. I guess Harry Gold offered him a deal he couldn't refuse,
for he closed his own office and joined Gold Marshak and
Associates and put together an important list there.

In 1993, however, Mike decided to return to his own business and
the *new* Rosen Group opened its doors.

Mike represents writers, directors and producers of one kind or
another. Writing clients work across the board in theater, film and
television. Chris Trumbo ("Dark Justice") and Robert Pucci and
Alanna Hamill ("Justice Calhoun") are representative of the list of
25 writing clients.

Agents
Mike Rosen.
Client List
25
Clients
Robert Pucci, Alanna Hamill and others.
Notes

Rosenstone/Wender

3 E 48th Street
E of 5th Avenue
New York, NY 10017
212-832-8330

Howard Rosenstone started in the business with William Morris in 1963. Originally an agent representing actors, Howard decided quickly that he preferred to handle directors and playwrights. In 1977 he left WMA to start his own agency (Howard & Company) and in 1980 he teamed with Phyllis Wender to form Rosenstone/Wender.

Partners, Wender and Rosenstone each maintain their own lists and function alone, so I assume that means that if you get Rosenstone, you don't get Wender and vice-versa.

Rosenstone represents directors, orchestrators, screenwriters, playwrights, composers and lyricists. He doesn't take on that many new clients so query letters need to be sensational and support high caliber work. Rosenstone represents writers from all over the world. Besides having such famous clients as David Mamet and Shel Silverstein, Howard represents the Tennessee Williams estate.

Agents
Howard Rosenstone and Phyllis Wender.
Client List
Confidential.
Clients
Check WGA listing.
Notes

The Schechter (Irv) Company, The

9300 Wilshire Blvd. #201
at Rexford
Los Angeles, CA 90024
310-278-8070

In 1984, after 15 years at The William Morris Agency, Irv Schechter opened a celebrated literary agency that has grown to include not only writers and directors, but actors and below the line personnel. Vice-President Debbee Klein was assistant to Norman Lear and Al Burton at Tandem Productions before joining Irv shortly after he opened his doors. She become a theatrical and literary agent at 21.

The literary department at Schechter covers every base: Andrea Simon heads the animation and Saturday morning department, Victoria Michaels handles game shows, and writers and directors in off-network cable and talk shows while Irv, Debra Lieb (Triad) and Charlotte Savavi preside over the film department. Debbee and fellow VP Don Klein (no relation) and Michael Margules represent the primetime television department. Direct, informed, easy to talk to and very hands on, Debbee is forward thinking and on top of every writing trend. Debbee speaks to her clients weekly, attends tapings and believes agents should earn their 10%.

Agents
Irv Schechter, Debbee Klein, Don Klein, Charlotte Savavi, Debra Lieb, Andrea Simon, Victoria Michaels and Michael Margules.
Client List
100
Clients
Check WGA listing.
Notes

Shapiro-Lichtman, Inc.

8827 Beverly Blvd. # C
W of La Cienega
Los Angeles, CA 90048
310-859-8877

If you become a client of Shapiro-Lichtman, rest assured that your phone calls will be returned. Marty Shapiro was still at the office at 8 o'clock at night when he returned my call. This is definitely the guy I would want representing me.

Shapiro and Mark Lichtman were colleagues at General Artists Corporation in 1968. Marty left when GAC merged with the forerunner of ICM, CMA. He worked at both the Phil Gersh and William Morris Agencies before rejoining with Lichtman to open Shapiro-Lichtman on Independence Day in 1969.

Marty wouldn't name any clients lest he leave someone out, but gave me permission to peruse the list and name some of his distinguished clients. They include David Webb Peoples ("Unforgiven," "Hero"), E. Nick Alexander ("Dark Justice," "The New Mike Hammer") as well as Emmy winning director Joseph Sargent (Miss Rose White) and nominee, Nancy Malone ("Trials of Rosie O'Neil"). Emmy nominated cinematographer Kees Van Oostrum ("Miss Rose White"), Donald A. Morgan ("Home Improvement"), costume designer Jerry Skeels ("PS I Luv U") and visual effects wizard Robert Legato ("Star Trek: The Next Generation") are only a sampling of their below the line personnel.

When I asked Marty the size of his list, he was both evasive and articulate, *Not too large to devote individual and personal attention to our clients and large enough that we can do all right.* In a constantly shifting marketplace, S-L clients write everything from film to reality programming to interactive projects.

Other agents at S-L are Mitchell Stein, Christine Foster, Bob Shapiro (Marty's father), Michael Lewis, Peggy Patrick and Lisa Sullivan. Respected theatrical agent Bud Moss has also joined the lineup bringing a list of eminent actors and expanding packaging capabilities.

Agents
Marty Shapiro, Mark Lichtman, Mitchell Stein, Christine Foster, Bob Shapiro, Michael Lewis, Peggy Patrick and Lisa Sullivan.
Client List
Not too large to devote individual and personal attention to our clients and large enough that we can do all right.
Clients
David Webb Peoples, E. Nick Alexander, Nancy Malone, Kees Van Oostrum and others.
Notes

Ken Sherman & Associates

9507 Little Santa Monica Blvd.
Writers & Artists Bldg.
at Rodeo Drive
Beverly Hills, CA 90210
310-271-8840

If you feel you can read people by their environment, you'd have to have Ken Sherman for an agent just on style, because his office is in the coolest building around. The legendary Writers & Artists building in Beverly Hills has Dan Petrie, Ray Bradbury and Digby Diehl (just for starters) as tenants and makes you feel like all the great screenplays from your past must have been written there.

A native Angelino, Ken says he always wanted to be in the business and though working toward a psychology degree from Berkley, he managed to spend summers as a production manager for an Academy Award winning educational film company. Opting for life experience instead of the job the film company offered, Ken went to Europe, made crepes in a restaurant, dubbed English into foreign films, worked on films, and wrote and researched a guide to Paris before returning to Los Angeles and becoming a reader for Columbia pictures.

When he interviewed with The William Morris Agency in 1975, he was hired immediately for a stint in the mailroom. He became an agent at WMA representing both actors and directors. Before opening his own office in 1989, he worked at The Lantz Office and The Kohner Agency. His list of 25-30, features writers with famous names as well as writers with that potential.

Ken does not accept unsolicited material and is not interested in expanding his client list, but he has very instructive quotes throughout the book.

Agents
Ken Sherman.
Client List
25-30 writers.
Clients
Check WGA listing.
Notes

H.N. Swanson, Inc.

8523 Sunset Blvd.
½ block W of La Cienega
Los Angeles, CA 90069
310-652-5385

If set dressing means anything, H.N. Swanson wins the prize. Stepping from the hustle-bustle of the Sunset Strip into the historic offices of H.N. Swanson is a trip back in time. I felt as though I had entered writers' heaven. Life-size pictures of clients William Faulkner and Raymond Chandler as well as a larger-than-life poster of founder H.N. Swanson's book, "Sprinkled with Ruby Dust," mahogany walls and leather arm chairs sitting on deep green carpet make you feel that even if you didn't write particularly well, somehow great writing would just jump on you while you were visiting your agent.

It would certainly mean something to me if my agency had represented Pearl Buck, F. Scott Fitzgerald, Elmore Leonard and Ernest Hemingway — and Swanson did.

Although originally a magazine publisher, H.N. Swanson (Swanie) was brought to California by David Selznick as an advisor and a producer. It didn't take Swanie long to realize there was no west coast representation for all the writers that kept getting off the trains from New York, so he sought to fill the void.

In 1934 he opened H.N. Swanson, Inc. and in 1936, he moved a couple of blocks down the road to erect the building that still bears his name. Swanson's list of clients, past and present, is impressive. HNS represents the screenwriter with the longest career in Hollywood, Charles Bennett. Bennett, who wrote many of Alfred Hitchcock's films, wrote Hitchcock's first film, "Blackmail" in

1929. When Twentieth Century Fox recently decided to resurrect the script and update it with two young writers, they found that Charles was still writing and he is now working on the project.

Writers of original television material were not courted until Swanie's stepson, Thomas Shanks, joined the business in 1989 and HNS was dragged, kicking and screaming into the television arena. Although Shanks' area of expertise was not agenting (he was a New York City Opera performer) he had been around Swanie's business all his life and demonstrates not only a keen organizational proficiency, but the ability to attract strong agents with equally strong client lists.

The list of agents at Swanson is distinguished. David Murphy's educational background at UCSD, AFI, the LA City College Film School and Truby's Writer's Studio give him a unique perspective into scriptwriter's problems. Before coming to Swanson, he worked at ICM in both the motion picture and television departments. Michelle Wallerstein arrives with a background from agencies as varied as Preferred Artists, Bloom Levy Shore and Associates Artist Career Management and she also ran her own agency, The Wallerstein Company. Gail Barrick was director of development for Jessica Lange's Prairie Films at Orion and at Wild Street Pictures and has spent time in story development at CAA.

Annette van Duren not only ran her own company before partnering at Warden-White-Van Duren, she road managed for Phyllis Diller and worked at United Features Syndicate. Steve Fisher's previous job history includes jobs in local news in New York as well as a daytime drama for NBC and a talk-information show hosted by Phil Donahue. He was head of research for "ABC World News Tonight," an off-air reporter, a writer and a field producer for CNN. In 1988, he came to LA as a reader and story researcher for both Paragon Motion Pictures and Catalina Production Group. He trained in the agency business in television at ICM and Harris & Goldberg (now Innovative Artists).

The agency has survived and prospered with the changes and now represents not only famous book authors and their estates, but a good stable of film and television writer clients. Representative of the list are Christopher Lofton ("Scarlett), Michael McGreevey ("Fame"), Barry Strugratz and Mark Burns ("Married to the Mob"), Michael Levine and Laura Kavanaugh ("Deep Cover"), Chuck Hughes ("Ed and His Dead Mother"), Rocky Lang ("Nervous Ticks"), Steve Kunes ("First Comes Love") and Carl Binder ("Neon Rider II").

Swanie died in 1991 after having a major stroke preceded by a few *strokelets* as he termed them, but his influence is everywhere.

Agents
Thomas Shanks, Michelle Wallerstein, Gail Barrick, Annette van Duren, Steve Fisher and David Murphy.
Client List.
100+
Clients
Chuck Hughes, Christopher Lofton, Michael McGreevey, Barry Strugratz and Mark Burns, Steve Koonis, Michael Levine and Laura Kavanaugh, Carl Binder, Dorothy Uhnak and many others.
Notes

Talent East

340-A E 58th Street
btwn 1st & 2nd Avenues
New York, NY 10022
212-838-7191

Bob Donaghey started Talent East in February of 1992 and says the
agency has taken on a life of its own. Bob's career began from the
moment he got off the bus from Michigan with a theater degree.
He worked as a page for CBS during the week and as Ed Sullivan's
assistant on the weekends. The Sullivan job involved dealing with
all the talent and their agents and managers. While attending to the
comforts of Frank Sinatra and the like for Sullivan, he was
promoted from page to Program Coordinator on *all the shows after
Cronkite till 11 p.m* at CBS. That job entailed screening shows and
negotiating with advertising agencies.

Stints at Grey Advertising, D'Arcy McManus, J. Michael Bloom
and Zoli whetted Bob's appetite for agenting and after starting a
short-lived agency representing models, Bob opened Talent East
repping actors. He's recently added a literary department. The list
is small, so there might be room for you.

Agents
Bob Donaghey, Carole Davis, H. Shep Pamplin and Johnny Puma.
Client List
Free lance only
Clients
Free lance only
Notes

The Turtle Agency

12456 Ventura Blvd.
at Whitsett
Studio City, CA 91604
818-506-6898

Between owner Cindy Turtle and colleague Beth Bohn, The Turtle Agency seems to have all the bases covered. Cindy's background includes television production in New York and Los Angeles plus a stint at the distinguished Eisenbach-Greene-Duchow agency where she became their first female agent representing writers, producers and directors for features and television. She was Director of Development for Showtime from 1980-1983 before starting the literary department for LA agent Harry Gold. She left Harry to form a partnership with Mike Rosen (The Rosen/Turtle Group). In 1990 Cindy started The Turtle Agency. Beth Bohn's background in sales and marketing perfectly complements Cindy's industry connections so that The Turtle Agency (which calls itself a full service agency) benefits from the synergistic combination. Beth is obviously a woman who finds a problem and fixes it. When she was dissatisfied with her earlier career, she consulted a career doctor to help point her talents toward a more rewarding life. Turtle and Bohn represent writers, directors and producers in all areas. Writers make up about two-thirds of their list of 45 clients.

Agents
Cindy Turtle and Beth Bohn.
Client List
45
Clients
Check WGA listing.
Notes

United Talent Agency (UTA)

9560 Wilshire Blvd. #500
at Rodeo Dr.
Beverly Hills, CA 90212
310-273-6700

Originally billing themselves as an intimate William Morris when James Berkus (IFA), Robert Stein and Gary Cosay (WMA) founded Leading Artists in 1983, LA's merger with important literary agency Bauer Benedek created United Talent Agency, an agency that is hot on the heels of their larger better known conglomerate competitors in the literary field.

Bauer Benedek principals, former WMA agent Marty Bauer and entertainment lawyer Peter Benedek, formed their agency in 1986. Other partners at UTA are Jeremy Zimmer (ICM) and Martin Hurwitz (New World Entertainment).

This fearless group has benefitted from the demise of InterTalent and the merger of Triad with William Morris. UTA picked up not only talented agents, but their clients as well. The main strength here is writers, producers and directors, but their list of actors continues to grow in stature and size.

Clients include most of the staff of "Roseanne;" executive producer, Bruce Helford; producer, Sy Dukane; story editors, Deann Heline and Eileen Heisler; producer, Denise Moss, plus staffers, Michael Gandolfi and Janice Jordan-Nelson, plus Lynn Latham (the pilot of "Homefront") and John Mattson ("Milk Money").

Agents
Robert Stein, James Berkus, Gary Cosay, Robb Rothman, Toby
Jaffe, Marty Bauer, Peter Benedek, Jeremy Zimmer, Martin
Hurwitz, Marty Adelstein, Pat Dollard, Christopher Harbert, Dana
Cioffi and Ilene Feldman.

Client List
Growing daily.

Clients
Bruce Helford, Sy Dukane, Deann Heline, Michael Gandolfi, Janice
Jordan-Nelson, Eileen Heisler, Denise Moss, Lynn Latham,
Bernard Lechowick, John Mattson and others.

Notes

Warden, White and Kane

8444 Wilshire Blvd. 4th Floor
Wilshire Theater Bldg.
1 block E of La Cienega
Beverly Hills, CA 90211
213-852-1028

In 1989, TV packager Dave Warden and WMA mailroom graduate/APA agent Steve White decided to start a motion picture literary agency with crossover into television. In 1992, Michael Kane (another WMA mailroom grad, class of '76) joined the group. His history includes working with prestigious literary agent Merrily Kane (his mother) as well as with Adams, Ray, Rosenberg (before and after they joined with Triad). Michael also headed the literary department at Triad and at Innovative Artists (aka Harris & Goldberg). One of the coolest guys you will meet, Michael is an articulate communicator who along with partners Warden and White is interested in the careers of his clients, not individual jobs.

WW&K represent about 60 writers and directors with just as many women on the list as men. WW&K's clients write for films and television, Jeff Arch ("Sleeping in Seattle"), Sam Hamm ("Batman") and Jeff Reno and Ron Osborn ("Moonlighting," "Flintstones" etc.)

Agents
Dave Warden, Steve White and Michael Kane.
Client List
60 writers and directors.
Clients
Jeff Arch, Sam Hamm, Jeff Reno, Ron Osborn and others.
Notes

Peregrine Whittlesey Agency

345 E 80th Street #31F
at 1st Avenue
New York, NY 10021
212-737-0153

Although at first glance, one might think this is an agency run by
Mr. Peregrine and Mr. Whittlesey, in fact, this is a successful
literary agency run by one woman whose name is Peregrine
Whittlesey. An actress who continually found herself producing
and working with writers developing material, Peregrine was one of
the founding members of The Manhattan Theater Club.

The native New Yorker developed the voucher program for TCG
and was Elaine May's assistant for three years during which time
she read for Ms. May as well as helped edit material. From 1980-
83, Whittlesey was Literary Manager for The Goodman Theater in
Chicago. At the Goodman, she developed writers and arranged
readings when necessary.

After a go at producing and a successful experience helping a friend
get his play produced at Long Wharf, Peregrine decided to take all
her contacts, her ability to work with playwrights and her instincts
and open her own agency. An agent who does not *represent
projects, but people,* Peregrine only takes on those playwrights she
believes in strongly.

Although some of her playwrights also write screenplays, her
interest lies in the theater. She is drawn to people who have
interesting lives rather than people who are just good writers. She
has a liaison with British agents and reps 10 playwrights from that
country. Since she is also fluent in French, she finds herself
working with artists from that country as well. Her Los Angeles

connection is the newly merged paradigm.

Some of the interesting people on Whittlesey's list are Darrah
Cloud ("The Stick Wife," "The House Across the Street"),
Migdalia Cruz ("Lucy Loves Me," "Frida"), Anthony Dimurro
("Coyote Ugly," "Moe Greeen Gets It in the Eye"), Gary Leon Hill
("Food from Trash"), Joel Drake Johnson ("School's Out"),
Romulus Linney ("Holy Ghosts," "April Snow," "Sand Mountain,")
Heather McCutchen ("A Walk on Lake Erie," "3 AM"), Marlane
Meyer ("The Geography of Luck," "Kingfish"), Sara Miles
("Charlemagne"), Yannick Murphy ("Blue Is the Color You Don't
See Anymore"), Dakota Powell ("Harry Black"), Dalt Wonk ("Rio
Seco") and Tug Yourgrau ("The Song of Jacob Zulu").

Peregrine responds to everything people send to her, but be patient,
she works alone and these things take time.

Agents
Peregrine Whittlesey.
Client List
24
Clients
Darrah Cloud, Migdalia Cruz, Anthony Dimurro, Gary Leon Hill,
Joel Drake Johnson, Romulus Linney, Heather McCutchen,
Marlane Meyer, Sara Miles, Yannick Murphy, Dakota Powell, Dalt
Wonk and Tug Yourgrau.
Notes

Wile Enterprises, Inc.

2730 Wilshire Blvd. #500
at Harvard Street
Santa Monica, CA 90403
310-828-9768

Shelly Wile is one of the few graduates of William Morris University who did not start in the mailroom. Shelly says he was a failed actor when a friend led him by the hand to WMA where he started as a secretary in the literary department in television live dramatic action. More than getting their money's worth to score a secretary with a background in theater, WMA made Shelly an agent within a year.

CMA (forerunner of ICM) eventually hired him away to run their literary department. He withdrew from the agency business to become VP of development of feature films for television for Cinema Center Films. In 1971 Shelly left CCF to develop shows for Talent Associates with David Susskind and Leonard Stern. By 1974 he was lured back to the agency business by Adams Ray Rosenberg. Thought by many to be the most prestigious boutique literary office in Los Angeles, ARR merged with Triad in 1984 and Shelly went with them. Triad has now merged with William Morris and Shelly started his own company in 1989.

Although Shelly was adamant about not mentioning the size of his client list or any names, a quick check at the WGA will reveal a list of heavy hitters. Sharon A. (Sam) Markevich (CAA, WMA) is Shelly's colleague.

At one time Shelly read all submissions, but that day has passed. If you are interested in representation from this office, important industry referrals by someone who has read your work is the only entree.

This office represents writers, producers and directors although the major thrust is definitely writers.

Agents
Shelly Wile and Sharon A. Markevich.
Client List
Confidential.
Clients
Check WGA listing.
Notes

Dan Wright

136 E 56th Street 2C
btwn 3rd & Lexington Avenues
New York, NY 10022
212-832-0110

Although many of Dan Wright's clients end up with motion picture deals, many of them are novelists. His list of 80 includes playwrights and screenwriters as well. Long associated with his wife Ann's successful commercial agency, Dan's literary department now dominates as Ann has dropped on camera clients in favor of voice overs.

Dan's clients include Patricia McConnell ("Sing Soft, Sing Loud") and Bryan Reich who won the prestigious Nichols Award for his screenplay, "Baubles" now being directed by Jonathan Demme. Sean Breckenridge's novel, "Yuppie Scum," will be published by St. Martins Press. Dan's international list includes Ed McNaughton from Paris ("McCabe") and Bob Mendes from Holland.

Queries with a sase will receive a reply. Dan wants information about the author's background and a brief description of the property.

Agents
Dan Wright.
Client List
80
Clients
Sean Breckenridge, Ed McNaughton, Bob Mendes, Bryan Reich and others.
Notes

Writers & Artists

11726 San Vicente Blvd. #300
just W of Barrington
Los Angeles, CA 90049
310-820-2240

Writers & Artists' name reflects the esteem in which this agency (launched in New York in 1971) holds its writers. And well it should, some of the most successful writers in the business call W&A home: Pulitzer prizewinner Robert Schenkkan, Polly Walker and Josie Lawrence ("Enchanted April"), Monte Merrick ("Memphis Belle"), Greg Taylor ("Prancer") and Jim Strain ("Bingo").

The literary department at W&A is headed by Rima Greer in Los Angeles and Bill Craver in New York. Rima came to Writers & Artists in 1983 after working as assistant to the executive director of the Writers Guild and a stint as a secretary at William Morris. Other agents for writers and directors at this agency are owner Joan Scott, Michael Stipanich, Jeff Robinov, Rob Golenberg, Byrdie Lifson-Pompan (Triad), Marti Blumenthal and Scott Hudson. A heavy hitter in all departments, W&A combines prestige with hands on service. Rima tells me she speaks to every one of her clients daily. About 75% of the list are writers who direct.

As with most of the other agencies I interviewed, although W&A has stars, they also continually start new talent. They don't look at unsolicited material. Check out Rima's quotes elsewhere in the book for ideas on how to get agents' attention. Rima stresses that it's not a good idea to submit your own material to studios and producers without an agent as this will retard your progress when you are represented.

Writers & Artists

19 W 44th Street
just W of 5th Avenue
New York, NY 10036
212-391-1112

Rima's assistant is David Higgins.

Agents
Los Angeles: Joan Scott, Rima Greer, Michael Stipanich, Jeff Robinov, Rob Golenberg, Marti Blumenthal and Byrdie Lifson-Pompan
New York: Bill Craver and Scott Hudson.
Client List
88 (NY/LA)
Clients
Robert Schenkkan, Monte Merrick, Greg Taylor, Jim Strain and others.
Notes

Stella Zadeh & Associates

11759 Iowa Avenue
at Barrington
Los Angeles, CA 90025
310-207-4114

When Stella Zadeh was an executive for CBS years ago, several colleagues told her she had too much energy for CBS and suggested she start her own business. A year later in 1985 Richard Lawrence (Abrams, Rubaloff & Lawrence) gave her a start. In 1986 she acquired a Talent and Literary license and the world will never be the same. Somehow with the help of two assistants, she manages to represent a base list of 80 clients and helps many more.

The queen agent of reality-based producers/writers/directors, Stella didn't want me to name names, but says she has someone on almost every major talk or magazine show on television.

Don't rush to the mail box. She only accepts industry referrals, but she will accept query letters. Although she handles a few traditional scriptwriters, they are all clients whose major thrust is reality-based programming. If you ask me, CBS should have harnessed the energy themselves.

Agents
Stella Zadeh.
Client List
80+
Clients
Check WGA listing.
Notes

Glossary

above the line
> A budgetary term referring to talent, advertising and other negotiable expenses involved in making a film. This includes writers, directors, actors and producers.

associate producer
> Performs one or more producer functions as delegated by the producer.

below the line
> A budgetary term referring to production costs including such personnel as gaffers, grips, set designers, make-up, etc. Generally those fees that are non negotiated.

bible
> Projected series story with ideas for progression from pilot forward.

buzz
> Industry term meaning exciting information that everybody is talking about.

calling card
> A spec script that gets you in the door. As The New York Times says, *Most often, a calling card is a script that everybody wants to read but nobody wants to make.*

clout
> Power.

connected
> To be in the system and to have entree to helpful relationships. If I am Mike Ovitz's secretary, I am connected to him and could get a project to him, etc.

co-producers

Two or more producers who perform the producer functions as a team.

coverage

Report supplied by reader to the buyer.

development

Process involving writers presenting work and/or ideas to producers who oversee the developing script through various stages.

The Dramatists Guild, Inc.

Playwrights collective. Not a union in the strict sense of the word, the DG, Inc. still manages to protect its members by offering collective bargaining agreements and contracts covering those producers and theater owners as well as guidelines relative to agency agreements and agents.

The Dramatists Guild Quarterly

Provides information regarding agents, conferences and festivals, artists colonies, fellowships and grants, membership and service organizations, residencies, workshops plus an index of honors (Pulitzers, Obies, Oscars, etc.).

element

According to The New York Times, *an element is the basic building block of Hollywood, without which any project is simply an empty space pierced only by the phone calls of agents. Elements may be actors, directors, occasionally producers. They are never writers.*

executive producer

Supervises one or more producers.

half-hour

Situation comedy.

interactive television

Programming involving audience participation via computer/television sets. Still in its infancy. Said to be the next big thing.

line producer

Supervises physical production of project and is supervised by another producer who handles other duties.

long form television

Movies of the week.

New Dramatists

Organization dedicated to finding gifted playwrights and giving them the time, space and tools to develop their craft, so that they may fulfill their potential and make lasting contributions to the theater.

outline

Written scene by scene diagram of script.

pitch

Term used to define the process where a writer meets with producer(s) to tell the story (pitch) of his idea in hopes he will be hired to write a script.

plugged in

Industry slang implying close associations or relationships with those in power.

producer

Person who initiates, coordinates, supervises and controls all aspects of the process from inception to completion.

query letter

A brief letter that introduces the writer, synopsizes an idea a la TV Guide and invites further contact.

reader

A person employed by a buyer to weed through many scripts to select what the reader thinks warrants closer scrutiny.

sase

Self addressed stamped envelope - needs to accompany query letters and manuscripts.

spec scripts

A script written on speculation without any financial remuneration up front or any prior interest from a prospective buyer.

story analyst

See reader.

think
Industry slang term meaning a way of thinking.
the trades
Daily Variety, The Hollywood Reporter and Weekly Variety are all newspapers that deal with the entertainment business. Available at newsstands or by subscription.
treatment
A detailed written breakdown of a script, usually scene by scene.
The Writers Guild of America
Screenwriters guild - negotiates collective bargaining for screenwriters, arbitrates, provides services of all kinds.
WGA Directory
Listing of Writers Guild members delineating contacts (agents/managers/lawyers) and credits.

Index to Agents & Agencies

Abrams, Harry 161
Abrams-Rubaloff 161
Abrams/Harris & Goldberg 161
Adams Ray Rosenberg 258, 261
Adams, Bret 162
Adelstein, Marty 257
Adler, Jerry 238
Agency, The 163, 168
Alessi, Anna Maria 165
Alexander, Barbara 36, 49, 51, 102, 104, 125, 138, 146, 221, 222
Aloni, Dan 192
Amsterdam, Marcia 166
Anonymous Agent 15, 23, 24, 50, 51, 62, 63, 106
APA 116, 117, 164, 170, 174
Arlook, Richard 192
Arnovitz, Scott 203
Artists Agency 167, 184, 242
Artists Group 164, 168
Ashley-Famous 176, 198, 202
Aspland, Dennis 216
Badgeley and Connor 182
Bankoff, Lisa 203
Barrett, Chris 223
Barrick, Gail 253
Bauer Benedek 120, 256
Bayer, Deborah 186
Becsey, Larry 163

Benjamin, Ben 203
Bennahum, Michael 165
Benson, Jeffrey 219
Berg, Phil 215
Berg-Allenberg Agency 215
Berko, Raphael 42, 50, 95, 147, 149, 221
Berkus, James 257
Berman, Richard 163
Bernstein, Ron 192
Bernstein, Shirley 234, 235
Bickel, Glenn 181
Bickoff, Yvette 184
Block, Bill 119, 202
Blumenthal, Marti 264, 265
Boatwright, Boaty 203
Bohn, Beth 255
Bormann, Jim 217
Brandt, Geoffrey 170
Brandt, Jeffrey 170
Bresler, Sandy 167
Bresler, Wolff, Cota and Livingston 167
Broder • Kurland 172
Broder, Bob 172
Broder•Kurland•Webb•Uffner 16, 47, 96, 123, 133, 136, 146, 148, 149, 161, 172
Brodex, Doug 233
Brunswick, Glen 18, 19, 37, 107, 108, 137, 174
Buchwald, Don 174
CAA 116, 117, 202, 252
Cairns, Diane 203
Caroline Leonetti Agency 221
Champoux, Caron 163
Charlotte Gusay Literary Agency 196
Christopher Nassif Agency 174
Cioffi, Dana 257
CMA 172, 202, 261
CNA 174
Cohen, Lee 225

Cohn, Sam 202
Connolly, Justin 181
Contemporary Artists 210
Cooper Agency 176
Cooper, Bryan 177
Cooper, Frank 176, 177
Cooper, Jeff 177
Corday, Evan 194
Cosay, Gary 256, 257
Cota, Jim 167
Craver, Bill 264
Creative Artists Agency 112, 180, 202
Curren, Ellen 193
Curtis Brown 194
Dade-Rosen 244
Dardis, Justen 164
Davey, Tricia 203
Davis, Carole 254
Detroit, Patty 203
DGRW 63, 182
Dollard, Pat 257
Don Buchwald & Associates 193
Don Kopaloff Agency, Inc. 212
Donaghey, Bob 254
Douglas, Barry 182
Douglas, Mitch 203
Dreyfus, Barbara 203
Durham, Kirk 30, 189
Eastman, Andrea 203
Eisenbach, Greene, Duchow 255
Emannuel, Ariel 203
Epstein, Gary 183
Everett, Judith 201
Famous Artists 187
Felber, William Agency 183
Feldman, Ilene 257
Feldman, Richard 203
Ferris, Amy 203

Field, Jeff 225
Field, Maggie 91, 99, 131, 139, 186
Fields, Marje 187
Fifi Oscard Agency 229
Fineman, Ross 161
Fisher, Steve 253
Foster, Christine 248
Fraser, Diane 219
Fredda Rose/Candy Monteiro 125
Freiberg, Mickey 167
Gabler, Lee 203
Gage Group 20, 29, 30, 86, 104, 106
Gage, Martin 189
Gaines, John 164
Garon, Jay 34
Gelff, Laya 82, 190
General Artists Corporation 247
Gersh Agency 247
Gersh Agency New York 193
Gersh, David 192
Gersh, Phil 192, 193
Gluck, Suzanne 203
Gold, Dodie 225
Gold, Harry 194, 255
Gold, Harry & Associates 168
Goldberg, Howard 200
Goldstone, Ed 168
Golenberg, Rob 264
Gomez, Rhonda 173
Gores, Sam 232
Gores/Fields 232
Gorman, Fred 63, 182
Gotler, Joel 236, 240
Graham Agency 199
Graham, Earl 199
Gray, Stephen 195
Green, Richard 24, 146, 237
Greenblatt, David 119, 203

Greenblatt, Ken 16, 222
Greenspan, Alan 203
Greenstein, Ian 173
Greer, Rima 17, 21, 66, 83, 95, 99, 124, 132, 133, 134, 138, 264
Grisham, John 34
Gross, Ken 233
Guc, David 193
Gumer, Bob 203
Gusay, Charlotte 196
Haas, Paul 203
Haber, Bill 203
Haber, Will 180
Hamilburg, Mitchell J. 217
Hanzer, Leonard 172
Harbert, Christopher 257
Harden, Mary 162
Harris & Goldberg 252, 258
Harris, J. J. 119
Harris, Mark R. 219
Harris, Todd 225
Harrison, Harvey 239
Henderson, Scott 184
Higgins, David 265
Hofflund, Judy 119
Hogenson, Barbara 214
Hohman, Bob 22, 83, 84, 87, 94, 114, 115, 141, 142, 143, 145, 147, 242, 243
Howard and Company 245
Hudson, Scott 264
Hyler, Joan 90
ICM 116, 119, 167, 172, 174, 202, 230, 247, 252, 261
IFA 172
Innovative Artists 200, 252
International Creative Management 119
InterTalent 119, 202, 256
Irv Schechter Company 99, 246
Jacobs, Stuart 18, 37, 104, 105, 107, 108, 137, 174
Jacobson, Mark 240

Jaffee, Michael 161
Jay Garon-Brook Associates 34
JHR 189
Joel Gotler, Inc. 240
Jones, Kerry 233
Josephson, Nancy 203
Joyce Ketay Agency 209
Kamins, Ken 203
Kane, Merrily 167
Kane, Michael 258
Kaplan Stahler Agency 139
Kaplan, Ken 201
Kaplan, Mitch 205, 206
Kato, Gordon 203
Kaufman, Bruce 173
Kelly, Maryann 223
Ken Sherman Agency 52
Kennar, Larry 186
Kimble, John 116
Klein, Debbee 22, 99, 102, 131, 246
Klein, Don 246
Klein, Marty 164
Koerner, Todd 205
Kohner Agency 210
Kohner, Inc. (Paul) 135
Kohner, Paul Inc. 105, 131, 132, 136, 210, 249
Kopaloff, Don 212
Korman, Tom 164, 168
Krentzman, Adam 181
Kroll, Lucy 213, 214
Kumen-Olenick 168
Kurland, Norman 172, 173
La Via, Carmen 229
Lantz Office 215, 249
Lantz, Robert 215, 216
Laster, Owen 225
Lawrence, Richard 266
Laya Gelff Associates 82

Leading Artists 256
Lee, Harris, Draper 229
Leibman, Sue 203
Leif, Ron 210
Leslie B. Kallen Literary Agency 204
Lew Weitz and Associates 238
Lewis, Michael 248
Lichtman, Mark 247
Lieb, Debra 246
Liebowitz, Phil 225
Lifson-Pompan, Byrdie 264, 265
Limato, Ed 202
Livingston, Mike 167
Lonner, David 181, 203
Loosemore, Lisa 203
Lucille Phillips Agency 229
Lucy Kroll Agency 213
LWA 238
Lyne, Jennifer 193
Mabank, Bayard 243
Major Talent 172
Malcolm, Robert 168
Mardigian, Ron 225
Margules, Michael 246
Marje Fields/Rita Scott 187
Markevich, Sharon A. 262
Marks, Stephen 219
Marshak, Darryl 194
Martino, Paul 203
Masser, Larry 164, 168
MCA 163
McIlvain, David 219
McNeal, Tom 203
McShame, Kevin 229
Meager, Mary 193
Media Artists Group 49, 51, 104, 146
Melnick, Jeffrey 194
Merrill, Helen 228

Metropolitan Talent Agency 223, 240
Metzger, Ed 190
Meyer, Ron 180
Michaels, Victoria 246
Miller, Robin Moran 19, 21, 25, 44, 50-53, 68, 147
Miller, Stuart 164
Millner, Joel 173
Mitchell J. Hamilburg Agency 217
Mitchell, Sharon 163
Monteiro Rose 17, 102, 131, 133, 138
Monteiro Rose Agency 226
Monteiro, Candy 82, 102, 126, 131, 133, 138, 227
Montiero-Rose 138
Moon, Nancy 168
Moore, Chris 203
Morris, Susan 193
Morris, William 176, 224
Morris, William Agency 246
MTA 223
Mulert, Carl 209
Nassif, Christopher 174
Neisser, Ken 192
Nethercott, Gayla 173
Neuwald, Ellen 208
Nevins, Alan 240
Newberg, Esther 203
Nides, Tina 181
Nigrosh, Nancy 192
O'Connor, David 181
Oscard, Fifi 229
Ostler, Bruce 229
Ostroff, Daniel 41, 51, 103, 230, 231
Ostrov, Danny 179
Ovitz, Mike 112, 180
PAA 205
Pamplin, H. Shep 254
paradigm 63, 86, 98, 126, 134, 136
Paramuse Artists Associates 234

Patman, Andy 167
Patrick, Peggy 248
Paul Kohner, Inc. 105
Pearl, Gary 233
Peretzian, Mike 225
Perkins, Rowland 180
Pitt, Lou 203
Pleshette & Green 84, 236
Pleshette, Lynn 16, 17, 24, 33, 84, 87, 98, 106, 134, 136, 145, 146, 147, 236, 237
Posner, Marcy 225
Powers, Ray 187, 188
Preferred Artists 238
Preminger, Jim 20, 89, 90, 93, 114, 140, 141, 142, 239
Progressive Artists Agency 205
Puma, Johnny 254
Rapke, Jack 181
Reilly, Tim 179
Renaissance Literary Talent Agency 240
Richland, Dan 242, 243
Richland, Joe 243
Richland/Wunsch/Hohman 87, 114, 189
Riordan, Monica 239
Robinov, Jeff 264, 265
Robinson, Stu 63, 86, 91, 98, 99, 126, 134, 136, 232, 233
Robinson, Weintraub and Gross 232
Rose, Fredda 17, 82, 102, 126, 131, 133, 138, 143, 227
Rose, Stephen 219
Rosen Turtle Group 255
Rosen, Mike 244, 255
Rosenberg, Joe 203
Rosenfield, Michael 180
Rosenfield, Sonya 181
Rosenstone, Howard 245
Rosenstone/Wender 245
Rossen, Mark 203
Rothaker, Flo 182
Rothman, Robb 257

Russo, Jonathan 184
Rutter, Art 168
Salomon, Barry 168
Salt, Gary 105, 131, 132, 135, 136, 211
Sanders, Howard 15, 65, 237
Sanford, Steve 203
Saperstein, Richard 203
Savavi, Charlotte 246
Schechter, Irv 174, 246
Schiff, David 119
Schwartz, Joel 240
Schwartz, Mort 183
Schwartz, Scott 203
Scott, Joan 258, 264, 265
Shanks, Tom 253
Shapiro, Bob 248
Shapiro, Martin 84, 137, 247
Shapiro, Marty 35, 84, 85, 93, 94, 99, 102, 124, 132, 149, 247
Shapiro-Lichtman 247
Shepherd, Dick 167
Sherman, Ken 17, 52, 85, 87, 88, 94, 98, 249
Shorr, Stille & Associates 232
Simon, Andrea 246
Slocum, Charles B. 79
Smith and Associates 210
Smith Stevens 210
Smith, Susan 164
Smith, Todd 181
Solo, Matt 192
Soloway, Arnold 168
Stahler, Elliot 30, 83, 84, 87, 114, 120, 139, 140, 142, 205, 206
Stalmaster, Hal 168
Stanford Beckett and Associates 242
STE 232
Stein, Mitchell 248
Stein, Robert 257
Stille, Lucy 232, 233
Stipanich, Michael 264, 265

Stockfish, Tammy 173
Stone, Ivy 229
Strickler, Tom 203
Strull, Roger 238
Stutz, Lucy 233
Sullivan, Lisa 248
Susan Smith & Associates 168
Sutton, Laura 163
Swanson, H. N. 251
Swedlin, Rosalie 181
Talent Associates 261
Talent East 254
Tenzer, David 181
The Agency 164
The Brandt Company 170
Triad 119, 242, 258, 261
Turtle, Cindy 255
Uffner, Beth 173
United Talent 117, 119, 120, 205
United Talent Agency 256
UTA 116, 256
Van Duren, Annette 253
Van Dyke, Mike 163
Vorce, Roger 164
Wakefield, Karen 183
Wald, Malvin 190
Wallerstein, Michelle 252, 253
Warden, Steve 258
Warden, White and Kane 258
Webb, Elliot 16, 47, 123, 133, 136, 146, 149, 172, 173
Webb, Irene 203
Weinberg, Sandy 201
Weiner, Barry 184
Weintraub, Bernie 233
Weissman, Susie 238
Weitzman, Lew 238
Weston, Richard 219
Westover, Jonathan 20, 29, 86, 104, 106, 133, 144, 189

Wexler, Pearl 210
White, Steve 258
Whittlesey, Peregrine 259, 260
Wiatts, Jim 202
Wile Enterprises, Inc. 261
Wile, Shelly 261
Wilhelm, Jim 182
William Morris 170, 215, 261
William Morris Agency 115, 163, 168, 180, 205, 224, 247, 249, 256
Williams, Jeanne 203
Wirstchafter, David 203
WMA 91, 112, 116, 117, 119, 202, 223, 236, 240, 245
Wolff, Don 167
Wood, Audrey 198
Worsley, Joe 195
Wright, Dan 263
Writers & Artists 20, 21, 83, 95, 134, 184, 230, 264
Writers and Artists 258
Wunsch, Bob 242, 243
Wunsch/Ostroff 230
Wyckoff, Craig 183
Yoselow, Scott 193
Yumkas, Carol 225
Zadeh, Stella 266

Index to Los Angeles
Agents & Agencies

Abrams, Harry 161
Adelstein, Marty 257
Adler, Jerry 238
Agency, The 163
Alexander, Barbara 36, 49, 51, 102, 104, 125, 138, 146, 222
Aloni, Dan 192
APA 164
Arlook, Richard 192
Arnovitz, Scott 203
Artists Agency 167
Artists Group 168
Bankoff, Lisa 203
Barrett, Chris 223
Bauer Benedek 120, 256
Bayer, Deborah 186
Benson, Jeffrey 219
Berko, Raphael 42, 50, 95, 147, 149, 221
Berkus, James 257
Bernstein, Ron 192
Blumenthal, Marti 265
Bohn, Beth 255
Brandt, Geoffrey 170
Bresler, Sandy 167
Broder●Kurland●Webb●Uffner 16, 47, 92, 96, 123, 133, 136, 146, 148, 149, 161, 172
Brodex, Doug 233
Brunswick, Glen 19, 37

Champoux, Caron 163
Cioffi, Dana 257
CNA 174
Cohen, Lee 225
Cooper Agency 176
Cooper, Frank 176
Coppage Agency 178
Corday, Evan 194
Cosay, Gary 256, 257
Davey, Tricia 203
Detroit, Patty 203
Dollard, Pat 257
Dreyfus. Barbara 203
Durham, Kirk 30
Emannuel, Ariel 203
Everett, Judith 201
Feldman, Ilene 257
Ferris, Amy 203
Field, Jeff 225
Field, Maggie 91, 131, 186
Fineman, Ross 161
Fraser, Diane 219
Gage, Martin 189
Gelff, Laya 35, 82, 190
Gersh, David 192
Gersh, Phil 192
Gold, Dodie 225
Gold, Harry 194
Gold/Marshak 194
Goldberg, Howard 200
Goldfarb, Robert 187
Goldstone, Ed 168
Gores, Sam 232
Gores/Fields 232
Gotler, Joel 240
Gray, Stephen 195
Green, Richard 24, 237
Greenblatt, David 203

Greenblatt, Ken 16, 222
Greenspan, Alan 203
Greer, Rima 14, 17, 20, 21, 83, 85, 95, 99, 124, 134, 138, 264
Gross, Ken 232
Gumer, Bob 203
Gusay, Charlotte 196
H. N. Swanson, Inc. 251
Haas, Paul 203
Harbert, Christopher 257
Harris, Mark R. 219
Harris, Todd 225
Harrison, Harvey 239
Hohman, Bob 22, 83, 84, 86, 87, 94, 145, 147, 242
Hyler, Joan 90
Innovative Artists 200, 258
InterTalent 119, 256
Irv Schechter Company 22, 131
Jacobs, Stuart 18, 37, 104, 105, 107, 108, 137, 174
Jacobson, Mark 240
Jaffee, Michael 161
Jim Preminger Agency 89, 239
Kallen, Leslie B. 204
Kamins, Ken 203
Kane, Michael 258
Kaplan Stahler 83, 87, 205
Kaplan, Mitch 205
Kelly, Maryann 223
Ken Sherman & Associates 249
Kennar, Larry 186
Klein, Debbee 22, 99, 102, 131, 246
Klein, Don 246
Koerner, Todd 205
Kohner, Paul 148
Kopaloff, Don 212
Lichtman, Mark 247
Limato, Ed 202
Mabank, Bayard 243
Mardigian, Ron 225

Markevich, Sharon A. 262
Marks, Stephen 219
Marshak, Darryl 194
McIlvain, David 219
McNeal, Tom 203
Media Artists Group 49, 104, 146
Metropolitan Talent Agency 223, 240
Mitchell, Sharon 163
Monteiro Rose 17, 102, 131, 138
Monteiro Rose Agency 226
Monteiro, Candy 82, 102, 126, 131, 133, 138, 227
Montiero-Rose 138
Moore, Chris 203
MTA 223
Neisser, Ken 192
Nevins, Alan 240
Nigrosh, Nancy 192
Ostroff, Daniel 230
Ovitz, Mike 180
paradigm 86, 98, 134, 136, 232
Pearl, Gary 233
Peretzian, Mike 225
Pitt, Lou 203
Pleshette & Green 84, 236
Pleshette, Lynn 16, 17, 24, 33, 84, 87, 98, 105, 106, 145, 236, 237
Preferred Artists 238
Preminger, Jim 20, 85, 87, 89, 90, 93, 140, 239
Renaissance Literary Talent Agency 240
Richland, Dan 242
Richland/Wunsch/Hohman 83, 84, 86, 87, 114
Riordan, Monica 239
Robinov, Jeff 265
Robinson, Stu 63, 86, 91, 98, 99, 126, 232
Rose, Fredda 17, 82, 102, 126, 131, 133, 138, 143, 227
Rose, Stephen 219
Rosenberg, Joe 203
Rossen, Mark 203

Rothman, Robb 257
Salomon, Barry 168
Salt, Gary 105, 148, 210, 211
Sanders, Howard 15, 18, 65, 237
Sandy Bresler Agency 167
Sanford, Steve 203
Saperstein, Richard 203
Schechter (Irv) Company, The 246
Schwartz, Joel 240
Shapiro, Martin 94
Shapiro, Marty 35, 84, 85, 93, 99, 102, 124, 132, 149, 247
Shapiro-Lichtman 84, 132, 247
Sherman, Ken 17, 52, 80, 85, 87, 88, 92, 94, 98, 249
Solo, Matt 192
Stahler, Elliot 30, 83, 84, 87, 205
STE 232
Stein, Robert 257
Stella Zadeh & Associates 266
Stille, Lucy 233
Stipanich, Michael 265
Strickler, Tom 203
Strull, Roger 238
Stutz, Lucy 233
Sutton, Laura 163
Swanson, H. N. 251
Swanson, H. N., Inc. 251
Triad 119
Turtle Agency, The 255
Turtle, Cindy 255
UTA 256
Van Dyke, Mike 163
Wakefield, Karin 183
Warden, Dave 258
Warden, White & Kane 258
Webb, Elliot 16, 47, 92, 148
Webb, Irene 203
Weintraub, Bernie 232, 233
Weissman, Susie 238

Weitzman, Lew 238
Weston, Richard 219
Westover, Jonathan 20, 29, 86, 104, 106, 133, 144
White, Steve 258
Wiatts, Jim 202
Wile Enterprises, Inc. 261
Wile, Shelley 261
William Morris Agency 246, 249, 256
Williams, Jeanne 203
Wirstchafter, David 203
WMA 240, 245
Worsley, Joe 195
Writers & Artists 20, 83, 85, 264
Wuliger, Frank 201
Wunsch, Bob 242
Wyckoff, Craig 183
Yumkas, Carol 225
Zadeh, Stella 266
Zadeh, Stella & Associates 266
Zeitman, Jerome 163

Index to New York
Agents & Agencies

Adams, Bret 162
Alessi, Anna Maria 165
APA 164
Bennahum, Michael 165
Bernstein, Shirley 234, 235
Boatwright, Boaty 203
Bormann, Jim 217
Craver, Bill 264
Davis, Carole 254
DGRW 182
Donaghey, Bob 254
Douglas, Gorman, Rothaker & Wilhelm 182
Eastman, Andrea 203
Fields, Marje 187
Gage, Martin 189
Garon, Jay 34
Gluck, Suzanne 203
Gorman, Fred 63, 182
Graham Agency 198
Graham, Earl 198
Harden, Mary 162
Helen Merrill 228
Hogenson, Barbara 214
Innovative Artists 200
Jay Garon-Brook Associates 34
Josephson, Nancy 203
Kato, Gordon 203

Ketay, Joyce 208
Lantz Office 215
Lantz, Robert 215, 216
Laster, Owen 225
Leibman, Sue 203
Liebowitz, Phil 225
Lifson-Pompan, Byrdie 264, 265
Literarium, The 217
Loosemore, Lisa 203
Lucy Kroll Agency 213
Lyne, Jennifer 193
Marcia Amsterdam Agency 166
Marje Fields/Rita Scott 187
Miller, Robin Moran 19, 21, 25, 44, 50-53, 68, 147
Morris, Susan 193
Mulert, Carl 208
Newberg, Esther 203
Oscard, Fifi 229
Pamplin, H. Shep 254
paradigm 86, 232
Paramuse Artists Associates 234
Peregrine Whittlesey 259
Posner, Marcy 225
Powers, Ray 187
Puma, Johnny 254
Robinov, Jeff 264
Rosenstone, Howard 245
Rosenstone/Wender 245
Scott, Rita 187
STE 232
Stevens, Clifford 232
Talent East 254
Wender, Phyllis 245
Whittlesey, Peregrine Agency 259
Wood, Audrey 198
Wright Agency, Dan 263
Writers & Artists 264
Yoselow, Scott 193

Index to Everything Else

90%-10% 129
Above the line 267
Access 91
Access - film/televison 28
America's Best - address 54
Associate producer 267
Below the line 267
Bible 267
British Alternative Theatre Directory 61
Buzz 267
Career guidance - Donie Nelson 49
Chanticleer Films 57
Chanticleer Films - address 57
Chesterfield Program 54
Clout 267
Co-producers 268
Conglomerate agents - training 93
Connected 267
Contests 53
Coverage 268
Decision - star agent or independent 115
Development 268
Diane Thomas Contest - address 54
Directors Guild - address 74
Discovery Program 57
Discovery Program - address 57
Divorce 122

Donie Nelson 49
Dramatists Guild 268
Dramatists Guild - membership requirements 155
Dramatists Guild Quarterly 156, 268
Education 92
El Mariachi 12
Ending the meeting 109
Ensemble Studio Theater 58
Episodic television 29
Executive producer 268
Field, Syd 66
Format guide 154, 155
Franchised Agents 81
Freelance Screenwriter's Forum 57
Freelance Screenwriter's Forum - address and membership info 57
FYI 73
Gotham Writers Workshop 68
Graham, Bruce 27
Grisham, John 34
Half-hour 268
Hauge, Michael 67
Hollywood Reporter - address 70
Hollywood Writers' Report 1993 3
IFP 55
Independent Features Projects 55
Interactive 268
International Information 60
International Information Resources 60
International Theater Institute 60
International theater resources 61
Iwanter, Sydney 48
Leavetaking 127
Line producer 269
Litwak, Mark 118
Long form television 269
Make a home for yourself 37
Marjorie Ballentine Studio 44, 69
McKee, Robert 67

Miller, Robin Moran 69
Minority - statistics 11
Money 2
Nelson, Donie 49
New Dramatists 58, 269
Nicholl Fellowships - address 54
Original British Theater Directory 61
Outline 269
Peoples, David Webb 34
Performing Arts Yearbook 61
Pitch 269
Playwrighting 68
Playwrighting - contest resource info 61
Playwrights Horizons 58
Plugged in 269
Producer 269
Producers 28
Public Theater 58
Query letter 269
Reader 269
Readers 47
Reading List 70
Reading scripts for money 47
Reel Power 89
Reference Library 70
Relationships - writer/agent 130
Robert Rodriguez 12
Robin Moran Miller 69
Rodriguez, Robert 12
Sase 269
Schenkkan, Robert 264
Screen and Television 28
Screenplay contests 54
Screenwriting Contests 53
Script Analysts 48
Scriptwriter's Forum - address 56
Scriptwriters Network/Los Angeles 56
Size 90

Spec scripts 269
Speculative scripts 269
Star agencies - shakeup 116
Statistics 2
Stature 91
Story Analysts 48, 269
Study 65
Subterfuge 44
Support groups 39, 55
Support groups - filmmakers 56
Support groups - theater 58
Synergistic relationship 139
Tartikoff, Brandon 31
Telling/Shopping 126
The Meeting 106
Theater 25, 58
Theater Communications Group 62
Theaters - Ensemble Studio Theater 58
Theaters - Playwrights Horizons 58
Things you can do to help your career 142
Time 80
Tolins, Jonathan 19, 46
Too much to expect 136
Trades 270
Treatment 270
Trottier, Dave 68
TV Market Page 72
Variety - address 70
Walter, Richard 66
WGA - resources 150
WGA Directory 270
Who makes the money 3
Who works? 3
Why agents? 77
Writer's Aid - address 55
Writers Guild - address 150
Writers Guild - format guide 154
Writers Guild - membership fee 151

Writers Guild - membership requirements 151
Writers Guild - minority programs 151
Writers Guild - registration service 150
Writers Guild of America 270
Writers Guild/East - address 151
Zucker, Laura 27

Come on Over

Gooseberry Patch
2500 Farmers Dr., #110
Columbus, OH 43235

www.gooseberrypatch.com

1·800·854·6673

Copyright 2004, Gooseberry Patch 978-1-61821-067-6
Seventh Printing, January, 2012

Do you have a tried & true recipe...

tip, craft or memory that you'd like to see featured in a **Gooseberry
Patch** cookbook? Visit our website at **www.gooseberrypatch.com**,
register and follow the easy steps to submit your favorite family recipe.
Or send them to us at:

Gooseberry Patch
Attn: Cookbook Dept.
2500 Farmers Dr., #110
Columbus, OH 43235

Don't forget to include the number of servings your recipe makes,
plus your name, address, phone number and email address.
If we select your recipe, your name will appear right along
with it...and you'll receive a **FREE** copy of the cookbook!

Contents

Breezy
Breakfasts
5

Appetizers 1-2-3
35

Snappy Soups
& Salads
73

Simply Delicious
Sides & Breads
105

Quick from the
Cupboard Mains
137

Desserts in
a Dash
181

Dedication

For everyone who enjoys cozy get-togethers around the table.

Appreciation

To our friends who shared their recipes that make everyone feel like family...thank you!

Breezy Breakfasts

Welcome!

Overnight Coffee Cake

Jennie Wiseman
Coshocton, OH

Company on their way? Bake right away, it's not necessary to chill.

1 c. all-purpose flour
1/4 c. sugar
1/4 c. brown sugar, packed
1/2 t. baking soda
1/2 t. baking powder

1/2 t. cinnamon
1/2 c. buttermilk
1/3 c. margarine
1 egg

Combine all ingredients; mix well. Spread in a greased 9" round cake pan; cover with plastic wrap and refrigerate overnight. Sprinkle with topping; bake at 350 degrees for 20 to 25 minutes. Drizzle with glaze. Serves 8.

Topping:

1/4 c. brown sugar, packed
1/4 c. chopped nuts

1/2 t. cinnamon
1/4 t. nutmeg

Toss all ingredients together.

Glaze:

1/2 c. powdered sugar
1/4 t. vanilla extract

3 to 4 t. milk

Combine powdered sugar and vanilla; stir in enough milk to reach desired consistency.

Breezy Breakfasts

Sunrise Cinnamon Loaves

Nichole Martelli
Alvin, TX

Make 'em mini loaves so every guest has their own. This recipe will make five, 6"x3" mini loaves...just shorten bake time to 35 minutes.

18-1/2 oz. pkg. yellow cake mix
   with pudding
4 eggs
3/4 c. oil

3/4 c. water
1 t. vanilla extract
1/2 c. sugar
3 T. cinnamon

Blend the first 5 ingredients together on high speed of an electric mixer for 3 minutes; divide batter in half. Equally divide one half and pour into 2 greased and floured 8"x4" loaf pans; set aside. Combine sugar and cinnamon in a small bowl; sprinkle half evenly over the batter in each loaf pan. Spread remaining batter evenly into each loaf pan; sprinkle loaves with remaining sugar and cinnamon. Use a knife to gently swirl sugar and cinnamon into batter; bake at 350 degrees for 45 minutes. Cool on wire racks. Makes 16 servings.

A glassful of fresh-squeezed orange juice is always
a treat at breakfast. Set out a juicer along with
a bowl of oranges cut in half so guests can take
a turn at squeezing their own.

Yummy Caramel French Toast

*The Doubleday Inn
Gettysburg, PA*

*Slice bread into sticks before baking...the kids will love
dipping them into syrup.*

1 c. brown sugar, packed
1/2 c. margarine
2 T. corn syrup
8 slices Italian bread
6 eggs, lightly beaten

1-1/2 c. milk
1 t. vanilla extract
1/8 t. salt
Garnish: warm syrup

Combine the first 3 ingredients in a saucepan; bring to a full boil.
Reduce heat; simmer until thickened, about 2 to 3 minutes. Pour in
a greased 13"x9" baking pan; arrange bread slices in a single layer on
top. Set aside. Combine eggs with remaining ingredients; mix well.
Pour over bread slices; cover with aluminum foil and refrigerate
overnight. Uncover and bake at 350 degrees until golden, about
45 minutes; drizzle with syrup before serving. Makes 8 servings.

Hosting a Mothers' Day Brunch or a Girls' Tea Party?
Dress up the table by tying pretty scarves around chair
backs, then tuck a tulip in each knot.

Breezy Breakfasts

German Apple Pancake

Marilyn Williams
Westerville, OH

Jonathan or McIntosh apples are the tastiest to use in this recipe.

1/4 c. butter
1-1/2 t. cinnamon, divided
2 apples, cored, peeled and
    thinly sliced
3 eggs, beaten
1/2 c. frozen apple juice
    concentrate, thawed

1/2 c. all-purpose flour
1/4 c. half-and-half
1-1/2 t. vanilla extract
1/4 t. nutmeg
1/8 t. salt

Melt butter with 1/2 teaspoon cinnamon over medium heat in a
10" oven-proof skillet; add apples. Sauté until tender, about 4 minutes;
set aside. Place eggs, apple juice concentrate, flour, half-and-half,
vanilla, remaining cinnamon, nutmeg and salt in a food processor;
process until smooth. Pour over apples; bake at 450 degrees until set,
about 10 minutes. Cut into wedges; place on serving plates. Spoon
apple cream on top before serving. Makes 6 servings.

Apple Cream:

1/2 c. plain yogurt
1/2 t. vanilla extract

2 T. frozen apple juice
    concentrate, thawed

Whisk all ingredients together until smooth.

Having friends over for
breakfast? Set the
table the night before...
one less thing
to think about in
the morning!

Best Brunch Casserole

Lita Hardy
Santa Cruz, CA

My family & friends have been enjoying this dish for over 30 years!

4 c. croutons
2 c. shredded Cheddar cheese
8 eggs, beaten
4 c. milk
1 t. salt

1 t. pepper
2 t. mustard
1 T. dried, minced onion
6 slices bacon, crisply cooked
    and crumbled

Spread croutons in the bottom of a greased 13"x9" baking pan; sprinkle with cheese. Set aside. Whisk eggs, milk, salt, pepper, mustard and onion together; pour over cheese. Sprinkle bacon on top; bake at 325 degrees until set, about 55 to 60 minutes. Serves 8.

Sausage & Egg Muffins

Rhonda Jones
Rocky Mount, VA

Egg-ceptionally easy!

1 lb. ground sausage
1 onion, chopped
12 eggs, beaten
2 c. shredded Cheddar cheese

1 t. garlic powder
1/2 t. salt
1/2 t. pepper

Brown sausage with onion; drain. Combine with remaining ingredients in a large mixing bowl; mix well. Spoon into greased muffin cups, filling 2/3 full; bake at 350 degrees until a knife inserted in the centers removes clean, about 25 minutes. Makes 12 to 15.

Breezy Breakfasts

Raisin-Oat Muffins

Denise Picard
Ventura, CA

I love making these muffins when friends stop by because I always have the ingredients on hand.

1 c. whole-wheat flour
3/4 c. long-cooking oats,
   uncooked
1/2 c. raisins
1/4 c. brown sugar, packed
1 T. baking powder

1/2 t. baking soda
1 t. salt
1/4 t. nutmeg
1 egg, beaten
1 c. milk
1/4 c. oil

Combine the first 8 ingredients in a large mixing bowl; set aside. Whisk egg, milk and oil together; mix into oat mixture until just moistened. Fill greased muffin cups half full with batter; bake at 400 degrees until golden, about 20 to 25 minutes. Makes one dozen.

Greet early-morning guests with flowers. Glue a ribbon to the bottom and up the sides of a tin can, then bring the ribbon ends up and tie in a bow. Fill the can with water and several fresh blooms and hang right on the doorknob.

Cappuccino Cooler

Dianne Gregory
Sheridan, AR

A perfect pick-me-up drink!

1-1/2 c. prepared coffee, cooled
1-1/2 c. chocolate ice cream,
　softened
1/4 c. chocolate syrup

crushed ice
1 c. frozen whipped topping,
　thawed

Blend coffee, ice cream and syrup together until smooth; set aside.
Fill 4 glasses 3/4 full with ice; add coffee mixture. Top with a spoonful
of whipped topping; serve immediately. Makes 4 servings.

Espresso Whirl

Patsy Roberts
Center, TX

Serve this refreshing drink at brunch or after dinner
in place of dessert.

1/2 c. prepared espresso, cooled
2 c. milk

1/4 c. sugar
1-1/2 c. crushed ice

Combine all ingredients in a blender; blend well. Pour into chilled
serving glasses; serve immediately. Makes 2 servings.

Offer guests fun toppers for their
coffees...vanilla powder,
mini chocolate chips, mini
marshmallows and whipped
topping. Yum!

Breezy Breakfasts

Fabulous Fruit Slush

Pam Klocke
Spicer, MN

An a.m. treat that's sure to delight friends.

1 c. water
1 c. sugar
2 T. lemon juice
12-oz. can frozen orange juice
   concentrate
12-oz. can crushed pineapple,
   drained

17-oz. can fruit cocktail, drained
16-oz. pkg. frozen strawberries,
   thawed and sliced
2 bananas, chopped
6-oz. jar maraschino cherries,
   drained and chopped

Combine water and sugar in a saucepan; heat until sugar is dissolved.
Add lemon and orange juice; heat until completely melted. Remove
from stove; stir in remaining ingredients. Pour mixture into 4 to
6 freezer-proof containers; freeze until solid. Remove containers from
freezer one hour before serving. Makes 4 to 6 servings.

A bowl filled with bright Lemons and Limes Looks so cheery
on a breakfast table...prick them a few times with a fork
to reLease their deLightful scent.

Early-Riser Breakfast

*Patty Laughery
Moses Lake, WA*

*This has become a tradition at Easter and Christmas because it's so
easy to prepare the night before and everyone loves it!*

8 slices bread, cubed
1 c. shredded Cheddar cheese
1 c. shredded Monterey Jack
　cheese
1-1/2 lbs. ground sausage,
　browned

4 eggs, beaten
3 c. milk, divided
10-3/4 oz. can cream of
　mushroom soup
3/4 t. dry mustard

Arrange bread in an ungreased 13"x9" baking pan; sprinkle with
cheeses and sausage. Set aside. Mix eggs and 2-1/2 cups milk
together; pour over bread. Cover with aluminum foil; refrigerate
overnight. Combine remaining ingredients; pour over bread mixture.
Bake, uncovered, at 300 degrees for 1-1/2 hours. Serves 8.

Tiny berry baskets filled with fresh fruit look charming at
each place setting. Stick a toothpick through a placecard
and prop up inside. Brunch guests will love it!

Breezy Breakfasts

Jump-Start Pizza

Mari MacLean
Bonita, CA

Add your own special toppings before baking.

8-oz. tube refrigerated crescent
   rolls, separated
28-oz. pkg. frozen shredded
   hashbrowns with peppers
   and onions, slightly thawed
   and divided

6 slices bacon, crisply cooked
   and crumbled
4-oz. can diced green chiles,
   drained
1/2 to 1 c. shredded Cheddar
   cheese
5 eggs, beaten

Arrange crescent rolls to cover the bottom of an ungreased pizza pan;
press seams together and pinch edges to form a slight rim. Spread
half the hashbrowns evenly over the crust, reserving remaining for
another recipe; sprinkle with bacon, chiles and cheese. Carefully pour
eggs on top; bake at 375 degrees for 30 to 35 minutes. Slice into
wedges to serve. Makes 8 servings.

Surprise overnight guests by leaving special treats in their
room...wrap up fragrant soaps in plush terry washcloths,
leave a few mints on their pillow or set up a small
coffee maker with mugs and individual coffee
packets for them to enjoy.

Frozen Fruit Squares

Kristine Marumoto
Sandy, UT

A fresh addition to any breakfast or brunch.

8-oz. pkg. cream cheese,
  softened
1 c. sugar
1-1/2 c. mayonnaise
1 c. chopped pecans
2 bananas, sliced
3 c. frozen whipped topping,
  thawed

2 8-oz. cans crushed
  pineapple, drained
2 10-oz. pkgs. frozen
  strawberries, thawed and
  drained
12-oz. pkg. mini marshmallows
1 c. grapes, halved

Blend cream cheese, sugar and mayonnaise together; fold in remaining ingredients. Spread in an ungreased 13"x9" freezer-safe pan; cover with aluminum foil and freeze. Remove from freezer and allow to soften before cutting into squares. Makes 18 servings.

So fun! Turn Frozen Fruit Squares into circles. Before freezing, spoon mixture into clean 12-ounce juice cans. Once they're frozen, just push fruit mixture from the can and slice into circles.

Breezy Breakfasts

Blueberry-Almond Muffins

Rochelle Sundholm
Eugene, OR

There's nothing so comforting and delicious as a blueberry muffin warm from the oven.

2 c. all-purpose flour
1 T. baking powder
1/4 t. salt
2/3 c. sugar
2 t. lemon zest

1/2 c. milk
1/2 c. butter, melted and cooled
2 eggs
1-1/2 c. blueberries

Combine first 5 ingredients in a large mixing bowl; form a well in the center. Set aside. Whisk milk, butter and eggs together; pour into well, stirring until just moistened. Fold in blueberries; fill greased muffin cups 2/3 full with batter. Sprinkle with topping; bake at 400 degrees for 15 to 20 minutes. Remove from muffin cups immediately. Makes 20.

Topping:

1/4 c. all-purpose flour
1/4 c. sugar

2 T. chilled butter, sliced
1/3 c. chopped almonds

Combine flour and sugar in a mixing bowl; cut in butter with a pastry cutter until crumbly. Add almonds; mix well.

Southern Country Casserole

Michelle Garner
Tampa, FL

There won't be any leftovers!

2 c. water
1/2 c. quick-cooking grits,
  uncooked
3-1/2 c. shredded Cheddar
  cheese, divided
4 eggs, beaten

1 c. milk
1/2 t. salt
1/2 t. pepper
1 lb. ground sausage, browned
1 T. fresh parsley, chopped

Bring water to a boil in a large saucepan; add grits. Return to a boil; reduce heat and simmer for 4 minutes. Mix in 2 cups cheese; stir until melted. Remove from heat; add eggs, milk, salt, pepper and sausage, mixing well. Pour into a greased 13"x9" baking pan; bake at 350 degrees for 45 to 50 minutes. Sprinkle with remaining cheese and parsley; return to oven until cheese melts, about 5 minutes. Serves 6 to 8.

Make your gatherings fit your home. Have a tiny dining area but a roomy patio or deck? Plan to invite friends over when you can serve casual meals outdoors.

Breezy Breakfasts

Baked Garden Omelet

Kathy Unruh
Fresno, CA

Here's one omelet you don't have to flip!

8 eggs, beaten
1 c. ricotta cheese
1/2 c. milk
1/2 t. dried basil
1/4 t. salt
1/4 t. fennel seed, crushed
1/4 t. pepper

10-oz. pkg. frozen spinach,
   thawed and drained
1 c. tomatoes, chopped
1 c. shredded mozzarella cheese
1/2 c. green onion, sliced
1/2 c. salami, diced

Whisk eggs and ricotta cheese together in a large mixing bowl; add milk, basil, salt, fennel seed and pepper. Fold in remaining ingredients; spread in a greased 13"x9" baking pan. Bake at 325 degrees until a knife inserted in the center removes clean, about 30 to 35 minutes; let stand 10 minutes before serving. Serves 6 to 8.

Mini Ham Muffins

Linda Stone
Cookville, TN

You can't eat just one!

1 c. self-rising flour
1/4 c. mayonnaise

1/2 c. milk
1 c. cooked ham, chopped

Stir all ingredients together; spoon into greased mini muffin cups. Bake at 350 degrees until golden, about 15 minutes. Makes one dozen.

The ornament of a house is
the friends who frequent it.
- Ralph Waldo Emerson

Crispy French Toast

Kathy Murray-Strunk
Mesa, AZ

This French toast is unlike any I've ever had. It's truly delicious,
attractive on a breakfast table and always a favorite.

4 eggs, beaten
1/2 c. milk
1/2 t. cinnamon
1 t. vanilla extract
1/8 t. salt

2 c. corn flake cereal, crushed
1 loaf French bread, cut into
   10 slices
Garnish: maple syrup

Whisk first 5 ingredients together in a shallow dish; set aside. Spread
crushed cereal on a plate; set aside. Dip bread slices into egg mixture;
turn once to coat both sides. Place in crushed cereal; turn once
to coat both sides. Arrange on a buttered baking sheet; bake at
450 degrees for 5 minutes. Flip bread slices; bake 5 additional
minutes. Drizzle with syrup; serve warm. Makes 10 servings.

No time to spend on folding napkins? Simply pull each
through the hole of a bagel, then set one
on each plate...oh-so clever!

Breezy Breakfasts

Gooey Caramel Rolls

Maureen Seidl
Inver Grove Heights, MN

*Years ago I owned a cafe where we perfected this simple recipe.
They can be prepared the day before and cooked the next morning...
just be sure to serve them piping hot!*

1-1/2 c. brown sugar, packed
3/4 c. whipping cream

2 loaves frozen bread dough,
   thawed

Whisk brown sugar and whipping cream together; pour into an
ungreased 13"x9" baking pan. Tip to evenly coat bottom; set aside.
Roll out one bread loaf into a 12"x6" rectangle; roll up jelly-roll style
beginning at a short side. Slice into 6, one-inch thick pieces; arrange
in baking pan. Repeat with remaining bread loaf. Cover with plastic
wrap; set aside until dough rises to top of pan. Uncover and bake at
350 degrees for 35 to 45 minutes; let cool slightly. Place a serving
plate tightly over pan; invert to remove rolls. Spoon any remaining
syrup on top; serve warm. Makes one dozen.

A quick & easy breakfast
or brunch
centerpiece... just fill
each muffin cup half
full of coffee
beans, then nestle
a small votive candle
in each. So simple!

Sweet Berry Popover

Elisabeth Macmillan
British Columbia, Canada

Use the freshest berries of the season.

1 c. milk
1 T. butter, melted
1/2 t. vanilla extract
1/4 c. plus 1 T. sugar, divided
1/4 t. salt

1/8 t. nutmeg
1 c. all-purpose flour
2 eggs, beaten
1 c. berries
1/4 t. cinnamon

Whisk milk, butter, vanilla, 1/4 cup sugar, salt and nutmeg together; blend in flour. Gradually mix in eggs; set aside. Butter a 9" pie plate; add berries, leaving a wide border around the rim. Gently pour batter on top; set aside. Combine remaining sugar with cinnamon; sprinkle over the batter. Bake at 450 degrees for 20 minutes; lower heat to 350 degrees without opening the oven door. Continue baking until popover is golden, about 20 additional minutes. Slice into wedges; serve immediately. Makes 8 servings.

Thread cranberries and grapes through wooden skewers and serve with any breakfast beverage...Looks really pretty in orange juice or white grape juice.

Breezy Breakfasts

Strawberry Scones

Jennifer Wickes
Pine Beach, NJ

*I created this recipe after tasting spectacular scones at an
Amish bake sale...these are top-notch!*

2 c. all-purpose flour
1/3 c. sugar
2 t. baking powder
1/4 t. salt
1/3 c. butter
1 egg, beaten

1 t. vanilla extract
1/4 c. whipping cream
1/4 c. buttermilk
1 c. strawberries, hulled and
   sliced
Optional: sugar

Combine flour, sugar, baking powder and salt in a large mixing bowl;
cut in butter with a pastry cutter until coarse crumbs form. Form
a well in the center; set aside. Whisk egg, vanilla, cream and
buttermilk together; stir into dry mixture until just moistened. Fold
in strawberries; gently knead dough on a lightly floured surface until
smooth, about 10 seconds. Pat into a 7-inch circle about one-inch
thick; slice into 8 wedges. Arrange on a parchment paper-lined baking
sheet; brush with glaze and sprinkle with additional sugar, if desired.
Bake at 375 degrees until golden, about 15 minutes. Cool on a wire
rack. Makes 8 servings.

Glaze:

1 egg, beaten

1 T. whipping cream

Whisk egg and cream together.

No-Eggs Breakfast Casserole

Loree Matson
Fort Wayne, IN

A real crowd-pleaser.

30-oz. pkg. frozen shredded
   hashbrowns, thawed
16-oz. container French onion
   dip

1 lb. ground sausage, browned
2 c. sour cream
2 c. shredded Cheddar cheese,
   divided

Combine first 4 ingredients and one cup cheese; mix well. Spread in a greased 13"x9" baking pan; bake at 350 degrees for 45 minutes. Sprinkle with remaining cheese; bake for 15 additional minutes. Serves 4 to 6.

Cheese, Please Pie

Stefan Szabo
Richfield, OH

Try stirring in diced sun-dried tomatoes, red pepper or green chiles.

1 egg
3/4 c. all-purpose flour
1/2 t. garlic salt

pepper to taste
1 c. milk, divided
1 c. shredded Muenster cheese

Whisk egg, flour, garlic salt, pepper and 1/2 cup milk together until smooth; gradually blend in remaining milk. Stir in cheese; pour into a greased 9" glass pie plate. Bake at 425 degrees until puffed and set, about 25 to 30 minutes. Cut into wedges; serve warm. Serves 4.

All happiness depends on a leisurely breakfast.
– John Gunther

Breezy Breakfasts

Chef's Baked Oatmeal

Laura Leeper
Altoona, IA

A yummy way to warm up tummies on chilly mornings.

3 c. quick-cooking oats,
   uncooked
2 t. baking powder
1 t. salt

1/2 c. butter, softened
2 eggs
2 c. milk

Stir together oats, baking powder and salt in a mixing bowl; set aside. In a separate bowl, combine butter, eggs and milk; blend into dry ingredients. Pour into an ungreased 13"x9" baking pan; bake at 375 degrees for 25 minutes. Serves 6 to 8.

Top off each bowl of Chef's Baked Oatmeal with a dainty edible flower...they add eye-catching color along with a delightful flavor. Grow them yourself or look for pesticide-free blooms in the supermarket. For a sweet taste, try roses, squash blossoms, daylilies or violets.

Sweet Apple Rolls

Mary Morrison
Zanoni, MO

I like to use gooseberries, strawberries and rhubarb too!

2 c. all-purpose flour
3/4 c. shortening
2-1/2 c. water, divided
5 apples, cored, peeled and
   chopped

2 c. sugar
1/2 c. margarine

Mix flour and shortening together; stir in 1/2 cup water. Roll out into 1/2-inch thick rectangle; sprinkle with apples. Roll up jelly-roll style; cut into twelve slices. Arrange in an ungreased 13"x9" baking pan; set aside. Combine remaining water, sugar and margarine in a saucepan; heat until sugar is dissolved. Pour over rolls; bake at 350 degrees for 50 minutes. Makes one dozen.

Puffy Pancakes

Stephanie Herrel
Oswego, IL

Cut into squares and drizzle your favorite syrup over top.

1/2 c. butter
1 c. milk
1 c. all-purpose flour

4 eggs, beaten
Garnish: powdered sugar

Place butter in a 13"x9" baking pan; heat in a 425-degree oven until melted. Whisk remaining ingredients together; pour over butter, without mixing. Bake at 425 degrees for 20 minutes; sprinkle with powdered sugar before serving. Makes 8 to 10 servings.

Lay pancakes on a baking sheet and place in a low oven to keep warm until all the batter is used.

Breezy Breakfasts

Pear Pancake

Jo Ann

Top each slice with a sprinkling of powdered sugar...yum!

4 pears, cored, peeled and sliced
1/4 c. brown sugar, packed
1/4 c. lemon juice
1 c. all-purpose flour
1 c. milk

3 T. sugar
1 t. vanilla extract
1/4 t. salt
3 eggs, beaten

Combine pears, brown sugar and lemon juice; stir well. Pour into a 12" skillet; sauté until pears are golden, about 5 minutes. Remove from heat; set aside. Place flour in a large mixing bowl; set aside. Whisk remaining ingredients together; pour into flour, mix well. Pour batter into an ungreased 12" oven-proof skillet; bake at 425 degrees until golden and puffy, about 25 minutes. Spoon warm pear mixture into the center before serving. Serves 4.

Add a simple, yet elegant touch to a brunch with friends. Stick whole cloves into firm pears to spell the first initial of each guest's name. Tie a sheer ribbon around each stem and stand the pears up at place settings.

Get Up & Go Granola

Nicole Shira
New Baltimore, MI

Sprinkle over yogurt for a satisfying breakfast treat.

zest of 2 oranges
1/3 c. maple syrup
1/2 c. oil
4 c. quick-cooking oats,
   uncooked
1 c. sliced almonds
2 c. mixed nuts

1/8 t. salt
1/3 c. honey
2-1/2 t. cinnamon
1/2 t. nutmeg
3/4 c. chopped dried apricots
3/4 c. chopped dried cherries
2 c. flaked coconut, toasted

Mix orange zest, maple syrup and oil together in a heavy saucepan;
bring to a boil. Boil for one minute; remove from heat. Stir in oats,
almonds, nuts, salt, honey, cinnamon, nutmeg, apricots and cherries;
spread onto an ungreased baking sheet. Bake at 350 degrees for 10
to 15 minutes; remove from oven. Sprinkle with coconut; cool. Break
into pieces; store in an airtight container. Makes 10 cups.

Create a cereal station for a quick & easy breakfast.
Set out 3 to 4 different kinds of cereal, Get Up & Go
Granola and pitchers of ice cold milk. Add a bowl of fresh
fruit to the spread along with O.J., coffee and hot cocoa.
You can even prepare oatmeal and keep it on the stove for
guests to serve themselves.

Breezy Breakfasts

Fruity Oatmeal Coffee Cake

Natalie Holdren
Topeka, KS

Best served with an icy glass of milk!

1 c. whole-wheat flour
3/4 t. baking powder
1/2 t. allspice
1-1/2 c. quick-cooking oats,
   uncooked and divided
1 c. brown sugar, packed and
   divided
1/2 t. salt
1/2 t. cinnamon

2 t. vanilla extract
1 egg
1/2 c. chopped nuts
1/2 c. raisins
1 c. strawberries, hulled and
   chopped
1 banana, sliced
1/4 c. margarine

Combine flour, baking powder, allspice, one cup oats, 3/4 cup brown sugar, salt and cinnamon; stir in vanilla, egg, nuts, raisins, strawberries and banana. Spoon into a greased 9"x9" baking pan; set aside. Mix remaining oats and brown sugar together; cut in margarine until crumbly. Sprinkle over fruit mixture; bake at 350 degrees for 35 minutes. Makes 9 servings.

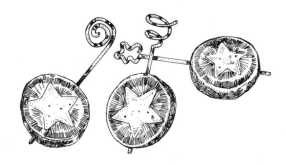

Bite-size beauties! Slice kiwi into 1/4-inch thick slices, then use a cookie cutter to cut out star shapes from the middle. Cut stars from melon slices, and fit the melon star into the opening in the kiwi.

Whole-Grain Jam Squares

Ellen Gibson
Orlando, FL

Stack on a jadite plate before serving...so pretty!

2 c. quick-cooking oats,
    uncooked
1-3/4 c. all-purpose flour
3/4 t. salt
1/2 t. baking soda

1 c. butter
1 c. brown sugar, packed
1/2 c. chopped walnuts
1 t. cinnamon
3/4 to 1 c. strawberry preserves

Combine the first 8 ingredients in a mixing bowl; stir until crumbly. Place 2 cups mixture to the side; press remaining mixture into the bottom of a greased 13"x9" baking pan. Spread preserves over the top; sprinkle with remaining oat mixture. Bake at 400 degrees for 25 to 30 minutes or until golden; cool. Cut into squares. Makes 2 dozen.

Butterscotch Banana Bread

Claire McGeough
Lebanon, NJ

My husband's favorite breakfast treat.

3-1/2 c. all-purpose flour
4 t. baking powder
1 t. baking soda
1 t. cinnamon
1 t. nutmeg
2 c. bananas, mashed

1-1/2 c. sugar
2 eggs
1/2 c. butter, melted
1/2 c. milk
12-oz. pkg. butterscotch chips,
    melted

Combine the first 6 ingredients together; set aside. Blend sugar, eggs and butter together in a large mixing bowl; gradually add flour mixture alternately with milk, mixing well. Fold in butterscotch chips; pour batter equally into 2 greased and floured 9"x5" loaf pans. Bake at 350 degrees for 60 to 70 minutes. Cool 15 minutes; remove from pans. Serve warm or cold. Makes 16 servings.

Breezy Breakfasts

Cinnamon-Apple Pancakes

Stephanie Moon
Silverdale, WA

Light and fluffy!

2 c. all-purpose flour
1 t. baking soda
2 t. baking powder
1 T. brown sugar, packed
1 t. salt
1 t. cinnamon

2 eggs
1-1/2 c. buttermilk
1/2 c. sour cream
1/4 c. margarine, melted
1 apple, cored, peeled and grated

Combine flour, baking soda, baking powder, brown sugar, salt and cinnamon in a large mixing bowl; set aside. Mix eggs, buttermilk, sour cream and margarine together; add to flour mixture. Fold in apple; pour 1/4 cup batter onto a greased hot griddle. Heat until golden on both sides, turning once. Serves 4 to 6.

Fun shapes for everyone! Spoon pancake batter into a plastic zipping bag, snip off one corner and gently squeeze batter onto a hot griddle into any shape...make cute animal shapes or alphabet letters.

3-Ingredient Sausage Squares

Shelley Wellington
Dyersburg, TN

This recipe can easily be halved and baked in an 8"x8" pan.

2 lbs. ground sausage
2 8-oz. pkgs. cream cheese,
  softened

2 8-oz. tubes refrigerated
  crescent rolls

Brown sausage in a 12" skillet; drain. Add cream cheese, stirring until melted and well blended; remove from heat and set aside. Press dough from one tube crescent rolls in a greased 13"x9" baking pan, being sure to cover bottom and part way up sides of pan; press perforations together. Pour sausage mixture over top; set aside. Roll remaining crescent roll dough into a 13"x9" rectangle; layer over sausage mixture. Bake at 350 degrees for 15 to 20 minutes or until golden; cut into squares to serve. Serves 6 to 8.

Zucchini Quiche

Rosemarie Rizzo
Toms River, NJ

Always a favorite!

4 eggs, beaten
1/4 c. grated Parmesan cheese
1/4 c. shredded mozzarella
  cheese
1/2 c. oil

1 c. biscuit baking mix
3 c. zucchini, thinly sliced
1/2 onion, chopped
1 t. fresh parsley, minced
1 t. garlic powder

Combine the first 5 ingredients; blend until smooth. Add remaining ingredients; stir well. Spread in a lightly greased 9" pie plate; bake at 350 degrees for 30 minutes. Makes 8 servings.

Breezy Breakfasts

Crustless Swiss Broccoli Quiche

Terri Dillingham
Windsor, NY

Serve with buttery toast.

4 eggs
3 T. all-purpose flour
1/2 t. dried oregano
1/8 t. pepper
1-1/2 c. milk
2 c. shredded Swiss cheese

1/4 c. green onion, sliced
10-oz. pkg. frozen broccoli,
   partially thawed
1/4 c. olives with pimentos,
   sliced

Blend first 5 ingredients together; gradually stir in the remaining ingredients. Pour into an ungreased 9" pie plate; bake at 350 degrees for 45 to 50 minutes. Makes 8 servings.

Make 'em mini! Bake Zucchini Quiche or
Crustless Swiss Broccoli Quiche in mini muffin cups for
individual servings...just decrease baking time by
10 minutes. Top each with a dainty dollop of sour cream
and a sprig of dill. So pretty!

Blueberry Pillows

Kristie Rigo
Friedens, PA

A delightful blend of cream cheese and blueberries stuffed inside French toast.

8-oz. pkg. cream cheese,
   softened
16 slices Italian bread
1/2 c. blueberries

2 eggs
1/2 c. milk
1 t. vanilla extract

Spread cream cheese evenly on 8 bread slices; arrange blueberries evenly over the cream cheese. Top with remaining bread slices, gently pressing to seal; set aside. Whisk eggs, milk and vanilla together in a shallow dish; brush over bread slices. Arrange on a hot griddle; heat until golden. Flip and heat other side until golden. Serves 8.

Sticky Buns

Catherine Smith
Champlin, MN

A quick & easy way to welcome morning guests.

18 frozen dinner rolls
3-1/2 oz. pkg. cook & serve
   butterscotch pudding mix

1/2 c. butter, melted
1/2 c. brown sugar, packed
1 t. cinnamon

Place rolls in a greased Bundt® pan; sprinkle with pudding mix. Set aside. Combine butter, brown sugar and cinnamon; pour over rolls. Cover tightly with buttered aluminum foil; let rise overnight. Uncover and bake at 350 degrees for 30 to 40 minutes; carefully invert onto a serving platter. Makes 18 servings.

Appetizers
1~2~3

Toasted Almond Party Spread

Karen Sweitzer
Columbus, OH

Delicious with assorted crackers and savory bread rounds.

8-oz. pkg. cream cheese,
   softened
1-1/2 c. shredded Swiss cheese
1/3 c. mayonnaise

2 T. green onion, chopped
1/8 t. nutmeg
1/8 t. pepper
1/3 c. sliced almonds, toasted

Combine all ingredients; mix well. Spread in an ungreased 9" pie plate;
bake at 350 degrees for 15 minutes. Serves 6.

Use mini cookie cutters to cut toasted bread
into charming shapes to serve alongside
savory dips and spreads.

Appetizers 1~2~3

Brie with Caramelized Onions

Kathleen Richter
Bridgeport, CT

Topped with cranberries and pistachios, this Brie is a hit at any holiday gathering. Serve with baguette slices for a very simple yet elegant appetizer.

5-oz. wheel Brie cheese
1 onion, chopped
2 T. butter
1/2 c. brown sugar, packed

1/2 c. dried cranberries
2 T. balsamic vinegar
1/4 c. chopped pistachios

Place Brie in a greased 9" pie plate; bake at 350 degrees for 10 minutes. Remove from oven; set aside. Sauté onion in butter until tender, about 5 minutes; add brown sugar, cranberries and vinegar. Heat until mixture caramelizes and thickens, about 5 minutes; pour over Brie. Sprinkle with pistachios; serve warm. Serves 6.

Group a selection of appetizers on a small table separate from the main serving tables so early-comers can nibble while the rest of the crowd gathers.

Cream Cheese Terrine

Amy Palsrok
Silverdale, WA

This is also known as $20 dip to my friends & family because it looks (and tastes!) like it's from a gourmet store. Serve with shaped crackers for the most impressive display.

4 8-oz. pkgs. cream cheese, softened and divided
2 cloves garlic, chopped
1/8 t. dried basil
7-oz. pkg. sun-dried tomatoes

3 T. green onion, sliced
1/8 t. dried parsley
4-oz. pkg. crumbled blue cheese
1/2 c. sliced almonds
7-oz. jar basil pesto

Combine first package cream cheese and garlic; spread into a plastic wrap-lined 8"x4" loaf pan. Sprinkle with basil; set aside. Mix second package cream cheese with tomatoes and green onion; spread over first layer. Sprinkle with parsley; set aside. Stir third package cream cheese with blue cheese and almonds; spread over tomato layer. Set aside. Combine remaining package cream cheese and pesto; spread over blue cheese mixture. Cover and refrigerate for at least one hour; remove to serving platter by gently pulling up on plastic wrap, invert onto platter and peel away plastic wrap. Serves 12.

When serving appetizers, a good rule of thumb for quantities is 6 to 8 per person if dinner will follow and 12 to 15 per person if it's an appetizer-only gathering.

Appetizers 1-2-3

Crab-Stuffed Mushrooms

Cindy Skinner
Hagerstown, MD

Your friends will think you spent the whole day in the kitchen!

15 mushrooms, stems removed
   and reserved
1 slice bread, crumbled
7-oz. can crabmeat, drained
salt and pepper to taste
1 egg, beaten

1/2 t. seafood seasoning
1/3 c. onion, chopped
Garnish: grated Parmesan
   cheese
2 T. butter, melted

Chop mushroom stems; combine with bread crumbs, crabmeat, salt, pepper, egg, seafood seasoning and onion. Mix well; spoon into mushroom caps. Sprinkle with Parmesan cheese; set aside. Coat bottom of a 13"x9" baking pan with butter; arrange mushroom caps on top. Broil for 2 to 4 minutes or until heated through and golden. Makes 15.

Add some sparkle to the table! Wrap inexpensive beaded bracelets around old canning jars. Set a tea light inside each jar or add simple arrangements of flowers. Guests can even take them home as favors.

Cucumber Canapés

Dawn Pryor
Jefferson, MD

*These are a favorite of my friends, family and co-workers. The fresh
dill and chives combine for a distinct and refreshing flavor.*

1 c. mayonnaise
3-oz. pkg. cream cheese,
   softened
1 T. onion, grated
1 T. fresh chives, minced
1/2 c. vinegar

1/2 c. Worcestershire sauce
1/8 t. garlic powder
1/8 t. dried parsley
1/8 t. fresh dill, chopped
1 to 2 baguettes, thinly sliced
2 cucumbers, sliced

Combine the first 9 ingredients together in a blender; blend until
smooth. Cover; refrigerate for 24 hours. Spread on bread slices; top
with a cucumber slice. Makes about 4 dozen.

To give cucumber slices a decorated edge, draw the tines
of a fork lengthwise down the side of a whole cucumber,
making grooves about 1/16-inch deep. Continue around
the cucumber, then cut into slices.

Appetizers 1~2~3

Delicious Dill Dip

Paula Dreessen
Merriam, KS

Serve in a round of pumpernickel bread...scoop out the inside and use for dipping!

8-oz. pkg. cream cheese,
   softened
1 c. sour cream
1 c. mayonnaise

1/2 c. green onion, chopped
2-1/4 oz. can sliced black olives,
   drained
1 T. dill weed

Blend together until smooth. Serves 6 to 8.

Turn ordinary cherry tomatoes into party favorites. Cut off
the top of each tomato, scoop out the seeds with a small
melon baller and turn over to drain on paper towels.
Pipe Delicious Dill Dip (or softened cream
cheese) into hollowed tomatoes and
sprinkle fresh dill over top.

Stuffed Jalapeños

Karen McGrady
Worthington, PA

Cool down these cheese-stuffed peppers by dipping them in sour cream.

8-oz. pkg. cream cheese,
    softened
1 c. shredded Cheddar cheese
1 c. mayonnaise
1 clove garlic, minced

18 jalapeños, halved
1 egg white
1 T. milk
1 c. corn flake cereal, crushed

Mix cream cheese, Cheddar cheese, mayonnaise and garlic together; spoon into jalapeños. Set aside. Combine egg white and milk; roll each jalapeño in egg white mixture. Coat with crushed cereal; arrange on an ungreased baking sheet. Bake at 375 degrees for 15 minutes. Makes 36.

Platters of food set on different levels make a more interesting presentation. Use books, a stack of plates or upside-down pots and bowls on a buffet table to create different heights, cover with a tablecloth and set serving dishes on top!

Appetizers 1~2~3

Festive Chicken Enchilada Dip

Jeannine English
Wylie, TX

Terrific served with crispy corn tortilla chips.

2 8-oz. pkgs. cream cheese,
  softened
1-1/3 c. shredded Cheddar
  cheese
1 t. minced garlic
1-1/2 T. chili powder
1 t. cumin
1 t. dried oregano

1 t. paprika
cayenne pepper to taste
3 boneless, skinless chicken
  breasts, cooked and chopped
1 bunch cilantro, chopped
4 green onions, chopped
10-oz. can diced tomatoes with
  green chiles

Mix cheeses together until well blended; add garlic, chili powder,
cumin, oregano, paprika and cayenne pepper. Mix well; stir in
remaining ingredients. Cover and refrigerate overnight. Serves 12.

A new way to serve Festive Chicken Enchilada Dip! Just
spread dip onto flour tortillas, roll up jelly-roll style
and cut into one-inch slices....add some kick by
topping each with a jalapeño pepper slice.

30-Minute Olive Appetizer

Joanne Walker
Ontario, Canada

Freeze baked squares until ready to use, then just heat up in the microwave...so easy!

8-oz. tube refrigerated crescent
  rolls
2 eggs, beaten
1 c. shredded Cheddar cheese

1/2 c. onion, minced
3 T. butter, softened
1 c. olives with pimentos, sliced

Spread crescent rolls to cover the bottom of a greased 13"x9" baking pan; set aside. Mix remaining ingredients together; spread over crust. Bake at 350 degrees for 15 to 20 minutes; cut into bite-size squares. Makes 4 dozen.

Here's a fun way to invite guests over:
Fill bouquets of balloons with helium and write the who,
what and where party information on each with a
permanent pen. Hand deliver or tie securely to doorknobs
with lengths of curling ribbon.

Appetizers 1~2~3

Denise's Meatballs

Audra Webb
Halifax, VA

*I first tasted these delicious meatballs at a family Christmas party.
They are so simple to make and are absolutely wonderful
any time of the year!*

3 lbs. ground beef
12-oz. can evaporated milk
1 c. quick-cooking oats,
    uncooked
1 c. crackers, crushed
2 eggs

1/2 c. onion, chopped
1/2 t. garlic salt
2 t. salt
1/2 t. pepper
2 t. chili powder

Combine all ingredients together, mixing thoroughly. Shape into
one-inch round balls; arrange in an ungreased 13"x9" baking pan.
Cover with sauce; bake at 350 degrees for one hour, basting
occasionally. Serves 15.

Sauce:

2 c. catsup
1 c. brown sugar, packed
1/2 t. liquid smoke

1/2 t. garlic salt
1/4 c. onion, chopped

Combine all ingredients; mix well.

Dining is and always was a great
artistic opportunity.
- Frank Lloyd Wright

Creamy Crab Dip

Regina Spencer
Olympia, WA

A delicious spread for toasted mini bagels.

1 c. mayonnaise-type salad
   dressing
8-oz. pkg. cream cheese,
   softened
2 T. lemon juice
1 stalk celery, chopped

8-oz. can crabmeat, drained
   and chopped
3 green onions, chopped
8-oz. can water chestnuts,
   drained and chopped

Blend salad dressing and cream cheese together until smooth and creamy; stir in remaining ingredients. Cover and refrigerate until firm. Makes 4 cups.

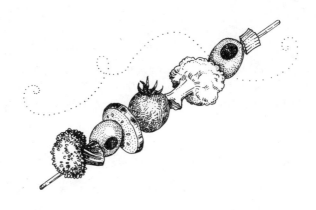

Guests will love these dippers. Thread carrot and celery slices, cauliflower and broccoli flowerets and olives onto small wooden skewers in different combinations...arrange around yummy dips and enjoy!

Appetizers 1-2-3

Slam-Dunk Vegetable Dip

Irene Putman
Canal Fulton, OH

This dip has been enjoyed at all kinds of events over the past 30 years...everyone always raves about it and asks for the recipe. My husband likes to use it as a condiment on sandwiches too!

2 c. mayonnaise
1/4 c. onion, chopped
3/4 t. paprika
3/4 t. Worcestershire sauce

1 t. prepared horseradish
8 drops hot pepper sauce
1/2 t. dry mustard
1/2 t. curry powder

Mix all ingredients together; chill. Makes about 2 cups.

Family Chip Dip

Geraldine Sherwood
Schererville, IN

Someone always volunteers to bring this to our family get-togethers. If it is ever forgotten, we'll go buy the ingredients and whip it up right then and there...it's a must-have!

8-oz. pkg. cream cheese,
   softened
1/3 c. catsup
1 T. milk

2 T. French salad dressing
2 t. Worcestershire sauce
1 onion, minced

Combine all ingredients together in a mixing bowl; blend until smooth and creamy. Makes about 1-1/2 cups.

So-Simple Hummus

Anne Girucky
Norfolk, VA

Serve with sliced pita rounds...it couldn't be easier!

15-1/2 oz. can chickpeas,
    drained
1 clove garlic, minced

1 T. olive oil
1 to 2 T. tahini paste or sesame
    seed paste

Combine chickpeas and garlic in a food processor; process until smooth. Gradually add remaining ingredients; blending until creamy. Makes 2 cups.

Dress up paper napkins in a snap! Trim napkin edges with decorative-edge scissors, then use permanent markers and rubber stamps to add polka dots, stripes or alphabet letters.

Appetizers 1-2-3

Pesto Packages

Jennifer Rudolph
Oakley, CA

For a bite-size snack...slice each crescent roll into 2 triangles before adding cheese and sauce.

Brie cheese, sliced
8-oz. tube refrigerated crescent
   rolls, separated

7-oz. jar pesto sauce

Place one slice Brie in the center of each crescent roll; spoon pesto sauce on top. Roll up crescents; pinch seams closed. Arrange on an ungreased baking sheet; bake according to crescent roll package directions. Makes 8.

Fresh Pesto Spread

Carol Burns
Delaware, OH

Spread over bread slices and broil until golden.

1/2 c. fresh basil, loosely packed
2 t. olive oil
1 t. lemon juice
1 clove garlic, minced

1 T. pine nuts
2 T. cold water
1 T. grated Parmesan cheese

Combine all ingredients except Parmesan cheese in a blender; pulse until smooth. Spoon into a glass bowl; stir in Parmesan cheese. Makes about 1/3 cup.

Keep a folder or drawer for clippings from magazines and newspapers...look for easy recipes, fun menus and party ideas you'd like to try.

Party Cheese Ball

Sarah Sommers
Atwater, CA

Everyone will be going back for more so be sure to have plenty of crackers...it's simply addicting!

2 8-oz. pkgs. cream cheese, softened
2 c. shredded sharp Cheddar cheese
1 t. pimento, chopped
1 t. onion, minced
1 t. lemon juice

1 t. green pepper, chopped
2 t. Worcestershire sauce
1/8 t. cayenne pepper
1/8 t. salt
Garnish: chopped pecans and fresh parsley, minced

Blend cream cheese until light and fluffy; add Cheddar cheese, pimento, onion, lemon juice, green pepper, Worcestershire sauce, pepper and salt. Shape into a ball; wrap in plastic wrap and refrigerate until firm. Roll in pecans and parsley. Serves 12 to 16.

Single servings! Roll Party Cheese Ball into mini balls and place in paper muffin cups. Fill more paper muffin cups with crackers and pretzels and arrange alongside mini cheese balls...guests can enjoy one of each!

Appetizers 1-2-3

Pepper-Swiss Cheese Log

Gail Prather
Isanti, MN

A big hit with any crowd!

2 3-oz. pkgs. cream cheese,
   softened
1/2 c. sour cream
1/4 t. garlic salt

1-1/2 c. shredded Swiss cheese
2 T. fresh parsley, minced
2 to 3 T. pepper

Blend cream cheese until smooth; add sour cream and garlic salt. Mix in Swiss cheese and parsley; cover and refrigerate for at least 2 hours. Shape into a log; sprinkle with pepper. Serves 8.

Jazzed-Up Cream Cheese Ball

Susie Kadleck
San Antonio, TX

A classic appetizer that's so easy to make.

3 8-oz. pkgs. cream cheese,
   softened
1 green pepper, chopped
8-oz. can crushed pineapple,
   drained

1 T. garlic salt
1 T. onion, minced
1 T. seasoned salt
1-1/2 c. chopped pecans

Combine first 6 ingredients together; mix well. Shape into a ball; roll in pecans. Wrap in plastic wrap; refrigerate until firm. Serves 18.

Creamy Artichoke-Garlic Dip

Jackie Smulski
Lyons, IL

We like it best with veggies and pita chips.

16-oz. jar marinated artichoke
    hearts, drained
2 T. fresh parsley, chopped
2 cloves garlic, minced
2 T. lemon juice

1-1/4 c. sour cream
1/4 c. mayonnaise
1/8 t. pepper
1/8 t. cayenne pepper

Place the first 4 ingredients in a food processor; process until smooth. Add remaining ingredients; process until well blended. Cover and refrigerate overnight. Makes about 3-1/2 cups.

Create quick chip 'n dip sets in no time. Spoon dips into pottery soup bowls and set each bowl on top of dinner plates which hold crackers, veggies, pretzels, chips and bread.

Appetizers 1-2-3

Baked Artichoke-Spinach Spread

Kelly Francis
Encino, CA

Serve with fresh French bread slices...delicious!

1 c. mayonnaise
1 c. shredded Parmesan cheese
16-oz. jar non-marinated
   artichoke hearts, drained
   and mashed

10-oz. pkg. frozen chopped
   spinach, thawed and drained
minced garlic to taste

Combine all ingredients; mix well. Spread in an ungreased 9" pie plate. Bake at 350 degrees until bubbly, about 40 minutes. Serves 8.

Add some whimsy to a wintertime gathering. Before guests arrive, fill a punch bowl with clean, fresh snow and nestle glasses inside to chill. Guests can grab a glass and fill with soda or punch...it's sure to stay extra cool!

Sweet Salsa

Traci Doxtator
Henderson, NV

My friend Marcia and I have had such fun entertaining each other's families every weekend...and we've built the most special friendship over salsa, chips and a deck of cards!

2 c. cantaloupe, peeled and
  finely chopped
2 c. cherry tomatoes, chopped
1/4 c. green onion, chopped
1/4 c. fresh basil, chopped

2 T. jalapeños, diced
2 T. lime juice
2 T. orange juice
1/4 t. salt
1/8 t. pepper

Stir all ingredients together; cover and refrigerate for at least 30 minutes. Makes about 4-3/4 cups.

Make your own tortilla chips to go with homemade salsas and dips...you won't believe how easy it is. Just slice flour tortillas into wedges, spray with non-stick vegetable spray and bake at 350 degrees for 5 to 7 minutes.

Appetizers 1-2-3

Black Bean Salsa

*Remona Putman
Rockwood, PA*

Excellent with chips or rolled up in flour tortillas.

16-oz. can black beans, rinsed
   and drained
7-oz. can corn, drained
2 cloves garlic, minced
1/2 c. Italian salad dressing
1/2 t. hot pepper sauce

3/4 t. chili powder
3 T. fresh cilantro, chopped
1 tomato, chopped
1/2 sweet onion, chopped
1/2 green pepper, chopped

Combine the first 7 ingredients; cover and refrigerate for 4 to 5 hours. Add remaining ingredients before serving; toss gently. Makes about 5 cups.

Easy Slow-Cooker Bean Dip

*Marni Senner
Long Beach, CA*

So easy to tote to potlucks and family gatherings.

4 16-oz. cans refried beans
1-lb. pkg. Colby Jack cheese,
   cubed
1-1/4 oz. pkg. taco seasoning
   mix

1 bunch green onions, chopped
1 c. sour cream
8-oz. pkg. cream cheese, cubed

Place all ingredients in a slow cooker; stir to mix. Heat on low setting until cheeses melt, about 2 to 3 hours. Stir often. Serves 12.

Everyone's Favorite Party Mix

Jennie Wiseman
Coshocton, OH

I like to package this mix in tins to hand out to family & friends...the empty tins often make their way back to me to be refilled!

5 c. doughnut-shaped oat cereal
5 c. bite-size crispy corn or rice cereal squares
9.4-oz. pkg. candy-coated chocolates

12-oz. jar peanuts
15-oz. pkg. mini pretzels
2 12-oz. pkgs. white chocolate chips
3 T. oil

Combine the first 5 ingredients in a large roasting pan; set aside. Place the chocolate chips and oil in a microwave-safe bowl; heat until melted, stirring often. Pour over cereal mixture; toss to coat. Spread mix on wax paper; let dry until firm. Break into pieces; store in an airtight container. Makes 20 servings.

For a cozy centerpiece, place a hurricane candle in the middle of the table, then surround it with small glass bowls filled with Everyone's Favorite Party Mix...the candlelight will make the treat bowls sparkle!

Appetizers 1~2~3

Sweet-Tooth Cheese Ball

*Joy Diomede
Double Oak, TX*

*Unbeatable when served with chocolate graham crackers and
vanilla wafers.*

8-oz. pkg. cream cheese,
  softened
1/2 c. butter, softened
1/4 t. vanilla extract

2 T. brown sugar, packed
3/4 c. powdered sugar
3/4 c. mini chocolate chips
3/4 c. chopped pecans

Blend cream cheese, butter and vanilla together until fluffy;
gradually mix in sugars. Fold in chocolate chips and pecans; wrap in
plastic wrap. Refrigerate for at least 2 hours before serving. Serves 8.

Fluffy Peanut Butter Dip

*Louise Grant
Glendale, AZ*

Serve with a platter piled high with fresh fruits.

1/2 c. creamy peanut butter
8-oz. container vanilla yogurt
1/8 t. cinnamon

1/2 c. frozen whipped topping,
  thawed

Mix the first 3 ingredients together; stir in whipped topping. Makes
2 cups.

*Instead of serving all the food in one room, try using
different rooms throughout the house for entertaining...set
up one for appetizers, one for dinner and one to serve
coffee and desserts.*

Spicy Buffalo Bites

Andrew Burns
Norwich, OH

Serve with additional hot sauce for those who really want to turn up the heat!

3/4 c. cooked chicken, shredded
4 t. hot pepper sauce
2 T. Dijon mustard
36 herb-flavored shredded
    wheat crackers

2 T. margarine, melted
4-oz. pkg. crumbled blue cheese
2 T. celery, minced

Combine first 3 ingredients together; mix well. Place one teaspoon mixture on each cracker; drizzle with margarine. Stir crumbled blue cheese and celery together; spread over chicken mixture. Arrange on ungreased baking sheets; bake at 400 degrees until cheese melts, about 4 minutes. Makes 3 dozen.

Honey-Glazed Chicken Wings

Janet McRoberts
Lexington, KY

A zippy appetizer just right for hungry teenagers!

12 chicken wings
1/2 c. barbecue sauce

1/2 c. honey
1/2 c. soy sauce

Arrange chicken wings in a greased 13"x9" baking pan; set aside. Whisk remaining ingredients together; pour over wings. Bake at 350 degrees for 50 to 60 minutes or until juices run clear when chicken is pierced with a fork. Serves 4.

Appetizers 1-2-3

Aloha Chicken Wings

Dianne Gregory
Sheridan, AR

A staple at summer cookouts and backyard gatherings.

1/4 c. butter
1/2 c. catsup
1 clove garlic, minced
3 lbs. chicken wings
1 c. bread crumbs
14-oz. can pineapple chunks,
   juice reserved

2 T. brown sugar, packed
1 T. whole ginger, minced
1 T. Worcestershire sauce
hot pepper sauce to taste

Place butter in a jelly-roll pan; heat in a 400-degree oven until melted. Stir catsup and garlic together; brush over wings. Coat with bread crumbs; arrange in jelly-roll pan, turning to coat both sides with melted butter. Bake at 400 degrees for 30 minutes. While baking, drain pineapple juice; place pineapple chunks to the side and reserve juice. Add enough water to juice to equal 3/4 cup liquid; pour into a small mixing bowl. Whisk in remaining ingredients; pour over wings. Continue baking until juices run clear when chicken is pierced with a fork, about 20 to 30 additional minutes; place pineapple around wings, baking until heated through. Serves 4.

Hosting a backyard gathering? Fill a wheelbarrow or a child's wagon with ice and tuck in bottles of soda and lemonade. Use colorful ribbon to tie a bottle opener to the handle so it stays near the drinks.

Baked Onion Dip

Debi DeVore
Dover, OH

Serve with a fun assortment of pretzels...rods, twists, bits and waffles.

1 c. mayonnaise
1 c. onion, chopped
1 T. grated Parmesan cheese

1/4 t. garlic salt
1 c. shredded Swiss cheese

Combine all ingredients; spread in an ungreased one-quart casserole dish. Bake at 350 degrees for 40 minutes. Makes about 3 cups.

Sausage-Cheese Dip

Margie Williams
Gooseberry Patch

Always a hit on those crisp, football tailgating days!

1 lb. ground beef
1 lb. ground sausage
1 t. cumin

2-lb. pkg. Mexican pasteurized
processed cheese spread,
cubed

Brown beef and sausage with cumin; drain. Place in a slow cooker; add cheese. Heat on low setting until cheese melts, about 2 to 3 hours. Serves 12.

Fill different baskets with dippers like pretzels,
bagel chips, veggies, bread cubes and potato chips.
Use a small riser (a book works well) to set under one side
of the bottom of each basket to create a tilt...looks so nice
and guests can grab dippers easily!

Appetizers 1~2~3

Flaky Sausage Wraps

Carmen Clever
Ashland, OH

Two of these hearty appetizers makes a meal!

6-oz. pkg. ground sausage
1/4 c. onion, chopped
1/4 c. green pepper, chopped
1 clove garlic, minced
1/4 t. mustard

3-oz. pkg. cream cheese,
    softened
1 T. green onion, chopped
8-oz. tube refrigerated crescent
    rolls, separated

Brown sausage with onion, green pepper and garlic; drain. Reduce
heat; add mustard, cream cheese and onion, stirring until cheese
melts. Cool slightly; place in a food processor. Process until smooth;
spread on crescent rolls. Roll up crescent-roll style; arrange on an
ungreased baking sheet. Bake at 350 degrees for 10 to 12 minutes.
Makes 8.

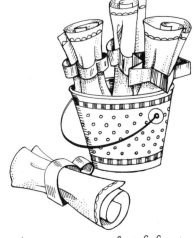

Designate a drawer or a shelf for keeping all the
little things you usually have to hunt down when expecting
guests. Be sure to include matches, toothpicks, a
corkscrew, coffee filters and birthday candles...you'll
be glad you thought ahead!

Strawberry-Tea Punch

Vickie

*Try making a batch using raspberries instead of strawberries too...
it's just as tasty!*

6-oz. can lemonade concentrate,
  partially thawed
1/2 c. sugar
1 t. vanilla extract

1 pt. strawberries, hulled and
  sliced
2 qts. brewed tea, cooled
ice cubes

Blend lemonade concentrate, sugar, vanilla and strawberries together;
pour into tea, stirring well. Pour over ice cubes in serving glasses.
Serves 10.

A sweet gesture! Sugar the rim of glasses before filling
with tea or punch. Just run a small lemon wedge around
the rim and place the glass upside down on a small plate
of sugar. Tap off any extra sugar before filling.

Appetizers 1~2~3

Pineapple Limeade Cooler

*Kelly delCid
Troy, OH*

Just right for those patio parties...the kids love it too!

1 c. sugar
6 c. pineapple juice, chilled
1 c. lime juice

2 ltrs. sparkling water, chilled
Garnish: lime wedges

Shake sugar and juices together until sugar is dissolved; cover and refrigerate. Stir in sparkling water before serving over ice; garnish each glass with a lime wedge. Makes 16 servings.

Mint Ice Cubes

*Melody Taynor
Everett, WA*

When served in iced tea, the tea becomes sweeter and mintier as the cubes melt.

6 c. water
1-1/2 c. sugar

1 t. lemon juice
48 mint leaves

Boil water, sugar and lemon juice together for 5 minutes; remove from heat and set aside to cool. Rub each mint leaf between your fingers to release its flavor; place one leaf in each of 48 ice cube compartments. Fill with sugar water; freeze. Makes 4 dozen.

Frozen grapes, strawberries and raspberries make flavorful ice cubes in frosty beverages. Freeze washed and dried fruit in a plastic zipping bag for up to 3 months...perfect for all the summer gatherings.

Basil-Mushroom Triangles

Mary Bettuchy
Duxbury, MA

Insert a toothpick into the top of each so guests can easily help themselves.

1/2 c. oil
6 fresh basil leaves
3 portabella mushrooms, sliced
   into wedges

salt and pepper to taste

Heat oil to sizzling in a small saucepan; add basil leaves. Turn off heat; set aside for 10 minutes. Strain oil into a 10" skillet, discarding basil leaves; reheat oil. Add mushroom pieces; sauté on both sides until golden, about 3 to 5 minutes. Remove from heat; sprinkle with salt and pepper. Serve warm. Serves 4 to 6.

Old dishes become tiered serving pieces when paired with a mug or candlestick. Center a mug on top of a dinner plate and top with a salad plate, gluing all if desired. Let dry, then serve up your favorite appetizers or desserts.

Appetizers 1~2~3

Snappy Asparagus Dip

Jane Gates
Saginaw, MI

Serve with crispy tortilla chips and fresh veggies.

1 lb. asparagus, trimmed,
   cooked and puréed
1 c. sour cream
1/2 c. salsa

1/8 t. lime juice
cayenne pepper, salt and pepper
   to taste

Combine all ingredients together; mix well. Cover and refrigerate until chilled. Makes about 2-1/2 cups.

Cheesy Potato Skins

Dolores Brock
Wellton, AZ

We love to dip these potato skins in ranch dressing.

4 potatoes, baked and halved
1/2 c. shredded Cheddar cheese
1/2 c. shredded mozzarella
   cheese

2 green onions, chopped
4 t. bacon bits

Place potatoes on a baking sheet; sprinkle with cheeses. Top with onions and bacon; heat under broiler until cheese melts. Serves 4.

If someone volunteers to pitch in with get-together preparations, or offers to bring a dish, let them! Just be sure to return the favor!

Baked Spinach Balls

Janet Pastrick
Fairfax, VA

To make ahead, just place spinach balls on baking sheets and freeze. Remove from freezer and place in heavy plastic zipping bags and return to freezer. When entertaining, remove from freezer, thaw on baking sheets and bake...so handy!

3 lbs. spinach, chopped, cooked
    and drained
2 c. herb-flavored stuffing mix
2 onions, minced
5 eggs, beaten
3/4 c. butter, melted

1/2 c. grated Parmesan cheese
2 cloves garlic, minced
1/2 t. salt
1 t. dried thyme
1/4 t. pepper

Combine all ingredients in a large mixing bowl; mix well. Shape into one-inch balls; arrange on ungreased baking sheets. Bake at 350 degrees for 15 minutes; serve warm. Makes 10 dozen.

When appetizers need to be served with a skewer, think beyond toothpicks...try sprigs of rosemary, bamboo picks or sugar cane spears.

Appetizers 1~2~3

Tortilla Roll-Ups

Kristin Freeman
Bixby, OK

Serve with salsa and guacamole for dipping.

8-oz. pkg. cream cheese,
   softened
1/3 c. salsa
1/4 c. green onion, chopped

1/2 t. garlic powder
1/2 t. chili powder
1/2 t. cumin
12-ct. pkg. flour tortillas

Blend cream cheese until light and fluffy; mix in salsa, onion, garlic powder, chili powder and cumin. Spread evenly over tortillas; roll up and refrigerate until firm, at least 2 hours. Cut into one-inch slices. Serves 12.

Carefree Cheese Spread

Bridget Dooley
Peru, IL

Whip up this tangy treat in no time. Serve with a loaf of French bread and crackers and guests can help themselves.

8-oz. pkg. cream cheese,
   softened
1 T. French salad dressing
1 T. chili sauce

3 to 4 drops Worcestershire
   sauce
garlic powder to taste

Blend all ingredients together until smooth. Makes one cup.

Laughter is brightest where food is best.
– Irish Proverb

Pizza by the Scoop

Tomi Russell
Algonquin, IL

Be sure to serve with sturdy crackers that can hold a lot!

15 to 20 pepperoni slices
2 c. shredded mozzarella cheese
2 c. shredded sharp Cheddar
  cheese

2 c. mayonnaise
1 sweet onion, chopped
4-1/2 oz. can diced green chiles

Arrange pepperoni slices on a paper towel and microwave for 20 to 30 seconds; pat with another paper towel and set aside. Combine cheeses, mayonnaise, onion and chiles in a mixing bowl; pour into a lightly greased 2-quart casserole dish. Layer pepperoni on top; cover and bake at 350 degrees for 45 minutes. Serves 8 to 10.

Please the whole gang by having an appetizer party! If your friends & family have different tastes, don't worry about deciding on the perfect main dish...just serve 4 to 5 different appetizers and everyone can choose their favorites.

Appetizers 1-2-3

Hearty Cheeseburger Bread

Marcy Venne
Russell, MA

Cut into one-inch slices for fun finger food.

2 lbs. ground beef, browned
1/2 t. garlic powder
1/4 c. butter
1 loaf French bread, cut in half
    horizontally

2 c. sour cream
3 c. shredded Cheddar cheese

Combine beef and garlic powder; set aside. Butter both halves of French bread; place on an ungreased baking sheet. Stir sour cream into beef mixture; spread onto bread. Sprinkle with cheese. Bake at 350 degrees for 15 to 20 minutes or until cheese melts; slice to serve. Serves 8 to 10.

Guests will love nibbling even more when appetizers are served on creative trays...try using a wooden cutting board, mirror, LP record, chessboard or an old-fashioned washboard. So fun!

Mini Manicotti

Emily Burns
Norwich, OH

A favorite Italian dish...in a new size!

1/2 lb. ground turkey, browned
1 clove garlic, minced
1 c. shredded mozzarella cheese
1/2 c. ricotta cheese
1/4 c. grated Parmesan cheese
1/2 t. dried Italian seasoning
1 t. lemon juice

1 egg, beaten
10-oz. pkg. frozen chopped
   spinach, thawed and drained
10 manicotti shells, cooked and
   rinsed
1-1/3 c. spaghetti sauce
2 T. shredded Parmesan cheese

Combine first 8 ingredients together in a large mixing bowl; stir in half
the spinach, reserving remaining for use in another recipe. Mix well;
spoon into shells. Slice each shell, diagonally, into 3 pieces; arrange in
an ungreased 13"x9" baking pan. Spoon spaghetti sauce on top; cover
with aluminum foil and bake at 350 degrees for 30 to 35 minutes.
Remove to a serving platter; sprinkle with Parmesan cheese.
Makes 30.

Quick and clever napkin rings! When serving pasta as an
appetizer or meal, use red & white checked napkins
(or just cut fabric into napkin-size squares) and slip each
through an uncooked manicotti shell.

Veggie-dillas

Glena Steele
Richfield, OH

An easy twist to a traditional quesadilla.

3/4 c. broccoli, chopped
1/4 c. carrots, shredded
1/4 c. green onion, sliced
2 T. water
6 6-inch flour tortillas

1 t. oil
2 c. shredded Cheddar cheese
Garnish: sour cream, salsa,
    sliced olives and sliced green
    onions

Combine broccoli, carrots, onions and water in a saucepan; heat until vegetables are crisp-tender. Drain; set aside. Brush one side of each tortilla with oil; place 3 tortillas oil-side down in an ungreased jelly-roll pan. Top with cheese; spread with vegetable mixture. Place remaining tortillas on top oil-side up; bake at 450 degrees until golden, about 6 minutes. Slice into wedges to serve; spoon desired garnishes on top. Serves 12.

Dress up a plain serving platter by arranging red and green cabbage leaves over the bottom of the plate...a lovely backdrop to the appetizer or main dish.

Easy Cheese Sticks

Margot Heinlein
Upper Arlington, OH

Melted cheese inside a crispy, golden shell.

1/3 lb. Monterey Jack cheese
1/3 lb. Cheddar cheese
1/3 lb. Swiss cheese
1/3 lb. mozzarella cheese
1 c. biscuit baking mix

1 t. paprika
1/2 c. milk
1 egg
oil for deep frying
marinara sauce

Cut cheeses into 3"x1/2" strips; place on a baking sheet. Wrap in plastic wrap; freeze for at least one hour. Blend baking mix, paprika, milk and egg together; set aside. Heat 2 inches oil in a deep stockpot to 375 degrees. Dip cheese strips in batter until coated; add to oil, heating until golden. Drain on paper towels; let stand 3 minutes before serving. Serve with marinara sauce on the side. Makes 2-1/2 dozen.

Ready-set-go snacks! When you need a little something extra for guests, but don't have any spare time, just pick up a few nibblers at the store. Assorted olives, fancy nuts, cream cheese and crackers, veggie sticks, cubed cheese and shrimp cocktail all make quick & easy treats.

Snappy Soups & Salads

Country Club Salad

Amy Jones
Buckhannon, WV

This salad recipe was shared with me by a good friend. A favorite recipe from their country club for parties and guests!

1-lb. pkg. bacon, crisply cooked
   and crumbled
1 head cauliflower, chopped

1 bunch romaine lettuce, torn
2 heads iceberg lettuce, torn
1 c. crumbled blue cheese

Toss all ingredients together in a large serving bowl; cover and refrigerate until chilled. Pour dressing on top before serving; refrigerating any excess dressing for later use. Toss gently. Serves 20.

Dressing:

1 c. cider vinegar
2 c. sugar
1 T. dry mustard

2 T. garlic powder
1/4 c. egg substitute
3 c. corn oil

Whisk all ingredients together.

When setting the table with stemmed glasses, open up colorful napkins, gather each in the middle and slip them, center down, into each glass...an instant dress-up for the table!

Snappy Soups & Salads

Wild Rice & Nut Soup

Linda Diepholz
Lakeville, MN

Toasted almonds add so much flavor to this special soup.

2 c. water
1/2 c. wild rice, uncooked
2 T. shallots, minced
2 T. butter
1/2 c. sliced mushrooms
1/4 c. all-purpose flour

4 c. chicken broth
1/4 c. carrots, grated
1/4 c. slivered almonds, toasted
1 c. half-and-half
Optional: 2 T. dry sherry
Garnish: fresh parsley, chopped

Bring water to a boil in a saucepan; add rice. Reduce heat; simmer, covered, for 45 minutes. Sauté shallots in butter in a 12" skillet until soft; add mushrooms and sauté for 2 additional minutes. Mix in flour; gradually stir in chicken broth until thickened. Add cooked rice, carrots and almonds; simmer for 5 minutes. Pour in half-and-half and sherry, if desired; heat through. Do not boil. Ladle into bowls; garnish with parsley. Serves 4.

It's a lovely thing; everyone sitting down together, sharing food.
- Alice May Brock

Oh-So-Quick Potato Soup

Flo Snodderly
North Vernon, IN

This recipe is perfect for just 2 but can easily be doubled or tripled!

1 cube chicken bouillon
1 c. water
1 c. mashed potatoes

1 T. butter
13-oz. can evaporated milk
   substitute

Combine all ingredients in a heavy saucepan; heat through without boiling, stirring until smooth. Makes 2 servings.

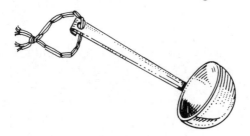

Traditional Clam Chowder

Amy Bachman
Waterville, PA

Bacon adds a smoky flavor to this rich dish.

2 c. red potatoes, peeled and
   cubed
1 c. onion, chopped
1/8 t. salt
1/8 t. pepper
2 c. water
4 6-1/2 oz. cans chopped clams,
   drained

4 c. milk
1 T. butter
8-oz. pkg. bacon, crisply cooked
   and crumbled
1 t. fresh parsley, chopped
2 T. all-purpose flour
3 cubes chicken bouillon

Place potatoes, onion, salt, pepper and water in a stockpot; boil until potatoes are tender, about 20 minutes. Add remaining ingredients; reduce heat. Simmer until thickened and heated through without boiling; stir often. Serves 4.

Snappy Soups & Salads

Broccoli-Cheese Soup

Donna Cloyd
Clinton, TN

*If I'm in a hurry, I use onion flakes instead of chopping up an onion...
quick and tearless!*

1/4 c. margarine
1/2 c. onion, chopped
1/4 c. all-purpose flour
3 c. chicken broth
2 10-oz. pkgs. frozen chopped
    broccoli, thawed

4 cubes chicken bouillon
1/2 t. Worcestershire sauce
3 c. shredded Cheddar cheese
1-1/2 c. half-and-half
1 c. milk

Melt margarine in a 12" skillet; add onion and sauté until tender.
Mix in flour; gradually add chicken broth, stirring until smooth.
Add broccoli, bouillon and Worcestershire sauce; heat over medium
heat until thickened and broccoli is tender, about 10 minutes. Mix in
remaining ingredients; stir until cheese is melted, about 10 additional
minutes. Makes 8 servings.

Get creative with placemats...try using mirror tiles,
colorful sheets of scrapbook paper, road maps, bandannas,
sheets of music or record album covers. Make them
different every time!

Spiral Pasta Salad

Irene Senne
Aplington, IA

This colorful salad brightens the buffet table.

16-oz. pkg. tri-colored spiral
    pasta, cooked
2 carrots, shredded
1 sweet onion, chopped
1 green pepper, chopped
2 stalks celery, chopped
1 c. mayonnaise

1 c. vinegar
14-oz. can sweetened
    condensed milk
3/4 c. sugar
1 t. salt
1/4 t. pepper

Place pasta in a large serving bowl; fold in vegetables and set aside. Combine remaining ingredients in a medium mixing bowl; blend well. Pour over pasta; stir until well mixed. Cover and refrigerate overnight. Serves 12 to 14.

Host friends in the garden this year. Greet everyone with fresh iced tea served from a sparkling new watering can and serve up salad using new garden trowels. So cute!

Snappy Soups & Salads

Picnic Spaghetti Salad

Ruth Cooksey
Plainfield, IN

After trying this recipe once, I knew it was perfect for taking to upcoming family reunions.

8-oz. pkg. spaghetti, coarsely
   broken
16-oz. pkg. coleslaw mix
1 onion, chopped

1 green pepper, chopped
1 c. mayonnaise
15-oz. jar coleslaw dressing

Prepare spaghetti according to package directions; drain and cool. Place in a large serving bowl; add remaining ingredients. Mix well; refrigerate until chilled. Serves 6 to 8.

Peanutty Crunch Salad

Carol Volz Begley
Beaver, PA

Wonderfully creamy and crunchy.

4 c. shredded cabbage
1 c. celery, chopped
1/2 c. sour cream
1/2 c. mayonnaise
1 t. salt
1/4 c. green onion, chopped

1/4 c. green pepper, chopped
1/2 c. cucumber, chopped
1 T. butter, softened
1/2 c. chopped peanuts
2 T. grated Parmesan cheese

Toss cabbage and celery together in a large serving bowl; cover and refrigerate until chilled. Whisk sour cream, mayonnaise, salt, onion, green pepper and cucumber together in a small mixing bowl; cover and refrigerate. Melt butter in a small skillet; sauté peanuts until golden. Right before serving, pour sour cream mixture over cabbage mixture; toss to coat. Sprinkle with peanuts and Parmesan cheese. Serves 6 to 8.

Black Bean Chili

Sharon Velenosi
Garden Grove, CA

This is my husband's favorite...and I never mind making it because it's so easy!

1 t. oil
2 onions, chopped
2 cloves garlic, minced
4-oz. can diced green chiles
2 t. chili powder
1 t. cumin

1 t. dried oregano
14-1/2 oz. can chopped
    tomatoes
2 15-oz. cans black beans,
    drained

Heat oil in a skillet; add onions and garlic. Sauté until soft; add remaining ingredients except for black beans. Mix well; bring to a boil over medium heat. Reduce heat; simmer for 10 minutes. Stir in beans; heat through. Serves 4 to 6.

3-Meat Slow-Cooker Chili

Beth Goblirsch
Minneapolis, MN

Spoon over a bed of rice or handful of taco chips...it feeds a crowd!

1 lb. ground beef, browned
1 lb. ground sausage, browned
1 lb. bacon, crisply cooked and
    crumbled

4 15-oz. cans tomato sauce
3 15-1/2 oz. cans kidney beans
chili seasoning to taste
15-1/4 oz. can corn, drained

Place first 3 ingredients in a greased slow cooker; stir in tomato sauce, kidney beans and chili seasoning. Heat on low setting for 4 to 6 hours; add corn during last hour of heating. Serves 8.

Snappy Soups & Salads

Cheeseburger Soup

Rhonda Gramstad
Brandon, SD

Serve with a juicy dill pickle on the side!

3/4 c. onion, chopped
3/4 c. carrots, shredded
1/2 c. celery, diced
1 t. dried basil
1/4 t. dried parsley
1/4 c. butter, divided
3 c. chicken broth
4 c. potatoes, peeled and diced

1/2 lb. ground beef, browned
1/4 c. all-purpose flour
8-oz. pkg. American cheese,
  cubed
1-1/2 c. milk
1/2 t. salt
1/4 t. pepper
1/2 c. sour cream

Sauté onion, carrots, celery, basil and parsley in one tablespoon butter in a 3-quart saucepan until tender, about 10 minutes; stir in broth, potatoes and ground beef. Bring to a boil; reduce heat and simmer, covered, for 10 minutes. Melt remaining butter in a small skillet; add flour, stirring until smooth and bubbly. Pour into soup; bring to a boil, stirring for 2 minutes. Reduce heat to low; stir in cheese, milk, salt and pepper. Continue stirring until cheese melts; remove from heat. Blend in sour cream before serving; serve warm. Serves 4 to 6.

It's the unexpected touches that make the biggest impressions. When serving soup or chili, offer guests a variety of fun toppings...fill bowls with shredded cheese, oyster crackers, chopped onions, sour cream and crunchy croutons then invite everyone to dig in!

Fabulous Feta Salad

*Jen Sell
Farmington, MN*

Make this salad into a main dish by topping with cooked chicken.

5-oz. pkg. spring-blend salad
   mix, divided
1/2 c. chopped pecans, toasted
3/4 c. crumbled feta cheese
6 slices bacon, crisply cooked
   and crumbled

11-oz. can mandarin oranges,
   drained and halved
grated Parmesan cheese to taste

Divide salad mix equally onto 4 serving plates; top each with equal
servings pecans, feta, bacon and mandarin oranges. Sprinkle with
Parmesan cheese; drizzle with poppy seed dressing. Serve
immediately. Serves 4.

Poppy Seed Dressing:

1/2 c. mayonnaise
1/3 c. sugar
2 T. cider vinegar

1/4 c. milk
1 T. poppy seed

Mix mayonnaise and sugar together; whisk in remaining ingredients.

Snappy Soups & Salads

Asian Chicken Salad

Tammy Rowe
Bellevue, OH

A wonderful combination of ingredients you probably already have on hand.

2 boneless, skinless chicken
  breasts, cooked and
  shredded
1 bunch green onions, thinly
  sliced

1 head lettuce, shredded
2 T. poppy seed
2-oz. pkg. slivered almonds
3-oz. pkg. chow mein noodles

Toss the first 5 ingredients together in a serving bowl; right before serving, sprinkle with chow mein noodles and pour dressing on top. Serves 4.

Dressing:

1/4 c. vinegar
1/2 c. oil
2 T. flavor enhancer

1/2 t. salt
1/2 t. pepper

Whisk all ingredients together.

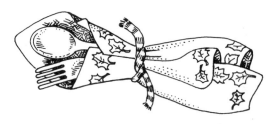

Balsamic vinegar really adds a zip to fresh salads. Pour some into a new spray bottle and set out for guests to use on their greens...spraying helps it go on easy without pouring too much!

Plaza Steak Soup

Jan Vaughn
Houston, TX

My mom would buy this soup "to go" so much at the Plaza III restaurant in Kansas City that the chef gave her the recipe.

1/2 c. butter, melted
1 c. all-purpose flour
2 qts. water
2 c. steak, cooked and cut into
    bite-size pieces
1 c. celery, chopped
1 c. onion, chopped

1 c. carrots, chopped
2 c. frozen mixed vegetables
28-oz. can stewed tomatoes
1 T. flavor enhancer
2 T. beef bouillon granules
1 t. pepper

Whisk butter and flour together until smooth in a large stockpot; stir in water and steak. Add remaining ingredients; bring to a boil. Reduce heat; simmer for 3 to 4 hours. Serves 6.

Stack up each guest's place setting, then tie it up
with homespun and tuck fresh blossoms in the knot...
everyone will feel like they're sitting down with
their own special gift!

Snappy Soups & Salads

Pepper Pot Soup

Weda Mosellie
Phillipsburg, NJ

Especially great on chilly evenings with a crisp loaf of bread and a fresh salad.

1 lb. ground beef
1 onion, chopped
10-oz. pkg. sliced mushrooms
16-oz. pkg. bowtie pasta,
  uncooked

5 c. chicken broth
1 T. fresh parsley, chopped
1 T. pepper

Brown ground beef with onion and mushrooms; drain and set aside. Boil bowtie pasta for 5 minutes; drain and set aside. Pour chicken broth into a 5-quart Dutch oven; add all the ingredients. Bring to a boil; reduce heat and simmer, covered, for 20 minutes. Serves 8.

Winter Ranch Dumplings

Fawn McKenzie
Wenatchee, WA

Drop these into a favorite soup recipe as a hearty addition to dinner.

4 eggs
1-1/2 c. milk
1-1/2 t. salt

1-1/2 t. baking powder
2 to 4 c. all-purpose flour
chopped parsley to taste

Combine ingredients together in the order listed; drop into a boiling soup recipe by tablespoonfuls. Cover and reduce heat; simmer for 15 minutes without removing cover. Serves 4.

The company makes the feast.
– English Proverb

Pineapple-Pretzel Fluff

Julie Giffen
Xenia, OH

My famous contribution to carry-ins.

1 c. pretzels, crushed
1/2 c. butter, melted
1 c. sugar, divided
8-oz. pkg. cream cheese,
  softened

20-oz. can crushed pineapple,
  drained
12-oz. container frozen whipped
  topping, thawed

Combine crushed pretzels, butter and 1/2 cup sugar; press into the bottom of an ungreased 13"x9" baking pan. Bake at 400 degrees for 7 to 9 minutes; set aside to cool. Break cooled mixture into coarse pieces; set aside. Blend cream cheese and remaining sugar together in a large mixing bowl until fluffy; fold in pineapple and whipped topping. Sprinkle with pretzel mixture; toss gently. Serve immediately. Serves 4.

Keep 'em cold! Fill a large galvanized tub with ice, then nestle 2 to 3 serving bowls of salads or other cold sides to keep chilled. Everyone can help themselves!

Snappy Soups & Salads

7-Fruit Salad

Laurie Parks
Westerville, OH

This salad is always a hit at summer get-togethers...and no one believes how easy it is!

1/2 c. lime juice
1/2 c. water
1/2 c. sugar
2 nectarines, peeled and thinly
   sliced
1 banana, thinly sliced
1 pt. blueberries

1 pt. strawberries, hulled and
   sliced
1-1/2 c. watermelon, scooped
   into balls
1-1/2 c. green grapes
1 kiwi, peeled and chopped

Whisk lime juice, water and sugar together in a medium mixing bowl until sugar dissolves; add nectarines and bananas, stirring to coat. Combine remaining ingredients in a 2-1/2 quart glass serving bowl; add nectarine mixture. Gently toss to mix; cover and refrigerate for one hour. Makes 8 to 10 servings.

Turn a strawberry pot into a garden-fresh centerpiece.
Place florist's foam in the center, then tuck
flowers in the openings that allow vines
to trail and arrange blooms on top.

Homemade Ham Salad

Marion Frisvold
Bloomington, MN

Try it with tuna or chicken instead of ham.

8-oz. pkg. spiral pasta, cooked
10-oz. pkg. frozen peas, cooked
2 lbs. cooked ham, diced
4 c. celery, thinly sliced
1-qt. jar mayonnaise-type salad
   dressing
3 t. salt

1 onion, minced
12 hard-boiled eggs, peeled and
   diced
2 4-oz. jars pimentos, drained
4-oz. pkg. chopped cashews
2 t. mustard
3 t. cider vinegar

Place all ingredients in a large serving bowl; mix well. Cover and refrigerate until chilled through. Serves 20.

Everyone loves a picnic and you don't need to head to the park to have one. Even if you don't have a deck or a patio, colorful blankets spread on the lawn (or in the living room!) create excitement for guests.

Snappy Soups & Salads

Light & Fruity Turkey Salad

Pat Habiger
Spearville, KS

A great way to use leftover turkey!

2-1/2 lbs. cooked turkey, diced
20-oz. can sliced water
   chestnuts, drained
2 lbs. seedless grapes, halved

2 c. celery, thinly sliced
20-oz. can pineapple chunks,
   drained
1-1/2 c. sliced almonds, toasted

Combine all ingredients together; mix well. Stir in dressing; cover and refrigerate overnight. Serves 8.

Dressing:

3 c. mayonnaise
1/2 T. curry powder

2 T. soy sauce
2 T. lemon juice

Whisk ingredients together.

A beachside centerpiece! Layer colored sand inside a clear glass vase or jar (use colors that match the tabletop) then tuck a taper candle inside.

Fix-Today, Better-Tomorrow Stew
Connie Carmack
Ballwin, MO

Serve with sourdough bread and sliced cheese...enjoy!

2 lbs. stew beef, cubed
2 14-1/2 oz. cans beef broth
2 10-3/4 oz. cans cream of
    mushroom soup
5 to 6 russet potatoes, cubed

1 c. baby carrots, halved
3 to 4 stalks celery, sliced
15-oz. can green beans, drained
2 onions, quartered

Place all ingredients in a Dutch oven; cover with aluminum foil. Bake at 325 degrees for 3-1/2 hours. Serves 4 to 6.

Thinking of a menu for guests? Let the season be your guide! Soups and stews chock full of harvest's bounty are just right for fall get-togethers, and juicy fruit salads are delightful in the summer. Not only will you get the freshest ingredients when you plan by the season, you'll get the best prices at the supermarket!

Snappy Soups & Salads

Hearty Vegetable-Beef Soup

Jennifer Rogers
Spotted Horse, WY

This good-for-you soup was handed down from my grandma. For family vacations we visited her in Ohio for two weeks and this soup was on the menu at least three times a week. I still make it in her old stockpot, always adding lots of love to each batch.

3 to 4-lb. bone-in chuck roast
1/2 onion, diced
3 potatoes, peeled and cubed
3 carrots, sliced
2 stalks celery, thinly sliced
15-oz. can cut green beans,
   drained
15-oz. can yellow wax beans,
   drained

15-oz. can butter or lima beans,
   drained
15-oz. can corn, drained
15-oz. can peas, drained
1/2 head cabbage, shredded
2 32-oz. cans cocktail vegetable
   juice

Place roast and onions in an 8-quart or larger stockpot; fill with enough water to just cover roast. Simmer until meat falls off bone, about one hour, adding additional water if necessary; set meat aside. Add potatoes, carrots, celery, beans, corn and peas to liquid in stockpot; bring to a boil. Stir in meat and reduce heat. Simmer until potatoes and carrots are tender, about 40 minutes; add cabbage and cocktail vegetable juice. Heat for 10 additional minutes; stir often. Serve warm. Serves 6 to 8.

Be sure to have plastic Containers on hand to send everyone home with Leftovers...if there are any!

Pumpkin Chowder

Sandy Westendorp
Grand Rapids, MI

This blend of everyday ingredients is anything but ordinary.

8-oz. pkg. bacon, diced
2 c. onions, chopped
2 t. curry powder
2 T. all-purpose flour
1-lb. pie pumpkin, peeled,
    seeded and chopped

2 potatoes, peeled and cubed
4 c. chicken broth
1 c. half-and-half
salt and pepper to taste
Garnish: toasted pumpkin seeds
    and sliced green onions

Brown bacon in a stockpot for 5 minutes; add onions. Sauté for
10 minutes; add curry and flour, stirring until smooth and creamy,
about 5 minutes. Add pumpkin, potatoes and broth; simmer until
potatoes are tender, about 15 minutes. Pour in half-and-half; season
with salt and pepper. Simmer for 5 minutes; do not boil. Spoon into
serving bowls; garnish with pumpkin seeds and onions. Serves 6.

Guests will love the smell of spicy pumpkin, and it's so
easy to create. Cut off the top of a pumpkin, scrape out
the insides and punch several holes in the pumpkin shell
with an apple corer. Rub cinnamon into the "walls"
of the pumpkin and place a tea light inside.

Snappy Soups & Salads

Veggie-Cheddar Chowder

Robin Outtrim
Camden, NY

Chock-full of goodness!

2 c. water
2 c. potatoes, diced
1/2 c. carrots, diced
1/2 c. celery, diced
1/4 c. onion, diced
1 t. salt

1/4 t. pepper
1/4 c. butter
1/4 c. all-purpose flour
2 c. milk
2 c. shredded Cheddar cheese
1 c. cooked ham, diced

Combine the first 7 ingredients in a large stockpot; bring to a boil. Boil until vegetables are tender, about 10 to 12 minutes. In the meantime, melt butter in a skillet; stir in flour until smooth. Gradually add milk, stirring until thickened; mix in cheese, stirring until melted. Pour into undrained vegetable mixture; add ham. Heat until warmed through, stirring constantly; do not boil. Serves 4.

There's nothing more cozy than a bowl of warm soup. For extra comfort, warm up oven-safe bowls in a 200-degree oven before filling...the soup (and guests) will stay warmer longer!

Family-Pleasing Coleslaw

Char Nix
Tustin, MI

For years I looked for a coleslaw recipe my family really liked...this one is a winner!

8 c. shredded cabbage
1/4 c. carrot, shredded
1/3 c. sugar
1/2 t. salt
1/8 t. pepper

1/4 c. milk
1/2 c. mayonnaise
1/4 c. buttermilk
1-1/2 T. white vinegar
2-1/2 T. lemon juice

Combine cabbage and carrots in a large serving bowl; gently mix. Set aside. Whisk remaining ingredients together; pour over cabbage mixture. Cover and refrigerate until chilled, about 4 hours; toss before serving. Serves 8 to 10.

Turn flower pot saucers into a set of colorful coasters. Use several shades of acrylic paint to brighten up the insides, let them dry and add to the tabletop or make stacks to give away as gifts.

Creamy Potato Salad

Francie Stutzman
Dalton, OH

A traditional classic with a twist.

2/3 c. Italian salad dressing
14 potatoes, baked, peeled
   and cubed
1-1/2 c. celery, chopped
2/3 c. green onions, sliced
8 hard-boiled eggs, peeled and
   separated

2 c. mayonnaise
1 c. sour cream
2-1/2 t. horseradish mustard
salt, pepper and celery seed
   to taste

Pour dressing over potatoes in a large mixing bowl; add celery and onions, tossing gently. Set aside. Chop egg whites; mix into potato mixture. Mash egg yolks in a medium mixing bowl; stir in mayonnaise, sour cream and mustard. Add to potato mixture; stir to coat. Season with salt, pepper and celery seed; cover and refrigerate until chilled, at least 4 hours. Serves 8 to 10.

Serve up slaw, salads and sides in colorful plastic or paper cups...clean up's a snap!

Slow-Cooker Chicken Chili

Erin Williams
Bayview, WI

This white chili really packs a punch!

1 lb. boneless, skinless chicken
    breasts, cubed
1 c. dried Great Northern beans,
    rinsed
1 clove garlic, minced
1 onion, chopped
2 t. dried oregano

1/2 t. salt
10-3/4 oz. can cream of chicken
    soup
5 c. water
1 t. cumin
4-oz. can diced green chiles
hot pepper sauce to taste

Combine all ingredients except cumin, chiles and hot pepper sauce in
a 4-quart slow cooker; mix well. Heat on low setting for 8 to 10 hours
or until juices run clear when chicken is pierced with a fork. Stir in
remaining ingredients; heat through. Serves 8.

Don't have a table big enough for guests? No worries!
Just make sure food you serve can be held in
one hand and eaten with a spoon or fork...chili, soups,
sandwiches, followed by brownies or
cookies are great!

Snappy Soups & Salads

Dutch Oven Stew

Jennifer Sens
Mason, OH

This recipe has been in our family for at least 100 years! When the cool days of Fall roll around, everyone looks forward to this stick-to-your-ribs stew served over a bed of warm egg noodles.

1 c. all-purpose flour
1 t. paprika
1-lb. pkg. stew beef, cubed
1 to 2 T. oil
20-oz. bottle catsup

6-1/2 c. water
1 onion, chopped
2 T. sugar
2 T. vinegar
2 T. pickling spices

Combine flour and paprika in a shallow bowl; add beef, tossing to coat. Place beef in a Dutch oven; brown in oil. Add catsup, water, onion, sugar and vinegar; bring to a boil. Tie pickling spices in a square of muslin; add to beef mixture. Reduce heat; simmer for 3 hours, stirring occasionally. Remove spice bundle before serving. Serves 4.

Planning a Fathers' Day Feast or celebrating a new job? Slip button-down shirts over the backs of chairs, knot a tie around the collar and slip placecards in the pockets. So fun!

Extra-Easy Taco Salad

Linda Day
Wall, NJ

*I sometimes like to add sliced black olives too...toss in
your favorite taco toppers!*

1 head lettuce, shredded
2 tomatoes, diced
1 onion, diced
1 green pepper, diced
3/4 lb. ground beef, browned
   and cooled

2 c. shredded Cheddar cheese
2 8-oz. bottles Catalina salad
   dressing
8-oz. pkg. nacho-flavored
   tortilla chips, coarsely
   broken

Mix all ingredients together in a large serving bowl. Serve
immediately. Makes 6 to 8 servings.

A large glass bowl is a must-have for entertaining.
Whether it's used as a salad bowl, pasta dish or
filled with water and floating candles, it
works beautifully!

Snappy Soups & Salads

Marinated Tomatoes

Mary Baker
Fountain, NC

Absolutely delicious with tomatoes freshly picked from the garden.

1 clove garlic, minced
1/2 t. dried thyme
1/4 c. green onion, chopped
1/4 c. fresh parsley, minced
1 t. salt

1/4 t. pepper
6 tomatoes, thickly sliced
1/4 t. vinegar
1/3 c. oil

Combine garlic, thyme, onion, parsley, salt and pepper; sprinkle over tomatoes. Set aside. Mix vinegar and oil; pour over tomatoes. Cover; refrigerate for at least 2 hours. Mix gently before serving. Serves 10.

Dressed-Up Cucumbers

Holly Sutton
Middleburgh, NY

This country-fresh recipe goes great with grilled entrées.

1 c. mayonnaise
1/4 c. sugar
1/4 c. vinegar

1/4 t. salt
4 c. cucumbers, sliced

Combine the first 4 ingredients; mix well. Fold in cucumbers; cover and refrigerate for at least 2 hours. Serves 6 to 8.

All cooks, like all great artists, must have
an audience worth cooking for.
– Andre Simon

Thumbs-Up Cornbread Salad

Jana Timmons
Hendersonville, TN

Be sure to get your share early...it'll be gone before you know it!

8-1/2 oz. pkg. cornbread mix
24-oz. can pinto beans, drained
2 15-oz. cans corn, drained
1/4 c. sweet onion, diced
1 c. cherry tomatoes, quartered
1/2 c. bacon bits, divided

2 c. shredded 4-cheese blend
   cheese, divided
1/3 c. celery, chopped
1 c. sour cream
2 c. ranch salad dressing

Prepare cornbread according to package directions; set aside to cool. Crumble cornbread into a large serving bowl; add beans, corn, onion, tomatoes, 1/4 cup bacon bits, 1-1/2 cups cheese and celery. Toss well; set aside. In another bowl, mix sour cream and ranch dressing together; pour over cornbread mixture. Sprinkle with remaining bacon bits and cheese. Serves 10.

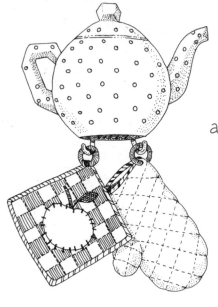

Try to arrange your grocery list according to the aisles in the supermarket... this will really cut down on time in the store running back & forth.

Snappy Soups & Salads

Bean & Ham Soup

Shannon Cronin
Hinton, IA

Comfort food!

1-lb. pkg. dried Great Northern
   beans, rinsed
8 c. water
1-1/2 lb. ham bone
2 potatoes, peeled and cubed
2 carrots, chopped

2 stalks celery, chopped
1 onion, chopped
3/4 t. dried thyme
1/2 t. salt
1/4 t. pepper
hot pepper sauce to taste

Combine beans and water in a large Dutch oven; bring to a boil.
Reduce heat; simmer for 2 minutes. Remove from heat; cover and
let stand for one hour. Bring beans to a boil again; add ham bone.
Reduce heat; simmer for one hour. Remove ham bone; cool and
remove meat from bone. Add meat to soup, discarding bone; stir in
remaining ingredients. Cover; simmer until vegetables are tender,
about 30 minutes. Serves 4 to 6.

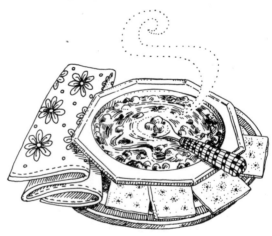

Getting the gang together for game day is fun and easy.
Celebrate with World Series Barbecue, Hoop Soups, or
Super Bowl Subs...they'll love it!

Cool Melon Salad

Jacqueline Kurtz
Reading, PA

There are so many pretty gelatin molds to use with this recipe.

3-oz. pkg. lime gelatin mix
2 c. warm water
1-1/2 c. cantaloupe, scooped
    into 1/2-inch balls

lettuce leaves
Optional: mayonnaise

Dissolve gelatin mix in warm water; pour into a lightly greased 4-cup mold. Fold in cantaloupe; refrigerate until firm. Unmold onto a serving platter lined with lettuce leaves; spread with mayonnaise, if desired. Makes 6 servings.

Make clever candleholders from melons to decorate for an afternoon gathering. Slice the top off of a cantaloupe, scoop out the insides and use cookie cutters to trace and cut designs on the outside. Set a tea light candle inside and enjoy!

Snappy Soups & Salads

Colorful Apple Salad

Jennifer Rudolph
Oakley, CA

Spoon this salad into a glass serving dish...it's so pretty!

6 Granny Smith apples, cored
    and chopped
6 Red Delicious apples, cored
    and chopped
3 stalks celery, diced

1/2 to 3/4 c. raisins
1 t. cinnamon
16-oz. container frozen whipped
    topping, thawed

Place apples in a large serving bowl; gently toss. Add remaining ingredients; stir gently. Serve immediately. Serves 12.

Frozen Cranberry Salad

Sue Dunlap
Huntsville, AL

Spoon into muffin cups and freeze for individual servings.

2 3-oz. pkgs. cream cheese,
    softened
2 T. mayonnaise
2 T. sugar
8-oz. can crushed pineapple

16-oz. can whole cranberry
    sauce
1/2 c. chopped pecans
1 c. frozen whipped topping,
    thawed

Blend cream cheese until light; mix in mayonnaise, sugar and pineapple. Fold in cranberry sauce and pecans; stir in whipped topping. Spread into an ungreased 11"x8" freezer-safe pan; cover with plastic wrap. Freeze; thaw slightly before serving. Cut into squares to serve. Makes 24 servings.

Fruity Marshmallow Salad

Kim Ripley
Elmira, NY

My family enjoys this salad at every holiday...and sometimes in between!

20-oz. can pineapple chunks, drained
14-1/2 oz. jar maraschino cherries, drained and halved
11-oz. can mandarin oranges, drained
1/2 lb. grapes, halved
10-1/2 oz. pkg. mini marshmallows

2 bananas, sliced
1 c. frozen orange juice concentrate, thawed
1/2 c. chopped walnuts
1-1/2 pts. whipping cream
1/4 c. sugar
1 t. vanilla extract

Combine pineapple, cherries, oranges, grapes and marshmallows; refrigerate overnight. Soak bananas in orange juice for 30 minutes; stir in walnuts. Set aside. Whip cream with sugar and vanilla, blending until stiff peaks form; spoon into a large serving bowl. Fold in fruit mixtures; stir gently. Serves 8.

Having girlfriends over for dinner? Tie different colors of satin bows to stemmed glasses before filling with bubbly. Easy and elegant beverage charms...cheers!

Simply Delicious Sides & Breads

Fabulous Baked Potato Casserole

Ginia Johnston
Greeneville, TN

This is my most requested recipe...it always goes first at every gathering.

6 to 7 potatoes, peeled and
   cubed
2 c. shredded Cheddar cheese
1 c. mayonnaise

1/2 c. sour cream
1 onion, diced
6 slices bacon, crisply cooked
   and crumbled

Place potatoes in a large saucepan; barely cover with water. Boil until fork tender, about 20 minutes; drain and set aside to cool. Combine cheese, mayonnaise, sour cream and onion together; mix in potatoes, tossing gently to coat. Spread potato mixture in a buttered 13"x9" baking pan; sprinkle bacon on top. Bake at 350 degrees until golden and bubbly, about 20 to 25 minutes. Serves 8.

What a welcome! Prop up a blackboard by the front door and use chalk to print the menu...guests will feel like they're dining in a charming bistro!

Simply Delicious Sides & Breads

All-Time Favorite Corn Casserole

Jackie Balla
Walbridge, OH

So good and easily doubled if expecting extras around the table.

2 15-oz. cans shoepeg corn,
   drained
10-3/4 oz. can cream of celery
   soup
1/2 c. onion, chopped

1 c. shredded Cheddar cheese
1/2 c. sour cream
1/2 c. butter, melted
1 sleeve round buttery crackers,
   crushed

Combine the first 5 ingredients in a buttered 2-quart casserole dish;
set aside. Mix butter and crushed crackers together; sprinkle over
corn mixture. Bake at 350 degrees for 45 minutes. Serves 4 to 6.

Green Beans in Garlic Butter

Carmen Turner
Key West, FL

Select the most slender green beans for the freshest taste.

1 c. chicken broth
salt and pepper to taste
2 lbs. green beans, trimmed and
   halved

4 cloves garlic, thinly sliced
1/4 c. butter, melted

Add chicken broth, salt and pepper to a stockpot; bring to a boil. Add
green beans; heat until tender, stirring often. Drain; place in a serving
bowl. Sauté garlic in butter in a small skillet until golden; pour over
green beans, tossing gently to coat. Serve warm. Makes 6 servings.

Tomato-Zucchini Casserole

Jeanne Hodack
Norwich, NY

This recipe has always been a hit at our church picnics. My family enjoys this as a main dish along with crusty bread and fresh fruit.

1 c. shredded Cheddar cheese
1/3 c. grated Parmesan cheese
1/2 t. dried oregano
1/2 t. dried basil
1 clove garlic, minced
3 zucchini, thinly sliced and divided

2 tomatoes, sliced and divided
1/4 c. butter
2 T. onion, minced
1/2 c. Italian-seasoned bread crumbs

Combine cheeses, oregano, basil and garlic; set aside. Spread half the zucchini and half the tomatoes in a greased 8"x8" baking pan; sprinkle with half the cheese mixture. Repeat layers; set aside. Melt butter in a small skillet; add onion and sauté until transparent. Remove from heat; stir in bread crumbs. Sprinkle over cheese layer; cover with aluminum foil. Bake at 350 degrees for 30 minutes; uncover and bake for an additional 25 minutes. Serves 8.

Find a great chandelier at a flea market? Add some new taper candles and set it in the center of the table for a quick centerpiece...no need for hanging!

Broccoli-Cauliflower Bake

Jo Ann

Frozen veggies make this dish a cinch.

16-oz. pkg. frozen broccoli cuts
16-oz. pkg. frozen cauliflower
   flowerets
1 c. onion, chopped
4 T. butter, divided
2 T. all-purpose flour
1 t. salt
1/2 t. garlic powder

1/2 t. dried basil
1/4 t. pepper
1-1/4 c. milk
2 3-oz. pkgs. cream cheese with
   chives, cubed
3/4 c. bread crumbs
3 T. grated Parmesan cheese

Prepare broccoli and cauliflower according to package directions; drain.
Place in a large saucepan; set aside. Sauté onion in 2 tablespoons
butter until tender; stir in flour, salt, garlic powder, basil and pepper.
Add milk; heat and stir until bubbly and thickened. Mix in cream
cheese; stir until melted. Pour over vegetables; stir to mix. Spread in
an ungreased 2-quart casserole dish; set aside. Melt remaining butter;
add bread crumbs and Parmesan cheese, mix until crumbly. Sprinkle
over casserole; bake at 400 degrees for 25 to 30 minutes. Makes
12 servings.

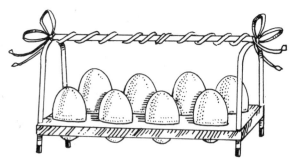

Quickly dress up a table by filling a glass bowl with
seasonal objects...pine cones and ornaments during
Winter, dyed eggs in Spring, seashells and sand in
Summer and shiny apples during Fall.

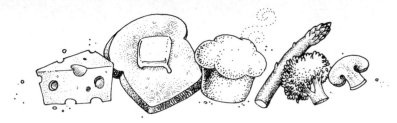

Parmesan & Basil Pull-Apart Bread
Judith Shipley
Camby, IN

Serve warm with extra butter or pizza sauce on the side for dipping.

25-oz. pkg. frozen roll dough
1 c. grated Parmesan cheese
1 T. dried basil
1 t. salt
1/2 c. butter, clarified

Thaw dough in the refrigerator overnight; slice each roll in half. Combine Parmesan cheese, basil and salt; set aside. Dip bread rounds in butter; roll in cheese mixture. Place in a greased Bundt® pan; let rise for 2-1/2 hours. Bake at 375 degrees for 20 to 25 minutes; invert on a serving plate. Makes 20 servings.

Tasty Garlic Bread
Renae Scheiderer
Beallsville, OH

A classic addition to spaghetti or lasagna.

1/3 c. butter
12 slices bread
1/2 t. garlic salt
3 T. grated Parmesan cheese

Spread butter equally on one side of each bread slice; cut each slice in half. Arrange butter-side up on an aluminum foil-lined baking sheet; sprinkle with garlic salt and Parmesan cheese. Broil 4 inches from the heat until lightly toasted, about one to 2 minutes. Makes 24 servings.

In cooking, as in all arts, simplicity is
the sign of perfection.
– Curnonsky

Herb Biscuits Supreme

La Verne Fang
Delavan, IL

You won't want to make biscuits any other way once you've tried these!

1-1/2 c. all-purpose flour	1 t. sugar
3 t. baking powder	1/2 t. dill weed
1/4 t. salt	1-1/2 t. dried chives
1/4 t. cream of tartar	1 c. whipping cream

Mix flour, baking powder, salt, cream of tartar and sugar together; stir in dill weed and chives. Mix well. Pour in cream; stir with a fork until just moistened. Place dough on a floured surface; knead. Roll out to a 3/4-inch thickness; cut into rounds with a biscuit cutter. Bake at 450 degrees on an ungreased baking sheet for 10 to 12 minutes. Makes 8.

Make a big impression with little effort. Cover the bottom of a salad plate with olive oil and drizzle a little balsamic vinegar on top...serve it alongside warm bread for dipping. Try filling saucers with oil and vinegar at each place setting for individual servings.

Asparagus-Onion Casserole

Joely Flegler
Edmond, OK

A tender and crunchy combination in one great dish.

1-lb. pkg. asparagus, trimmed
    and cut into one-inch pieces
2 onions, sliced
5 T. butter, divided
2 T. all-purpose flour
1 c. milk

3-oz. pkg. cream cheese, cubed
1 t. salt
1/8 t. pepper
1/2 c. shredded Cheddar cheese
1 c. bread crumbs

Sauté asparagus and onions in one tablespoon butter until crisp-tender, about 8 minutes; transfer to an ungreased 1-1/2 quart casserole dish. Set aside. Melt 2 tablespoons butter in a saucepan; whisk in flour until smooth. Gradually add milk; heat and stir until thickened, about 2 minutes. Reduce heat; mix in cream cheese, salt and pepper, stirring until cheese melts. Pour over asparagus and onions; sprinkle with Cheddar cheese. Melt remaining butter in a small skillet; remove from heat. Add bread crumbs; toss gently. Sprinkle over casserole; bake at 350 degrees for 35 to 40 minutes. Serves 4 to 6.

Dime-store treasures! Seek out vintage silver serving pieces...jazz them up by hot gluing beads, rhinestones, buttons or tiny silk flowers on the handles.

Crispy Wild Rice

Mary Jo Babiarz
Spring Grove, IL

Cheesy, crunchy and delicious!

2 6-oz. pkgs. long-grain and
    wild rice mix
8-oz. jar pasteurized processed
    cheese sauce
8-oz. can sliced water chestnuts,
    drained

6-oz. jar sliced mushrooms,
    drained
2-oz. jar diced pimentos,
    drained
2.8-oz. can French fried onions,
    crushed

Prepare rice mix according to package directions; place in a mixing
bowl. Mix in cheese sauce, water chestnuts, mushrooms and
pimentos; spread in a lightly buttered 11"x7" baking pan. Cover with
aluminum foil; bake at 325 degrees for 20 minutes. Uncover; top with
French fried onions. Bake 5 additional minutes. Serves 4 to 6.

Have a cupboard full of mismatched dishes and a drawer
full of mismatched flatware? A combination of different
colors and patterns makes fun settings for the table,
so go ahead and mix it up!

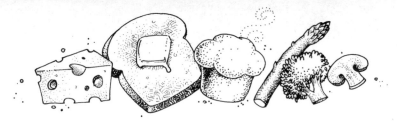

Grandma's Biscuits

Kristie Rigo
Friedens, PA

*When Grandma bakes these, my 2 teenage boys
eat them all in one sitting!*

3 c. biscuit baking mix   2/3 c. milk
2 3-oz. pkgs. cream cheese

Place baking mix in a large mixing bowl; cut in cream cheese until
crumbly. Add milk; mix until soft dough forms. Pat dough into a
circle, 1/2-inch thick, on a surface lightly dusted with biscuit baking
mix; cut into biscuits with a 2-inch biscuit cutter. Arrange on lightly
greased baking sheets; bake at 450 degrees until golden, about 8 to
10 minutes. Makes one dozen.

Try different toppers for Grandma's Biscuits. Before
baking, brush tops with melted butter then sprinkle on
treats like chocolate chips, cinnamon and sugar, chopped
nuts, shredded cheese or diced pepperoni.

Kitchen's Best Dinner Rolls

Marilyn Kent
Clontarf, MN

There's nothing quite like the smell of homemade bread.

4-1/2 to 5 c. all-purpose flour,
    divided
1/4 c. sugar
1 pkg. active dry yeast

1 t. salt
1 c. milk
1/2 c. water
1/4 c. margarine

Mix 1-1/2 cups flour, sugar, yeast and salt together in a large mixing bowl; set aside. Heat milk, water and margarine in a saucepan to 120 degrees as measured by a candy thermometer; blend into flour mixture. Add remaining flour, 1/2 cup at a time, until a soft dough forms; knead 2 to 3 minutes. Shape into 12 rolls; arrange in a greased 13"x9" baking pan. Set aside to rise until double in bulk; bake at 375 degrees for 20 to 25 minutes. Makes one dozen.

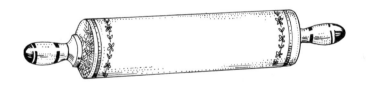

Make Kitchen's Best Dinner Rolls extra special. Just before baking, mix together 3 tablespoons flour, 3/4 teaspoon hot water and 3 tablespoons softened butter. Pipe mixture onto rolls in fun designs...flowers, snowflakes and smiley faces look great!

6-Bean Slow-Cooker Bake

Doreen DeRosa
New Castle, PA

Great for a crowd!

15-1/2 oz. can chickpeas
15-oz. can lima beans
15-1/2 oz. can hot chili beans
14-1/2 oz. can green beans
15-oz. can yellow wax beans
16-oz. can pork & beans
10-3/4 oz. can tomato soup
1-1/4 c. sugar

2 T. barbecue sauce
2 T. mustard
6-oz. can tomato paste
1 lb. bacon, crisply cooked and
  crumbled
1-lb. pkg. hot sausage, sliced
  and browned

Add all ingredients to a slow cooker; mix well. Heat on low setting
until warmed through, about 4 hours. Serves 10 to 12.

An instant hit! Core an apple, then scoop out
the insides, leaving at least 1/4-inch thick
sides...set each on a serving plate
and fill with baked beans.

Simply Delicious Sides & Breads

New England Baked Beans

Nelle Stinson-Smith
Mobile, AL

This All-American dish is a slow-poke in the oven, but it's definitely worth the wait!

8-oz. pkg. dried Great Northern beans	2 T. brown sugar, packed
1/2 lb. bacon, diced	1/4 c. molasses
2 t. salt	1/2 t. dry mustard
	2 t. Worcestershire sauce

Soak beans in cold water overnight; drain. Place in a large Dutch oven; cover with water. Boil until skins break; drain. Pour into a buttered roasting pan; stir in bacon. Pour boiling water on top until just covered; set aside. Mix remaining ingredients together; add one cup boiling water. Stir into beans; cover. Bake at 250 to 300 degrees for 6 to 8 hours, adding additional water to keep beans covered. Uncover during last half hour to brown the bacon. Serves 6 to 8.

Microwave "Baked" Beans

Andrea Kahlenbeck
Columbus, IN

A 5-minute side dish!

16-oz. can pork & beans	dried, minced onion
1/2 c. brown sugar, packed	pepper to taste
1 T. catsup	

Combine first 3 ingredients in a microwave-safe bowl; mix well. Sprinkle with enough dried onion to lightly cover the top; mix well. Add pepper to taste; cover and microwave on high until thickened, about 4 minutes. Stir after each minute. Serves 4.

Marvelous Mashed Potatoes

Janie Branstetter
Duncan, OK

Need a side dish in a hurry? This one couldn't be easier.

4 c. instant mashed potato
    flakes
8-oz. pkg. cream cheese, cubed
1 bunch green onions, chopped

2 T. fresh parsley, minced
1 T. butter
paprika to taste

Prepare mashed potatoes according to package directions, substituting cream cheese for butter; stir in onions and parsley. Spoon into a buttered one-quart casserole dish; dot with butter. Sprinkle with paprika; bake at 400 degrees for 30 minutes. Serves 6.

Easy Scalloped Potatoes

Dawn Miller
Mount Morris, MI

Cut down on prep time by leaving the peel on the potatoes...just as tasty!

7 potatoes, peeled, sliced and
    divided
1 onion, chopped and divided
10-3/4 oz. can cream of
    mushroom soup, divided

1/2 c. cooked ham, cubed and
    divided
Optional: 2 c. shredded Cheddar
    cheese

Arrange a third of the potato slices in the bottom of a lightly buttered 2-quart casserole dish; add a third of the onion, a third of the soup and a third of the ham. Repeat layers twice; sprinkle cheese on top, if desired. Bake for 350 degrees for 45 to 55 minutes. Serves 4.

Simply Delicious Sides & Breads

Buttermilk Hushpuppies

Liz Plotnick-Snay
Gooseberry Patch

Perfect for a BBQ!

2 c. cornmeal
1 c. all-purpose flour
1 T. sugar
1 T. baking powder
1/2 t. baking soda
1-1/2 t. salt
1 t. pepper

1 egg
1 t. hot pepper sauce
1-1/2 c. buttermilk
1 c. onion, minced
1 c. corn
oil for deep frying

Combine the first 7 ingredients in a medium mixing bowl; set aside. Whisk egg and hot pepper sauce together; stir in buttermilk. Add to cornmeal mixture; stir until just moistened. Fold in onion and corn; drop by tablespoonfuls into hot oil. Heat until golden, turning once; drain on paper towels. Makes 3 dozen.

Group several pillar candles on a tray or in a shallow bowl in the center of the table, then surround the bases with twigs, rocks and leaves...now you have a campfire indoors. Get out the s'mores!

Lemon-Rice Pilaf

Esther Robinson
Brownsville, TX

A complement to any main dish...garnish each serving with a lemon slice.

2 T. butter
1/2 c. long-grain rice, uncooked
1/2 c. vermicelli, uncooked and
    broken into 1-inch pieces

1-3/4 c. chicken broth
1 T. lemon zest
1 T. fresh parsley, chopped

Melt butter in a saucepan; add rice and vermicelli. Cook until golden; add broth. Bring to a boil; reduce heat. Cover; simmer for 15 to 20 minutes. Stir in lemon zest and parsley. Serves 4.

When garnishing with lemon slices, do it with a twist! Cut thin slices with a paring knife, then cut from center to rind. Hold edges and twist in opposite directions.

Marinated Carrots

Gloria Robertson
Midland, TX

Fresh carrots and green peppers team up in this vegetable side dish.

2 lbs. carrots, sliced
1 green pepper, chopped
1 onion, chopped
1 c. tomato juice
1/8 t. salt
1/8 t. pepper

1/3 c. white vinegar
1 c. sugar
1 t. mustard
1 t. Worcestershire sauce
1/2 c. oil

Boil carrots until crisp-tender; rinse in ice water and drain. Add pepper and onion; set aside. Combine remaining ingredients in a saucepan; heat over low heat until warmed through, stirring often. Pour over carrot mixture; cover and refrigerate overnight. Serves 8 to 10.

Escalloped Apples

Alison O'Keeffe
Westerville, OH

Dress up your dinner with this sweet side.

10 c. tart apples, cored, peeled
    and sliced
1/3 c. sugar
2 T. cornstarch

1 t. cinnamon
1/4 t. nutmeg
2 T. chilled butter, sliced

Place apples in a 2-1/2 quart microwave-safe bowl; set aside. Combine sugar, cornstarch, cinnamon and nutmeg; sprinkle over apples. Toss gently to coat; dot with butter. Cover and microwave on high until apples are tender, about 15 minutes, stirring every 5 minutes. Makes 8 to 10 servings.

Savory Corn

Jo Anne Hayon
Sheboygan, WI

This is my daughter's favorite recipe!

10-oz. pkg. frozen corn,
   partially thawed
1/4 c. butter
1 t. cornstarch
1/2 t. sugar

1/4 t. salt
1/4 t. dried tarragon or
   dried basil
1/8 t. pepper

Combine all ingredients in an ungreased one-quart, microwave-safe bowl; cover and heat on high for 6 to 7 minutes, stirring twice during heating. Serves 4.

Awesome Onion Casserole

Deborah Lamoree
Mesa, AZ

Your guests will be amazed by the flavor of this dish...just don't tell them how easy it is to prepare!

2 yellow onions, sliced,
   separated into rings and
   divided
1 red onion, sliced, separated
   into rings and divided
12 green onions, chopped and
   divided

1 t. pepper, divided
6-oz. pkg. crumbled blue cheese
10-oz. pkg. Havarti cheese,
   grated
3 T. butter, sliced
3/4 c. dry white wine or chicken
   broth

Layer half the yellow, red and green onions in a lightly buttered 13"x9" baking pan; sprinkle with 1/2 teaspoon pepper. Add blue cheese; layer remaining onions on top. Sprinkle with remaining pepper; layer Havarti cheese on onions. Dot with butter; pour wine or broth over the top. Bake at 350 degrees for one hour or until onions are tender. Serves 6.

Oh-So-Creamy Hashbrowns

Sandy Watters
Altoona, PA

A wonderful potato dish without having to peel a single potato!

30-oz. pkg. frozen shredded
   hashbrowns, partially
   thawed
1 c. sour cream
1 c. butter, melted and divided

2 10-3/4 oz. cans cream of
   chicken soup
1 onion, diced
50 to 60 round buttery crackers,
   crushed

Mix hashbrowns, sour cream, 1/2 cup butter, soup and onion
together; spread in a buttered 13"x9" baking pan. Set aside. Pour
remaining butter over crushed crackers; toss gently. Sprinkle over
potato mixture; bake at 350 degrees for one hour. Serves 8 to 10.

When shopping for cloth napkins, be sure to pick up an
extra one...use it to wrap around a flower pot, pitcher or
pail and you'll always have a matching centerpiece.

Homestyle Dressing

Therese Reid
Rhodesdale, MD

Moist and tasty!

1 onion, chopped
2 stalks celery, chopped
1/2 c. margarine
1/2 T. poultry seasoning
1-1/2 loaves bread, cubed
2 10-3/4 oz. cans cream of
    chicken soup

2 10-1/2 oz. cans chicken broth
4 eggs
1/4 t. dried sage
1/2 t. pepper
1 t. salt

Sauté onion and celery in margarine; set aside. Combine poultry seasoning with the bread; add remaining ingredients. Spread in a buttered roaster; cover and bake at 400 degrees for one hour. Serves 6 to 8.

There's nothing easier than sprucing up a table with flowers... Cluster a small bunch of garden roses in a teapot, add a bouquet of daffodils to an old-fashioned milk bottle or arrange fresh daisies in a watering can. It's so simple!

Herbed Onion Bread

Lorie McGuire
Erie, KS

Slice and serve with whipped butter.

1-1/2 c. onion, diced
2 T. butter
3 c. biscuit baking mix
1 egg

1 c. milk
1 t. dried basil
1 t. dill weed

Sauté onion in butter in a skillet until tender, about 5 to 7 minutes; remove from heat. Combine remaining ingredients in a large mixing bowl; stir in onion until just blended. Spoon into a greased 9"x5" loaf pan; bake at 350 degrees for 55 to 60 minutes. Cool; remove from pan. Makes 8 servings.

Clover Tea Rolls

Renae Scheiderer
Beallsville, OH

A classic you'll make again and again.

2 c. all-purpose flour
1/4 c. sugar
3/4 t. baking soda
1/2 t. salt

1/3 c. shortening
1/2 c. milk
3 T. lemon juice

Sift together flour, sugar, baking soda and salt in a large bowl. Cut in shortening until mixture resembles coarse crumbs. Combine milk and lemon juice; quickly stir into flour mixture to form a soft dough. Turn out onto a lightly floured surface; knead slightly. Form into small marble-size balls. Place 3 balls into each greased muffin cup; bake at 450 degrees for 15 minutes or until golden. Makes one dozen.

Garden Skillet

Vickie

Personalize with your favorite veggies...try broccoli, squash, tomatoes or carrots. Make it different every time!

2-1/2 c. bowtie pasta, uncooked
2 T. butter
1 t. minced garlic
2 zucchini, cut into 1/2-inch
   slices

1 red onion, sliced into thin
   wedges
1-1/2 T. fresh basil, chopped
8-oz. pkg. Cheddar cheese, diced
salt and pepper to taste

Prepare bowtie pasta according to package directions; drain and set aside. Melt butter in a 10" skillet; sauté garlic until golden. Add zucchini, red onion and basil; heat over medium heat until tender, about 4 to 6 minutes. Stir in pasta; heat through. Add cheese, salt and pepper; toss gently. Serve immediately. Serves 4 to 6.

Looking for a centerpiece to go with a garden-fresh meal? Slice a watermelon in half and use half as a vase...don't even bother to hollow it out! Simply tuck flower stems right in the melon, and the water inside will help keep them vibrant.

Simply Delicious Sides & Breads

Roasted Root Vegetables

Jennifer Wickes
Pine Beach, NJ

Roasting brings out the natural sweetness of vegetables.

4 red potatoes, quartered
4 turnips, quartered
2 parsnips, cut into one-inch
   slices
2 carrots, thickly sliced
1 yam, cut into one-inch slices

16 pearl onions, peeled
4 beets, quartered
8 cloves garlic
1/2 c. olive oil
2 T. fresh rosemary, chopped
salt and pepper to taste

Wash and rinse vegetables; spread on paper towels to drain, patting each piece dry. Place in a large plastic zipping bag; add remaining ingredients. Close bag; turn several times to coat vegetables evenly. Spread mixture in a roasting pan; bake at 450 degrees for one hour. Serves 8.

Be sure to place warm melted butter on the table for guests to brush over vegetables or rolls. Make a natural butter brush by bundling sprigs of fresh herbs such as thyme, oregano, parsley or rosemary, then bind them together with jute...adds extra flavor too!

Praline-Topped Butternut Squash

Nancy Kowalski
Southbury, CT

*When we're invited to a family gathering I'm always
asked to bring this dish.*

2 butternut squash, peeled and
   cubed
7 T. margarine, divided
1/2 t. salt
1/8 t. pepper

2 eggs, beaten
1/2 t. cinnamon
1/2 c. brown sugar, packed
1/8 t. nutmeg
1/2 c. chopped walnuts

Boil squash in water until soft; drain. Spoon into a blender; purée until
smooth. Transfer to a saucepan; stir in 4 tablespoons margarine, salt
and pepper. Warm through; remove from heat. Mix in eggs; spread
into a greased one-quart casserole dish. Set aside. Combine cinnamon,
brown sugar, remaining margarine, nutmeg and walnuts; sprinkle
over squash mixture. Bake at 350 degrees for 30 minutes. Serves 8.

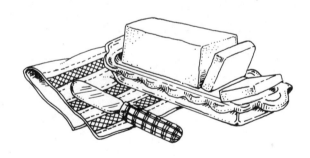

Oh-so clever! Invite friends over for a Fall gathering, and
before they arrive, go outside to collect large,
colorful leaves...place one under each glass
at the table to use as coasters.

Pineapple-Topped Sweet Potatoes   *Linda Littlejohn*
Greensboro, NC

My family won't eat sweet potatoes any other way!

2 c. sweet potatoes, boiled and
   mashed
1/4 t. salt
1/4 c. margarine, softened

1 c. sugar
2 eggs
1/4 c. milk
1 t. vanilla extract

Combine all ingredients together; spoon into an ungreased 2-quart casserole dish. Spoon on topping; bake at 350 degrees for 30 minutes. Serves 8.

Pineapple Topping:

1/4 c. all-purpose flour
1/2 c. sugar
1 egg

1/4 c. margarine, softened
8-oz. can crushed pineapple,
   drained

Combine flour and sugar; stir in egg and margarine. Fold in pineapple; mix well.

Dance fresh fruits
and veggies down
the center of the
table...decorating
is done!

Impossible Garden Pie

Suellen Anderson
Rockford, IL

It's just not possible that this delicious side dish is so quick & easy to make!

2 c. zucchini, chopped
1 c. tomatoes, chopped
1/2 onion, chopped
1/3 c. grated Parmesan cheese
1/2 t. dill weed

1 c. milk
1/2 c. biscuit baking mix
2 eggs
1 t. salt
1/4 t. pepper

Combine vegetables; spread in a greased 9" deep-dish pie pan. Set aside. Blend remaining ingredients together until smooth; pour over vegetables. Bake at 350 degrees for 35 to 45 minutes, until golden brown; cool for 5 minutes before serving. Serves 6 to 8.

Have a fun collection of pie birds? Use them for placecard holders! Just cut out cardstock, print on names, then nestle them right in the beaks. So cute!

Harvest Zucchini Pie

Jackie Smulski
Lyons, IL

This is a traditional fall favorite in my family.

8-oz. tube refrigerated crescent
   rolls
2 zucchini, sliced
1 clove garlic, minced
1 onion, chopped
2 T. olive oil
2 T. fresh parsley, minced

1/4 t. pepper
4-oz. can mushrooms, drained
4-oz. carton egg substitute
1/3 c. grated Parmesan cheese
1/2 c. shredded Monterey Jack
   cheese

Separate crescent dough into 8 triangles; line a greased 9" pie pan
with dough, facing points toward the center. Press seams together;
set aside. Sauté zucchini, garlic and onion in oil; add parsley and
pepper. Spoon into crust; add mushrooms and egg substitute. Sprinkle
with cheeses; bake at 375 degrees for 35 to 40 minutes. Let stand
5 minutes before serving. Makes 6 to 8 servings.

On a hot day, just before guests arrive, stand up bottles
of well-chilled soda and water in galvanized box
planters, then line arrange them down the center
of the table. Guests can help themselves
to refreshments throughout the meal!

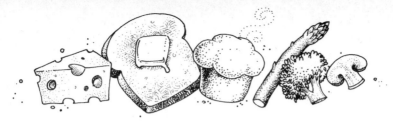

Spinach Mashed Potatoes

Vicki Ault
Syracuse, OH

Skip the gravy with these mashed potatoes...they're so flavorful, they don't need any!

6 to 8 potatoes, peeled and
    boiled
1/2 c. margarine
3/4 c. sour cream
1 t. salt
1/4 t. pepper

1 t. sugar
2 T. onion, chopped
1 c. shredded Cheddar cheese,
    divided
10-oz. pkg. frozen chopped
    spinach, cooked and drained

Mash potatoes with margarine; stir in sour cream, salt, pepper, sugar, onion and 3/4 cup cheese. Fold in spinach; spoon into a greased 13"x9" baking pan. Sprinkle with remaining cheese; bake at 350 degrees for 25 to 30 minutes. Serves 6.

Rosemary Potatoes

Gayle Burns
Bloomington, IN

So simple, yet extraordinarily delicious.

4 to 6 red potatoes, peeled and
    quartered
1 to 2 t. dried rosemary, crushed
2 cloves garlic, minced

salt and pepper to taste
1/4 c. olive oil
2 T. lemon juice

Mix all ingredients together; spoon into a greased 13"x9" baking pan. Bake at 350 degrees for one hour. Serves 4 to 6.

One-Dish Macaroni & Cheese

Carolyn Cote
Burlington, CT

So easy since the pasta isn't cooked first...allows plenty of time to relax before friends arrive!

14-oz. pkg. elbow macaroni,
    uncooked
4 c. shredded Cheddar cheese

2 10-3/4 oz. cans Cheddar
    cheese soup
3-1/2 c. milk

Combine all ingredients in a buttered 3-quart casserole dish; cover and bake at 350 degrees for one hour. Uncover and bake 20 additional minutes. Serves 8 to 10.

Save the memories! Be sure to take pictures at your gathering and send copies to friends as a thank-you for coming. Or use an instant camera and give pictures to guests on their way home.

Potluck Vegetable Casserole

Michelle Rooney
Gooseberry Patch

Be ready...your friends will surely request the recipe for this dish.

17-oz. can creamed corn
2 c. shredded Swiss cheese
10-3/4 oz. can cream of celery
  soup
17-oz. can corn, drained
10-oz. pkg. frozen cauliflower,
  cooked and drained

10-oz. pkg. frozen broccoli,
  cooked and drained
4-oz. can sliced mushrooms
2 T. butter, melted
1-1/2 c. bread crumbs

Combine creamed corn, cheese and soup; add corn, cauliflower, broccoli and mushrooms. Spoon into an ungreased 12"x7" baking pan; set aside. Mix butter and bread crumbs together; sprinkle over vegetable mixture. Bake at 375 degrees for 30 to 35 minutes. Makes 8 servings.

No time to bake bread for company on their way? Dress up store-bought refrigerated bread sticks in no time. Separate bread stick dough and lay flat; brush with olive oil and sprinkle sesame seeds and snipped parsley over top. Holding ends of bread sticks, twist 2 times; bake as directed.

Baked Spinach Casserole

Karen Pilcher
Burleson, TX

If you like spinach, you'll love this recipe!

3 T. onion, grated
16-oz. pkg. sliced mushrooms
3 T. butter
3 T. all-purpose flour
2 t. salt
1/4 t. white pepper

1/4 t. nutmeg
2 c. whipping cream
2 10-oz. pkgs. frozen chopped
   spinach, thawed, drained
   and divided
3 T. shredded Swiss cheese

Sauté onion and mushrooms in butter for 5 minutes; blend in flour, salt, pepper and nutmeg. Gradually stir in cream; heat to boiling, stirring constantly. Remove from heat; set aside. Place half the spinach in a greased 13"x9" baking pan; cover with half the mushroom mixture. Repeat layers; sprinkle with cheese. Set pan in a larger pan filled with 1/2 inch water; bake at 325 degrees for 40 minutes. Serves 6 to 8.

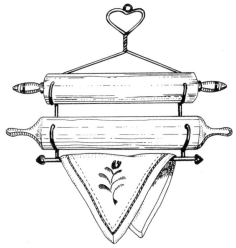

Cooking is at once child's play and adult joy.
And cooking done with care is an act of love.
    - Craig Claiborne

Lemon Biscuits

Jennifer Licon-Conner
Gooseberry Patch

So light...wonderful with chicken, seafood and garden salads.

2 c. all-purpose flour
1 T. sugar
2 t. baking powder
2 t. lemon zest
1/2 t. baking soda

1/2 t. salt
1/2 c. shortening
1/3 c. buttermilk
1/3 c. mayonnaise

Combine first 6 ingredients in a mixing bowl; cut in shortening with a pastry cutter until coarse crumbs form. Make a well in the center; set aside. Whisk buttermilk and mayonnaise together; pour into well, stirring until just blended. Place dough on a lightly floured surface; knead until smooth, 10 to 12 times. Pat into a 1/2-inch thick rectangle; cut into biscuits using a round glass or biscuit cutter. Arrange on ungreased baking sheets; bake at 450 degrees until golden, 10 to 12 minutes. Cool slightly before serving. Makes 8 to 10.

Paper plates and cups don't have to be plain and boring. Look for those that come in bright colors, then quickly dress them up with ribbons, rick-rack, flowers or stickers.

Quick from the Cupboard Mains

Cheddar Ziti Bake

Wendy Lee Paffenroth
Pine Island, NY

This recipe is easily doubled...a handy dish to offer friends for open houses, graduations and receptions.

1-lb. pkg. sweet Italian sausages
1 lb. ground beef
1 onion, chopped
2 29-oz. cans crushed tomatoes
1 c. red wine or beef broth
1 T. Italian seasoning
16-oz. pkg. ziti pasta, cooked
4 c. shredded Cheddar cheese

Place sausages in a saucepan; cover with water. Boil for 15 to 20 minutes; drain and rinse under cold water. Cut into 1/2-inch slices; brown with ground beef in a 12" skillet. Add onion; sauté until tender. Add crushed tomatoes and wine or broth; stir in seasoning. Heat until boiling; reduce heat and simmer until thickened. Remove from heat; pour 1/4 cup sauce in the bottom of a roasting pan. Add half the pasta, half the remaining sauce and half the cheese. Repeat layers. Bake at 325 degrees until bubbly, about 40 minutes. Serves 8.

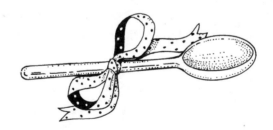

Delight dinner guests with a creative centerpiece. Stack several terra cotta pots, gluing inside each rim. Place floral foam inside the top pot and nestle a candle inside, then tuck small flowers around the candle base. Try making several in different heights and group together on the table.

Bowties & Blush Pasta Dish

Brooke Sottosanti
Columbia Station, OH

A restaurant-style meal in the comfort of your own home!

1 T. butter
1 onion, chopped
1 banana pepper, chopped
2 cloves garlic, chopped
1 T. all-purpose flour
3/4 c. milk
1/2 c. whipping cream

1/2 t. salt
1-1/4 c. spaghetti sauce
16-oz. pkg. bowtie pasta,
  cooked
1/4 c. grated Parmesan cheese
1/4 c. fresh basil, chopped

Melt butter over medium heat in a 12" skillet; add onion, pepper
and garlic. Sauté until tender; stir in flour. Gradually add milk, cream
and salt; bring to a boil. Mix in spaghetti sauce; heat for 10 minutes.
Remove from heat; pour into a serving bowl. Add pasta; mix gently.
Sprinkle with Parmesan cheese and basil; serve warm. Serves 8.

Use simple garnishes to dress up main dishes throughout
the year. Fresh mint sprigs add coolness and color to
summertime dishes while rosemary sprigs and
cranberries arranged to resemble holly add
a festive touch to holiday platters.

Oven-Baked Pineapple Pork Chops

Linda Patten
Lake Zurich, IL

Any side dish goes well with this main...we like buttered noodles sprinkled with Parmesan cheese.

8-oz. can pineapple slices,
    drained with juice reserved
2 T. soy sauce
1/2 t. ground ginger
1/2 t. garlic powder

4 pork loin chops
1/3 c. Italian-seasoned bread
    crumbs
1 t. paprika

Combine 4 tablespoons pineapple juice, soy sauce, ginger and garlic powder in a shallow bowl; add pork chops, turning once to coat. Marinate in the refrigerator for at least 4 hours. Gently toss bread crumbs and paprika in a pie pan; add pork chops, coating both sides. Arrange pork chops in a shallow ungreased 13"x9" baking pan; bake at 350 degrees for 25 minutes. Turn pork chops; place one pineapple slice on each pork chop. Bake 25 additional minutes; serve warm. Makes 4 servings.

Once you've planned a scrumptious menu for family & friends, be sure to take notes...you're likely to want to repeat it sometime down the road.

Pork Chop & Potato Bake

Lori Derham
Knoxville, IL

A simple dish with lots of flavor.

10-3/4 oz. can cream of celery
   soup
24-oz. pkg. frozen shredded
   hashbrowns, thawed
1/2 c. milk
1/2 c. sour cream
1/4 t. pepper

2.8-oz. can French fried onions,
   divided
6 pork chops, browned
1/2 t. seasoned salt
1 c. shredded Cheddar cheese,
   divided

Combine soup, hashbrowns, milk, sour cream, pepper and half
the French fried onions; spread into a buttered 13"x9" baking pan.
Arrange pork chops on top; sprinkle with seasoned salt. Cover with
aluminum foil; bake at 350 degrees for 40 minutes. Top with cheese
and remaining onions; bake, uncovered, 5 additional minutes.
Serves 6.

Add a warm glow to the party with a simple strand of
lights. Decorate the table with a string of white lights
folded inside a sheer table runner or strip
of fabric. Sparkly!

Chicken Salad Croissants

Arlene Smulski
Lyons, IL

Great for a quick supper or a casual weekend lunch.

2 c. cooked chicken, cubed
1/3 c. celery, diced
1/4 c. raisins
1/4 c. dried cranberries
1/4 c. sliced almonds
2/3 c. mayonnaise
1/8 t. pepper

1 T. fresh parsley, minced
1 t. mustard
1 T. lemon juice
4 to 6 croissants, split in half
    horizontally
4 to 6 lettuce leaves

Combine the first 10 ingredients in a large mixing bowl; mix well.
Cover and refrigerate for 2 to 3 hours. Spoon about 1/2 cup mixture
on the bottom half of each croissant; add a lettuce leaf and the top
croissant half. Makes 4 to 6.

Fast and fun! Whip up several different kinds of sandwiches (or stop at the local deli for a few!) and cut each one into 4 sections. Arrange them all on a large platter with chips and pickles... everyone will love the variety and it couldn't be easier.

Santa Fe Sandwiches

Deanne Birkestrand
Minden, NE

Add a fresh fruit salad for a quick & tasty meal with friends.

6 hoagie buns, split in half
   horizontally
1/2 c. mayonnaise
1/2 c. sour cream
1/2 t. chili powder
1/2 t. cumin
1/4 t. salt
6 tomatoes, sliced
8-oz. pkg. sliced cooked turkey

1/2 c. sliced black olives
1/3 c. green onion, sliced
3 avocados, pitted, peeled and
   sliced
8-oz. pkg. shredded Cheddar
   cheese
Garnish: shredded lettuce and
   salsa

Arrange hoagie buns open-faced on an ungreased baking sheet; set aside. Mix the next 5 ingredients together; spread equally over hoagie buns. Layer remaining ingredients in the order listed equally on top of each bun; bake at 350 degrees for 15 minutes. Slice each in half to serve; garnish with lettuce and salsa. Makes 12 servings.

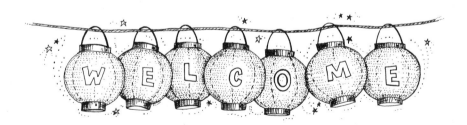

Wrap Santa Fe Sandwiches in parchment paper to keep them fresh before serving. Tie a gingham ribbon around each and tuck white daisies in the knots...guests will feel so special.

Fool-Proof Homemade Pizza

Vicki Vaughan
Franklin, MA

My mother's specialty was homemade pizza. It took her about 10 hours to make and the slightest error would lead to disaster in the kitchen! Through years of experimentation I now, thankfully, have the easiest, fool-proof pizza recipe to share with family & friends!

2 pkgs. active dry yeast
2 c. warm water
2 t. salt
6 T. olive oil

1 t. sugar
5 to 6 c. all-purpose flour,
    divided

Dissolve yeast in water; add salt, olive oil and sugar. Set aside until foamy. Place 5 cups flour in a large mixing bowl; add yeast mixture. Knead until a smooth dough forms, adding additional flour if necessary; place in a well-greased bowl, turning to lightly coat sides of dough. Cover and let rise in a warm place until double in bulk, about one to 2 hours; divide into 2 equal portions. Pat into 2 greased pizza pans; add toppings. Bake at 450 degrees for 10 minutes. Makes 16 servings.

Toppings:

15-oz. can tomato sauce
1 t. sugar
1/4 c. grated Parmesan cheese
5 c. shredded mozzarella cheese
1 t. dried oregano

1 t. dried basil
Optional: sliced pepperoni, sliced
    mushrooms, sliced tomatoes
    and additional cheese

Combine tomato sauce and sugar; spread evenly over both crusts. Sprinkle with remaining ingredients and any other desired toppings.

Crowd-Pleasing Potato Pizza

Marshall Williams
Westerville, OH

The slices disappear quickly!

3 potatoes, peeled and cubed
10-oz. tube refrigerated pizza
   crust
1/4 c. milk
1/2 t. salt
1-lb. pkg. bacon, diced
1 onion, chopped

1/2 c. red pepper, chopped
1-1/2 c. shredded Cheddar
   cheese
1-1/2 c. shredded mozzarella
   cheese
Optional: sour cream

Place potatoes in a large saucepan; barely cover with water. Boil until tender, about 20 to 25 minutes; drain and set aside. Flatten pizza dough on an ungreased 14" pizza pan; pinch edges to form a rim. Prick dough with a fork; bake at 350 degrees until golden, about 15 minutes. Cool on a wire rack. Transfer potatoes to a mixing bowl; add milk and salt. Mash until smooth; spread over crust. Slightly brown bacon; add onion and pepper and cook until tender. Drain and spread over potatoes. Sprinkle with cheeses; bake at 375 degrees for 20 minutes. Cut into wedges to serve; spread with sour cream, if desired. Makes 8 servings.

Have some fun at the dinner table. Cut out comic strips
from the newspaper, laminate them,
then use as napkin rings.

Potluck Casserole

Joan Macfarlane
Hillsboro, NH

Easy to make and yummy when reheated.

1 onion, chopped
1 green pepper, chopped
2 T. butter
1 lb. ground beef
16-oz. can whole tomatoes

1/2 c. long-cooking rice,
    uncooked
1-1/2 t. salt
1/2 t. pepper
1 t. chili powder

Sauté onion and green pepper in butter until tender; add ground beef. Brown; drain and remove from heat. Pour tomatoes in an ungreased 13"x9" baking pan; sprinkle with rice, salt, pepper and chili powder. Add ground beef mixture; stir to combine. Cover with aluminum foil; bake at 350 degrees for one hour. Serves 6.

Create a casserole topper. Unfold 2 refrigerated pie crusts; sprinkle one with pecans and sun-dried tomatoes (or any other goodies) and top with remaining crust. Roll crusts together and cut into shapes with cookie cutters. Bake at 425 degrees for 8 minutes and arrange on casserole before serving.

Saucy Meatloaf

Jennifer Inacio
York, PA

This has become a hit at informal dinner parties. I even made this for my friend who doesn't like meatloaf...she loved it so much, she asked for the recipe and she now makes it at least twice a month!

1-1/2 lbs. ground beef	1-1/2 t. salt
1/2 c. quick-cooking oats, uncooked	1 t. pepper
	1 c. tomato juice
1/2 c. onion, chopped	1 egg

Combine all ingredients; mix well. Pat into an ungreased 9"x5" loaf pan; pour sauce on top. Bake at 350 degrees for 1-1/2 hours; let stand 5 minutes before slicing. Makes 8 servings.

Sauce:

6-oz. can tomato sauce	3 T. brown sugar, packed
3 T. vinegar	2 t. Worcestershire sauce
2 T. mustard	

Stir all ingredients together; mix well.

My doctor told me to stop having intimate dinners for four.
Unless there are three other people.
– Orson Welles

Overnight Chicken Casserole

Cammi Kruse
Cosmos, MN

So easy because you don't have to cook the noodles!

2-1/2 c. cooked chicken, diced
2 c. elbow macaroni, uncooked
10-3/4 oz. can cream of chicken
    soup
1 c. plus 3 T. milk
14-1/2 oz. can chicken broth

8-oz. pkg. pasteurized processed
    cheese spread, cubed
1 t. salt
1 onion, chopped
1/4 c. celery, diced

Combine all ingredients together; spread in an ungreased
13"x9" baking pan. Cover with aluminum foil; refrigerate overnight.
Uncover and bake at 350 degrees for 1-1/2 hours. Serves 8.

Draw Here!

Kids coming for dinner too? Set up a separate table for
them and use a sheet of butcher paper for the tablecloth.
Place a flowerpot filled with markers, crayons and
stickers in the middle...they'll have a blast!

Feed-'Em-All Casserole

Tammy Rowe
Bellevue, OH

Expect ooh's and ahh's when you serve this hearty chicken dish.

3 boneless, skinless chicken
   breasts, cooked and cubed
16-oz. pkg. wide egg noodles,
   cooked
2 c. sour cream
15-oz. can mixed vegetables,
   drained

2-oz. jar pimentos, drained
1/4 c. grated Parmesan cheese
1 T. dried parsley, chopped
1 t. garlic powder
1/2 t. salt
1/2 t. pepper
2.8-oz. can French fried onions

Combine all ingredients, except French fried onions, in a large mixing
bowl; mix well. Spread in a buttered 13"x9" baking pan; bake at
350 degrees for 10 minutes. Sprinkle with French fried onions; bake
10 additional minutes or until bubbly and golden. Serves 8 to 10.

One-Skillet Chicken & Rice

Julie Heinze
Weston, OH

Clean up's a breeze!

1/4 c. all-purpose flour
1 T. seasoned salt
6 boneless, skinless chicken
   breasts
2 T. oil
2 14-1/2 oz. cans whole
   tomatoes, chopped

1-1/4 oz. pkg. taco seasoning
   mix
1 c. celery, chopped
1 c. long-cooking rice, uncooked
1/2 c. onion, chopped
1/2 c. parsley, chopped

Combine flour and seasoned salt in a plastic zipping bag; add chicken,
shaking to coat. Brown chicken in oil in a 12" skillet; add tomatoes,
taco seasoning, celery, rice and onion. Bring to a boil; reduce heat,
cover and simmer for 20 minutes. Sprinkle with parsley. Serves 6.

Sour Cream Taco Bake

Sheri Cazier
Black Diamond, WA

My husband always requests this special dish for his birthday.

1-1/2 lbs. ground beef
1-1/4 c. onion, chopped and
  divided
1-1/4 oz. pkg. taco seasoning
  mix
12-oz. can diced tomatoes
2 T. salsa

1/2 c. oil
12 corn tortillas
4 c. shredded Monterey Jack
  cheese
2 c. sour cream
1 t. seasoned salt
pepper to taste

Sauté ground beef and 1/2 cup onion until beef is browned; drain.
Add taco seasoning mix, tomatoes and salsa; reduce heat and simmer
for 20 minutes. Set aside to cool. Heat oil in 12" skillet; add tortillas,
one at a time, heating on both sides until just soft. Drain on paper
towels; set aside. Spoon 2 tablespoons meat sauce, 2 tablespoons
cheese and 2 tablespoons remaining onion in the center of each
tortilla; fold in half and arrange in a greased 13"x9" baking pan.
Spread any remaining meat sauce, cheese and onion on top; set aside.
Combine sour cream and seasoned salt; spread over tacos. Sprinkle
with pepper; bake at 325 degrees for 25 to 30 minutes. Makes
12 servings.

Clever condiments! When serving Mexican meals, slice the tops off peppers, rinse and remove seeds. Then fill with guacamole, sour cream and salsa. Cover with reserved tops and refrigerate until ready to serve. Works great for cookouts too...fill with mustard, mayo and catsup.

Black Bean Spaghetti Sauce

Cyndy Rogers
Upton, MA

Spoon over a heaping plate of warm spaghetti noodles.

1 onion, sliced
1 red pepper, sliced
1 yellow pepper, sliced
8-oz. pkg. sliced mushrooms
14-1/2 oz. can diced tomatoes

15-oz. can black beans, drained
  and rinsed
3-1/2 oz. jar capers, packed in
  water
2 t. dried Italian seasoning

Sauté the first 4 ingredients until crisp-tender in a 12" skillet sprayed
with non-stick vegetable spray over medium-high heat; stir
constantly. Add remaining ingredients; bring to a boil. Reduce heat
and simmer for 15 minutes; stir frequently. Makes 6 servings.

Use old serving dishes in a new way for a fresh look.
Handed-down cream and sugar sets can hold sauces,
bread sticks can be arranged in gravy boats and a trifle
dish can make a great salad bowl.

Bubble Pizza

Tracy Lindberg
Meridian, ID

So fun to make for a house full of young guests!

3 7-1/2 oz. tubes refrigerated
    buttermilk biscuits,
    quartered
14-oz. jar spaghetti sauce,
    divided
3 c. shredded mozzarella cheese,
    divided

1 clove garlic, minced
Optional: sliced pepperoni, sliced
    mushrooms, onion, ham,
    sausage or pineapple

Place biscuit pieces in a large mixing bowl; add half the spaghetti sauce, 2 cups cheese and garlic. Mix until biscuit pieces are well coated; spread in a greased 13"x9" baking pan. Pour remaining sauce on top; add any optional toppings. Sprinkle with remaining cheese; bake at 350 degrees for 40 to 45 minutes. Serves 8 to 10.

You don't have to spend a lot of time setting the table for casual gatherings. Just wrap colorful napkins around silverware and slip them into a glass at each place setting. It's so charming...and you don't have to remember where the forks, knives and spoons go!

Simple Stuffed Shells

Max Bentley
Waunakee, WI

A 3-cheese delight!

24-oz. carton cottage cheese
1/4 c. grated Parmesan cheese
1 t. garlic powder
2 eggs
salt and pepper to taste
12-oz. pkg. large shell pasta,
    uncooked

1 c. spinach leaves, torn
14-oz. can diced Italian
    tomatoes
14-oz. jar spaghetti sauce
2 c. shredded mozzarella cheese

Combine the first 5 ingredients in a medium mixing bowl; mix well.
Spoon into shells; arrange in a 13"x9" baking pan sprayed with
non-stick vegetable spray. Tuck spinach between shells; pour tomatoes
and spaghetti sauce on top, making sure all shells are well covered.
Cover with aluminum foil; bake at 375 degrees for 30 minutes.
Uncover and sprinkle with mozzarella cheese; bake 15 additional
minutes or until cheese is melted. Serves 6.

Sophistication in a snap! Fill 3 stemmed glasses half full
with water, float a tea light in each and group them
together in the center of the table.

Slow-Cooker Steak

Vickie Simpson
Norfolk, VA

The aroma will bring family & friends to the table in no time!

3 potatoes, peeled and quartered
4-oz. pkg. baby carrots
2 stalks celery, diced
1 onion, chopped
6 beef round steaks, browned
12-oz. jar beef gravy

10-3/4 oz. can cream of
    mushroom soup
1/8 t. curry powder
1/8 t. garlic salt
1/8 t. pepper

Combine vegetables; place in a slow cooker. Arrange steaks on top; set aside. Mix remaining ingredients together; pour over steaks, stirring to coat vegetables and steaks. Heat on low setting for 6 to 8 hours or on high for 3 to 4 hours. Serves 6.

Guests are sure to head to the powder room to wash up before dinner, so why not offer them individual handtowels. Just roll up small white washcloths and tuck them all in a pretty basket by the sink. They'll love the pampering!

Meatball Sub Casserole

Mary Kowaleski
Shawano, WI

All the yum of subs in one easy dish.

1/3 c. green onion, chopped
1/4 c. seasoned bread crumbs
3 T. grated Parmesan cheese
1 lb. ground beef
1-lb. loaf Italian bread, cut into
    one-inch thick slices
8-oz. pkg. cream cheese,
    softened

1/2 c. mayonnaise
1 t. Italian seasoning
1/4 t. pepper
2 c. shredded mozzarella
    cheese, divided
28-oz. jar spaghetti sauce
1 c. water
2 cloves garlic, minced

Combine onion, bread crumbs and Parmesan cheese in a large bowl; mix in ground beef. Shape mixture into one-inch meatballs; place in an ungreased jelly-roll pan and bake at 400 degrees for 15 to 20 minutes. Arrange bread slices in a single layer in a greased 13"x9" baking dish; set aside. Combine cream cheese, mayonnaise, Italian seasoning and pepper; spread over bread. Sprinkle with 1/2 cup mozzarella cheese. Combine sauce, water, garlic and meatballs; spread over cheese mixture. Sprinkle remaining mozzarella on top; bake at 350 degrees for 30 minutes. Serves 6 to 8.

No tablecloth? No problem! It's absolutely optional, so go without...or use creative tabletoppers like an old-fashioned quilt, favorite scarf or lengths of lace.

Reuben Casserole

Peggy Zahrt
Estherville, IA

The classic sandwich becomes a casserole.

16-oz. jar sauerkraut, drained
6 to 9 oz. corned beef slices,
   chopped
1-1/2 c. shredded Swiss cheese
1/2 c. mayonnaise

1/4 c. Thousand Island salad
   dressing
6 T. butter, melted
4 to 6 slices rye bread, cubed

Layer sauerkraut, beef and cheese in an ungreased 13"x9" baking pan; set aside. Combine mayonnaise and Thousand Island salad dressing; spread over cheese layer. Drizzle butter on top; sprinkle with bread cubes. Bake at 350 degrees for 30 minutes or until cheese is bubbly. Serves 6.

Dress up a one-dish dinner when serving on individual plates. A simple chopped herb around the edge of the plate will add a lot of color, and a complementary sauce that has been drizzled around the edge will give a nice frame to the meal. Your guests will think you've had dinner catered!

Quick Ham & Cheeses

Rosemarie Wasko
Portage, PA

Serve with tomato soup...ultimate comfort food!

2 12-oz. tubes refrigerated
    biscuits
5-oz. can minced ham
1 t. dried, minced onion

1 t. margarine
5 slices Swiss cheese
2 T. butter, melted
1 t. poppy seed

Flatten each biscuit; arrange 5 on an aluminum foil-lined baking
sheet, setting remaining biscuits to the side. Combine ham, onion and
margarine together; spread equally over 5 biscuits. Arrange one slice
Swiss cheese on top of each; place remaining biscuits on top of cheese.
Pinch top and bottom biscuits together to seal. Brush with butter;
sprinkle with poppy seed. Bake at 350 degrees until golden, about
15 to 18 minutes. Makes 5 servings.

Ham & Swiss Pie

Mary Rita Schlagel
Warwick, NY

Breakfast, lunch or dinner...this pie is a treat!

2 c. cooked ham, diced
1 c. shredded Swiss cheese
1/3 c. onion, chopped
4 eggs, beaten

2 c. milk
1 c. biscuit baking mix
pepper, paprika and dried
    parsley to taste

Spread ham, cheese and onion in the bottom of an ungreased
9" deep-dish pie pan; set aside. Place eggs, milk and biscuit baking
mix into a blender; mix for 15 seconds. Pour over ham mixture;
sprinkle with remaining ingredients. Bake at 400 degrees for 30 to
40 minutes or until a knife inserted in the center removes clean;
cool for 10 minutes before serving. Serves 6.

Chicken Casserole Supreme

Carol Rickard
Chardon, OH

You can't go wrong with this popular dish.

1 onion, chopped
1 c. green pepper, chopped
2 T. butter
16-oz. pkg. chicken-flavored
    stuffing mix
4 c. chicken broth

6 eggs, beaten
3 10-3/4 oz. cans cream of
    celery soup
8 c. cooked chicken, chopped
3 c. prepared rice

Sauté onion and green pepper in butter; set aside. Combine stuffing
mix and broth in a very large mixing bowl or roaster; stir in eggs,
soup, chicken, rice, onion and green pepper. Divide evenly between
2 lightly buttered 13"x9" baking pans; bake at 325 degrees for
30 to 40 minutes. Serves 16.

Everyone will love making toasts with these cute
beverage charms. Pick up several small bells in different
colors at a local craft store. Thread 2 or 3 onto
ribbon and tie to stemmed glasses.

Chicken in Cream Sauce

Louise Denton
Sacramento, CA

Every bite is moist and juicy!

8 boneless, skinless chicken
   breasts
1.05-oz. pkg. Italian salad
   dressing mix, divided
8-oz. pkg. cream cheese,
   softened and divided

10-3/4 oz. can cream of
   mushroom soup
1/2 c. green onion, chopped
1/3 c. white wine or chicken
   broth

Arrange chicken in a greased 2-quart baking pan; set aside. Heat half
the package Italian dressing mix, half the package cream cheese and
soup together in a microwave-safe bowl, stirring until well blended;
set remaining mix and cream cheese aside for use in another recipe.
Stir onion and wine or broth into cream cheese mixture; spread over
chicken breasts. Bake at 350 degrees for one hour or until juices run
clear when chicken is pierced with a fork. Makes 8 servings.

A special touch when serving seafood. Wrap lemon halves
in cheesecloth, tie with a colorful ribbon, attach a
placecard, if desired, and set one on each plate.
Guests can squeeze the lemon over their dishes...the
cheesecloth prevents squirting and catches seeds!

Scalloped Scallops

Cheryl Kiss
Kingsport, TN

A sure-fire winner!

3/4 c. butter, melted
2 c. round buttery crackers,
  crushed
1 c. bread crumbs
1-1/2 lbs. scallops, divided

1-1/2 c. half-and-half, divided
salt and pepper to taste
2 t. paprika
Garnish: 1 lemon, sliced into
  4 to 6 wedges

Combine butter, crushed cracker crumbs and bread crumbs; mix well.
Sprinkle one-third in the bottom of a buttered 1-1/2 quart casserole
dish; top with half the scallops. Pour on half the cream; salt and
pepper to taste. Repeat layers; top with remaining bread crumb
mixture. Sprinkle with paprika; bake at 350 degrees until scallops are
heated through, about 30 to 40 minutes. Spoon onto serving plates;
garnish each with a lemon wedge. Makes 4 to 6 servings.

Give a rose to everyone at the
table! Unfold a green napkin and
lay it across a drinking glass. Roll
up a white napkin (pink looks pretty
too) and slip it into the glass, so
the green napkin comes up over the
edges, and the white "rose" can
be seen in the middle.

Citrus-Cherry Pork & Pasta

Brad Daugherty
Gooseberry Patch

Guests are always excited when this dish is on the menu.

1 t. oil
1 lb. pork tenderloin, cubed
1/2 sweet onion, sliced
2 T. orange juice
2 T. balsamic vinegar
2 T. olive oil
1/4 t. salt

1/4 t. pepper
1 T. orange zest
8-oz. pkg. mostaccioli pasta,
  cooked and drained
3 c. broccoli flowerets
1/2 c. dried cherries
1/2 c. chopped walnuts

Heat oil over medium-high heat in a 12" non-stick skillet. Add pork and onion; sauté 3 to 4 minutes or until pork is browned and onion is tender; set aside. Shake orange juice, vinegar, olive oil, salt, pepper and orange zest in a small jar with a tight fitting lid; set aside. Toss pork and onion mixture, pasta, broccoli, cherries and walnuts together in a large serving bowl; pour orange juice mixture on top. Gently toss; serve immediately. Makes 6 servings.

Dinners at home don't have to be in the kitchen...and the outdoors isn't reserved for cookouts. Bake up a tasty dish inside, then lead everyone to the backyard to dine al fresco...they'll be so surprised!

So-Tender Barbecue Chicken

Christina Jones
Lebanon, TN

We pour any extra barbecue sauce over prepared rice for a speedy side.

4 boneless, skinless chicken
    breasts
1/2 c. catsup
1/4 c. vinegar
1/4 c. Worcestershire sauce
1/2 c. water

6 T. butter
2 t. salt
1/2 c. brown sugar, packed
2 t. dry mustard
2 t. paprika
1 t. chili powder

Place chicken in an ungreased 13"x9" baking pan; set aside. Mix remaining ingredients together; spread over chicken. Bake at 300 degrees for 2 hours or until juices run clear when chicken is pierced with a fork. Serves 4.

Oven-Crispy Barbecue Chicken

Margie Williams
Gooseberry Patch

Team up with cornbread and a crisp salad for a pleasing dinner.

18-oz. bottle barbecue sauce
4 to 6 boneless, skinless chicken
    breasts
4 c. crispy rice cereal, crushed
1 t. salt

1 t. pepper
1 t. garlic powder
1 t. onion powder
1 t. dried parsley

Pour barbecue sauce in a bowl; coat both sides of chicken breasts with sauce. Set aside. Combine remaining ingredients; roll chicken breasts in mixture. Lay on an aluminum foil-lined baking sheet; bake at 400 degrees for 30 minutes. Serves 4 to 6.

Salisbury Steak & Onion Gravy

Dawn Lawrence
Claremont, NH

It won't last long!

10-1/2 oz. can French onion
   soup, divided
1-1/2 lbs. ground beef
1/2 c. bread crumbs
1 egg, beaten
1/4 t. salt

1/8 t. pepper
1 T. all-purpose flour
1/4 c. catsup
1/4 c. water
1 t. Worcestershire sauce
1/2 t. mustard

Combine 1/2 cup soup, beef, bread crumbs, egg, salt and pepper in a large mixing bowl; shape into 6 patties. Brown in a skillet; drain and set aside. Gradually blend remaining soup with flour until smooth; add remaining ingredients. Pour into skillet; stir well. Cover; return to heat and simmer for 20 minutes, stirring occasionally. Serves 6.

Hand-written menus lend a personal touch to any table. Cut colored papers to fit the front of old-fashioned milk bottles or Mason jars. Write on details and wrap around the jars with a pretty ribbon...fill jars with water and flowers and arrange in the center of the table.

Rose Hill Chicken Spaghetti

Aliceson Haynes
Orange, TX

*Serve up spaghetti in a whole new way...you'll be
pleasantly surprised!*

1 onion, chopped
2 stalks celery, chopped
1/4 c. margarine
14-1/2 oz. can tomatoes with
　green chile peppers
10-3/4 oz. can cream of chicken
　soup
10-3/4 oz. can cream of
　mushroom soup

8-oz. pkg. pasteurized processed
　cheese spread, cubed
4-1/2 oz. can mushrooms,
　drained
seasoned salt to taste
4 boneless, skinless chicken
　breasts, boiled and chopped
12-oz. pkg. spaghetti, cooked

Sauté onion and celery in margarine until tender in a large stockpot;
add tomatoes, soups, cheese and mushrooms. Simmer until cheese
melts; sprinkle with salt. Add chicken; stir well. Simmer until heated
through; stir in spaghetti. Serves 8 to 10.

Cooking Rule: If at first you don't succeed,
order pizza.
– Unknown

Classic Lasagna

Naomi Cooper
Delaware, OH

Best when assembled the day before and refrigerated overnight.

2 lbs. ground beef
1 onion, chopped
2 cloves garlic, chopped
2-1/2 t. salt
1/4 t. pepper
1/2 t. dried basil
1 T. dried parsley
2 bay leaves
2 6-oz. cans tomato paste

1-1/2 c. hot water
2 c. cottage cheese
2 eggs, beaten
16-oz. pkg. lasagna noodles,
 cooked and divided
4 c. shredded mozzarella cheese,
 divided
1/4 c. grated Parmesan cheese

Brown beef, onion and garlic in a 12" skillet; season with salt, pepper, basil, parsley and bay leaves. Stir in tomato paste and hot water; bring to a boil. Reduce heat; simmer for 5 minutes. In a separate bowl, blend cottage cheese with eggs; set aside. Spread a thin layer of beef mixture in a greased 13"x9" baking pan; top with a layer of noodles. Spread half the cottage cheese mixture over noodles; sprinkle with half the cheese. Repeat layers; sprinkle with Parmesan cheese. Cover with aluminum foil; bake at 350 degrees for 30 to 45 minutes. Serves 8.

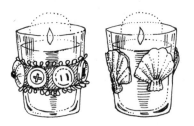

Brush hot glue on the sides of tea lights and decorate with buttons, ribbon, beads, small shells or hard candies. Arrange on a pedestal plate for a centerpiece or dance along the mantel...decorating is done!

Super Scrumptious Soft Tacos

Tina Stidam
Delaware, OH

Try these with crunchy taco shells too!

1 lb. ground beef
2/3 c. water
1 T. chili powder
1/2 t. salt
1/4 t. garlic powder
1/4 t. cayenne pepper
15-1/2 oz. can kidney beans,
   drained

1 head lettuce, torn
1 c. Cheddar cheese, shredded
2/3 c. olives, sliced
2 tomatoes, chopped
1 onion, chopped
8 10-inch flour tortillas
Garnish: avocado and sour
   cream

Brown ground beef in a 12" skillet, stirring occasionally; drain. Stir in water, chili powder, salt, garlic powder, cayenne pepper and kidney beans. Heat to boiling; reduce heat and simmer for 15 minutes, stirring occasionally. Remove from heat; set aside to cool for 10 minutes. Toss lettuce, cheese, olives, tomatoes and onion in large bowl. Spoon beef mixture down the centers of the tortillas; sprinkle with lettuce mixture. Garnish with avocado and sour cream. Serves 8.

Host a bring-your-favorite-topping taco party. Just provide the shells and the beef or chicken and everyone else can bring lettuce, tomatoes, olives, cheese, onion, salsa, sour cream and guacamole. Delicious!

Chicken Enchiladas

Michele Nance
Stevenson, WA

Add diced green chiles to enchiladas for extra zip!

28-oz. can green enchilada
   sauce
10-3/4 oz. can cream of chicken
   soup
2 c. sour cream
2-1/2 lbs. boneless, skinless
   chicken breasts, boiled and
   chopped

20 flour tortillas
4 c. shredded Colby Jack cheese,
   divided
4 c. shredded Cheddar cheese,
   divided

Mix sauce, soup and sour cream together; spread one-third in an
ungreased 13"x9" baking pan. Mix one-third with chicken; spoon
onto tortillas and sprinkle with half the cheeses. Roll up jelly-roll style;
place seam-side down on sauce. Spread with remaining sauce and
cheeses; bake, covered, at 375 degrees for 20 minutes. Uncover and
bake 10 additional minutes. Makes 20 servings.

Taco Pie Delight

Tina White
Charleston, IL

This hearty south-of-the-border bake is popular with everyone.

1 lb. ground beef, browned
1-1/4 oz. pkg. taco seasoning
16-oz. can refried beans
2 c. shredded mozzarella and
   Cheddar cheese mix

8-oz. jar taco sauce
9-inch pie crust, baked
1 tomato, chopped
Garnish: shredded lettuce,
   sour cream

Combine ground beef and taco seasoning mix together in a skillet;
simmer. Add refried beans; heat through. Layer ground beef mixture,
cheese and taco sauce in the pie crust. Bake at 350 degrees for
15 minutes; sprinkle with tomato. Slice into wedges; top with desired
garnishes before serving. Makes 8 servings.

Better-than-Ever Beef Stroganoff
Trisha MacQueen
Bakersfield, CA

You only need one skillet to whip up this favorite.

1-1/2 lbs. round steak, sliced
1/4 c. all-purpose flour
pepper to taste
1/2 c. butter
4-oz. can sliced mushrooms,
    drained
1/2 c. onion, chopped

1 clove garlic, minced
10-1/2 oz. can beef broth
10-3/4 oz. can cream of
    mushroom soup
1 c. sour cream
6-oz. pkg. medium egg noodles,
    cooked

Coat steak with flour; sprinkle with pepper. Brown in a 12" skillet with butter; add mushrooms, onion and garlic. Sauté until tender; stir in broth. Reduce heat; cover and simmer for one hour. Blend in soup and sour cream; heat on low for about 5 minutes. Do not boil. Spoon over warm noodles to serve. Serves 4.

Bring a whole new look to your table with a table runner you can make in a flash. Just tie 5 oversized cloth napkins together, corner-to-corner, and lay across the table.

Beef Stir-Fry with Couscous

Vickie Burns
Norwich, OH

No one's ever late for dinner when this is being served!

1-1/4 lb. boneless beef top
   sirloin steak
14-1/2 oz. can beef broth
1 c. couscous, uncooked
1 T. olive oil
1 red pepper, sliced

1/2 c. sweet onion, chopped
1 clove garlic, minced
1/2 c. honey Dijon barbecue
   sauce
1 T. fresh parsley, chopped

Cut steak lengthwise in half and then crosswise into 1/4-inch thick strips; set aside. Bring beef broth to a boil in a medium saucepan; stir in couscous. Cover; remove from heat. Heat oil over medium-high heat in a 12" non-stick skillet until hot; add half the beef. Stir-fry one to 2 minutes or until outside surface is no longer pink; remove. Repeat with remaining steak. In same skillet, stir-fry red pepper, onion and garlic for 2 to 3 minutes. Return beef to skillet; stir in barbecue sauce. Heat and stir one to 2 additional minutes or until heated through. Spoon over couscous to serve; sprinkle with parsley. Makes 4 servings.

So fun with an oriental dinner! Place a 6"x6" tile next to each guest's place and rest chopsticks on top... just be sure to have forks available too!

Easy-on-the-Cook Barbecue Ribs

Deb Bleick
Woodstock, GA

Be sure to have lots of napkins handy!

3 lbs. country-style pork ribs,
   browned
1/2 c. catsup
1-1/2 t. salt
1/8 t. chili powder
1/2 t. dry mustard

2 T. brown sugar, packed
2 10-3/4 oz. cans tomato soup
1 T. Worcestershire sauce
1/4 c. vinegar
1 onion, diced
1 T. lemon juice

Place ribs in large roasting pan; set aside. Combine remaining ingredients; mix well. Stir in one to 2 cups water; pour over ribs. Bake at 350 degrees until tender, about 2 to 3 hours. Serves 6.

Look beyond traditional napkins when hosting family & friends. Try using bandannas, colorful dishtowels, inexpensive fabrics from the craft store or, for especially saucy foods, use moistened washcloths...they'll love it!

Pantry Ham

Rosalia Burns
Delafield, WI

I remember how excited I was when my mother made this ham because it meant we were having company...and also one of her fabulous desserts!

8-lb. cooked ham with bone
4 12-oz. cans cola
2 15-1/4 oz. cans pineapple
    juice
1 T. whole cloves
1 c. brown sugar, packed

3 to 4 T. Dijon mustard
20-oz. can sliced pineapple,
    drained
6-oz. jar maraschino cherries,
    drained

Place ham, cola and pineapple juice in a large stockpot; simmer until ham is thoroughly warmed and the liquid is almost gone. Place ham in a large roaster; slice diamond cuts on top. Insert whole cloves in each diamond; set aside. Mix brown sugar and mustard together; rub over ham. Arrange pineapple rings and cherries over ham, keeping in place with toothpicks if necessary. Add juices from stockpot; bake at 350 degrees until warmed through, about 1-1/2 hours. Occasionally baste with juices; slice and serve. Serves 8 to 10.

Make-It-&-Go Ham Dinner

Kimber Bowersox
Morristown, TN

Simple and pleasing.

3 to 5-lb. smoked ham with
    bone

2 12-oz. cans cola
1 c. brown sugar, packed

Place ham in a slow cooker; set aside. Combine cola and brown sugar; pour over ham. Heat on high setting for 2-1/2 hours; baste occasionally. Serves 6.

Traditional Sunday Steak

Kathy Rudd
Lake Worth, FL

Sure to impress everyone at the table!

1-1/2 lb. beef flank steak
2 T. all-purpose flour
2 T. olive oil
salt and pepper to taste
1 cube beef bouillon

1 c. water
2 T. fresh parsley, chopped
1 t. sugar
3/4 t. dried thyme

Score steak on one side; coat both sides with flour. Place in a skillet with oil; heat until browned, turning to brown both sides. Season with salt and pepper; add bouillon, water, parsley, sugar and thyme. Cover; simmer for 1-1/2 to 2 hours or until beef is tender. Serve with steak gravy. Serves 4.

Steak Gravy:

pan juices
3 T. all-purpose flour

1/2 t. browning and seasoning
   sauce

Add water to pan juices to equal a total of 1-1/4 cups liquid; return to skillet and set aside. Whisk flour and 1/2 cup water together until smooth; gradually pour into pan juices, heating over low heat. Add browning sauce; stir and heat until thick and bubbly.

Baked Herb Chicken

Susan Young
Madison, AL

A quick & easy, one-pan meal.

6 boneless, skinless chicken
   breasts
1 c. fresh parsley, chopped
1/2 c. grated Parmesan cheese

1/2 c. chopped pecans
1/3 c. oil
3 T. lemon juice
3 T. dried basil

Arrange chicken in a greased 13"x9" baking pan; set aside. Combine remaining ingredients; pour over chicken. Bake at 350 degrees for 45 to 50 minutes. Serves 6.

Tomato-Olive Pasta

Donna Weidner
St. Augustine, FL

Be sure to make enough for extra helpings!

3 cloves garlic, minced
2 T. olive oil
1/3 c. sun-dried tomatoes,
   chopped
1-1/4 c. chicken broth

1/2 c. black olives, chopped
1/2 c. fresh parsley, chopped
16-oz. pkg. penne pasta, cooked
1 c. crumbled feta cheese

Sauté garlic in olive oil over medium heat for 30 seconds; add sun-dried tomatoes and chicken broth. Simmer for 10 minutes; stir in black olives and parsley. Pour tomato mixture over pasta; top with cheese, tossing lightly. Makes 8 servings.

Chicken with Basil Cream Sauce

Elaine Slabinski
Monroe Twp, NJ

*Whipping cream and Parmesan cheese add extra richness
to this easy chicken dish.*

1/4 c. milk
1/4 c. bread crumbs
4 boneless, skinless chicken
    breasts
3 T. butter
1 T. olive oil
1/2 c. chicken broth

1 c. whipping cream
4-oz. jar pimentos, drained
1/2 c. grated Parmesan cheese
1/4 c. fresh basil, minced
1/8 t. pepper
1 t. cornstarch

Place milk and bread crumbs in separate bowls; dip chicken in milk,
then coat with bread crumbs. Melt butter and oil in a skillet; add
chicken. Heat until browned; remove from pan. Place in oven to keep
warm. Pour broth in skillet; bring to a boil. Stir in cream and pimentos;
boil and stir for one minute. Reduce heat; mix in Parmesan, basil
and pepper. Cook until heated through; add cornstarch, stirring until
thickened. Pour over chicken before serving. Serves 4.

So quick & easy! Use
empty seed packs to hold
silverware...cut off the tops
of packets with pinking shears,
empty the seeds then slide the
silverware handles inside.

Quick from the Cupboard Mains

Mom's Stuffed Cabbage Rolls

Megan Pepping
Coshocton, OH

Every year we look forward to Fall when we get the huge heads of cabbage that have the perfect leaves for these rolls.

3 qts. plus 1/2 c. water, divided
3-1/2 lb. head cabbage
1 lb. ground beef
1/2 c. instant rice, uncooked
1 onion, minced
2 eggs, beaten
1 c. mushrooms, chopped
2 t. salt, divided

1/8 t. pepper
1/8 t. allspice
1 onion, sliced into rings
1/4 t. salt
16-oz. can tomato sauce
28-oz. can tomatoes
1/3 c. lemon juice
1/4 c. brown sugar, packed

Bring 3 quarts water to a boil in a large stockpot; add cabbage leaves and simmer 2 to 3 minutes or until leaves are pliable. Remove cabbage and drain. Place 12 of the largest leaves to the side. Combine beef, rice, onion, eggs, mushrooms, one teaspoon salt, pepper, allspice and 1/4 cup water; mix until well blended. Place 1/4 cup beef mixture into the center of each leaf; roll up beginning at the thick end of each leaf. Place a few remaining cabbage leaves in bottom of a Dutch oven; arrange rolls seam-side down on leaves and top with sliced onions. In a large mixing bowl, combine remaining salt, tomato sauce, tomatoes, lemon juice and remaining water together; pour over cabbage rolls. Bring to a boil over medium heat; sprinkle with brown sugar. Remove from heat; cover and bake at 350 degrees for 1-1/2 hours. Uncover and bake for 1-1/2 additional hours. Serves 12.

If you're planning on serving cold beverages with the main dish, put some freezer-proof cups in the freezer a few hours before guests arrive...a chilled glass makes all the difference!

Deluxe Chicken Bake

Lisa Peterson
Sabina, OH

Easy to make and always a hit!

8-oz. pkg. wide egg noodles,
   cooked
10 T. butter, divided
3-1/2 c. milk, divided
1/4 c. all-purpose flour
1/2 t. salt
1/8 t. pepper

2 10-oz. cans chicken gravy
4 c. cooked chicken, diced
2 T. pimento
1/2 c. seasoned bread crumbs
1/2 to 1 c. shredded Cheddar
   cheese

Combine noodles, 2 tablespoons butter and 1/2 cup milk; set aside. Mix 6 tablespoons butter, flour, salt and pepper in a heavy saucepan; heat and stir until smooth. Pour in remaining milk, whisking until thickened; add gravy, chicken and pimento. Stir in noodles; remove from heat. Spread into a greased 13"x9" baking pan; bake, covered, at 350 degrees for 25 minutes. Melt remaining butter; mix in bread crumbs and cheese. Sprinkle over noodle mixture. Bake, uncovered, for an additional 10 minutes. Serves 6.

Pick up inexpensive, glass salt & pepper shakers at flea markets. Dress them up by gluing on rhinestones or colorful beads. For the holidays, tie on a couple jingle bells...they'll ring with each shake!

Elegant Chicken Roll-Ups

*Teri Lindquist
Gurnee, IL*

Just right for a special occasion.

8 boneless, skinless chicken
   breasts
8 slices cooked ham
8 slices Swiss cheese
10-3/4 oz. can cream of chicken
   soup
1/2 c. dry white wine or chicken
   broth

1/2 c. sour cream
1 t. dried tarragon
1 t. pepper
2 c. cornbread stuffing mix,
   crushed
1 t. dried parsley

Wrap each chicken breast in a slice of ham; arrange in a greased
13"x9" baking dish. Lay one slice cheese over each chicken breast;
set aside. Whisk together soup, wine or broth, sour cream, tarragon
and pepper; pour over chicken. Cover with aluminum foil; bake at
325 degrees for 40 minutes. Remove foil; baste chicken. Sprinkle
with stuffing mix and parsley; bake, uncovered, for 15 additional
minutes. Serves 8.

It's easy to make eye-catching
floral arrangements by using
unexpected containers.
Instead of vases, try standing
flowers in jars of water, then
tuck the jars into simple paper
shopping bags, formal top hats,
or vintage purses.

Pizza Pasta Casserole

Maureen Rose
Lancaster, OH

Add any extra pizza toppings before sprinkling with cheese.

2 lbs. ground beef
1 onion, chopped
2 28-oz. jars spaghetti sauce
16-oz. pkg. spiral pasta, cooked

4 c. shredded mozzarella cheese, divided
8-oz. pkg. sliced pepperoni, divided

Brown ground beef with onion; drain. Stir in spaghetti sauce and pasta; spread equally in 2 greased 13"x9" baking pans. Sprinkle both with cheese; arrange pepperoni slices on tops. Bake at 350 degrees for 25 to 30 minutes. Makes 24 servings.

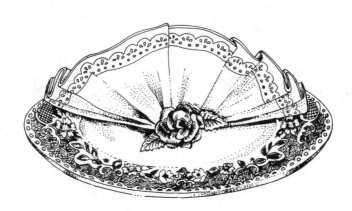

Host a progressive dinner with several friends. Each family serves one course at their house, as everyone travels from home to home. Start one place for appetizers, move to the next for soups and salads, again for the main dish and end with dessert!

Company Spaghetti Bake

Louann Rossman
Erie, PA

This dish reminds me of special visits to my grandparents' house when I was a young girl. It seems like we had this all the time...it's no wonder because it's so delicious and great to make ahead.

1 lb. ground beef
3/4 c. onion, finely chopped
1/2 c. green pepper, finely
   chopped
10-3/4 oz. can cream of
   mushroom soup
10-3/4 oz. can tomato soup
1-1/3 c. water
8-oz. can tomato sauce
1/2 t. salt
1 clove garlic, minced
8-oz. pkg. spaghetti, cooked
1-1/2 c. sharp Cheddar cheese,
   shredded and divided

Brown beef with onion and green pepper in a 12" skillet; drain. Add soups, water, tomato sauce, salt and garlic; simmer until heated through. Place spaghetti in a large mixing bowl; add sauce mixture and one cup cheese, mixing well. Spread into a greased 13"x9" baking pan; top with remaining cheese. Bake at 350 degrees for 45 minutes or until bubbly in center. Serves 6 to 8.

Out-of-town guests coming for the weekend? Make them feel at home by preparing a basket filled with in-season fresh fruit, snacks for late-night nibbles along with a local map and directions to favorite sites, shops and restaurants.

Beef & Sausage Empanada

Cheryl Lochmann
Powell, OH

A Mexican version of the Italian calzone that is sure to please family & friends. Make it up to 2 days in advance and refrigerate until baking.

1 lb. ground sausage
1 lb. ground beef
16-oz. jar medium salsa
3 c. shredded Cheddar cheese, divided
2 c. sour cream

1/4 t. cayenne pepper
1/2 t. cumin
6 10-inch flour tortillas, divided
29-oz. can enchilada sauce, divided
2 4-oz. cans green chiles

Brown first 2 ingredients together; drain. Stir in salsa and one cup Cheddar cheese; set aside. Combine sour cream, cayenne pepper, cumin and remaining Cheddar cheese together; set aside. Cover the bottom of an ungreased 13"x9" baking pan with 2 tortillas; spread with a layer of the sour cream mixture. Add a layer of meat mixture, then enchilada sauce. Repeat layers twice; sprinkle with chiles and remaining cheese. Cover with aluminum foil; bake at 350 degrees for 45 to 60 minutes. Uncover and bake 15 additional minutes; set aside for 20 minutes before serving. Makes 20 servings.

Make clean-up extra easy. Drape a paper tablecloth over the table, and use paper plates and plastic utensils. Decorate with wrapping paper strips, stickers and markers, then write guests' names right on the tablecloth for easy placecards. When dinner's done, just roll everything up and toss!

Desserts in a Dash

Creamy Peanut Butter Pie

Michelle Greeley
Hayes, VA

Whip up this no-bake dessert in minutes!

8-oz. pkg. cream cheese,
  softened
1/2 c. sugar
1/3 c. creamy peanut butter

1/3 c. frozen whipped topping,
  thawed
10 peanut butter cups, coarsely
  chopped and divided
9-inch chocolate pie crust

Blend cream cheese, sugar and peanut butter together until smooth;
fold in whipped topping and half the chopped peanut butter cups.
Spread into crust; sprinkle with remaining chopped peanut butter cups.
Refrigerate until firm. Serves 6 to 8.

Give pies extra pizazz when company's coming.
Pour melted chocolate onto wax paper, spread into
a 3-inch wide strip and let stand until cool but not
firm. Pull a vegetable peeler across chocolate
and arrange curls on top of pies.

Desserts in a Dash

Banana Cream Pie

Rachelle Santamaria-Lao
Moreno Valley, CA

Sometimes we top with whipped cream and chocolate jimmies.

1/4 c. sugar
3 T. cornstarch
1-1/2 c. milk
2 egg yolks

1 T. butter
1/2 t. vanilla extract
2 bananas, sliced
9-inch pie crust, baked

Combine sugar and cornstarch in a double boiler; add milk. Heat and
stir until mixture thickens; remove from heat. Slowly mix in egg
yolks; return to heat, stirring until thickened. Stir in butter and vanilla;
remove from heat. Set aside to cool. Layer banana slices over the
bottom of the pie crust; pour sugar mixture on top. Bake at
400 degrees until golden, about 10 minutes; set aside to cool.
Makes 8 servings.

Banana Cupcakes

Debbie Donaldson
Florala, AL

*Handed-down recipes are so special...this one is from my mother and
it's one of the very first desserts I ever made.*

1/3 c. butter
1 c. sugar
3 bananas, mashed
2 eggs, beaten

1/4 c. buttermilk
1 t. vanilla extract
1-1/2 c. self-rising flour
3/4 t. baking powder

Cream butter and sugar; mix in remaining ingredients. Fill paper-lined
muffin cups 2/3 full with batter; bake at 325 degrees for 15 to
20 minutes. Makes 1-1/2 dozen.

Rainbow Cake

Wendy Lee Paffenroth
Pine Island, NY

Serve with a spoonful of whipped cream and sprinkling of strawberries for an extra-special treat.

16-oz. pkg. angel food cake mix   Garnish: powdered sugar
red, blue, yellow and green food
    coloring

Prepare cake mix following package directions; do not pour into tube pan. Place one cup batter into each of 4 different bowls; tint one pink, one blue, one yellow and one green. Spread pink batter into a greased and floured tube pan; carefully spoon blue batter on top. Repeat with yellow and then green batters; carefully place on lowest rack of oven, baking according to package directions. Remove from oven; invert onto a serving platter. Let cool; sprinkle with powdered sugar. Serves 10.

Decorating dessert plates is so easy and fun.
Try drizzling fruity syrups along the edges or pipe on
melted chocolate in fun designs and words. You can also
use simple kitchen utensils (forks work great) as
stencils...just lay them on the plate, sprinkle cocoa
or powdered sugar over top and remove to
show off designs. Clever!

Desserts in a Dash

Mom's Special Occasion Cherry Cake
Roger Baker
La Rue, OH

Mom always made this cake for birthdays, showers, anniversaries and the church ice cream social. Many times someone would offer to buy the whole cake before it could be cut and served!

2-1/4 c. cake flour
2-1/2 t. baking powder
1/4 t. salt
1/2 c. shortening
1-1/3 c. sugar
3 egg whites, beaten

2/3 c. milk
10-oz. jar maraschino cherries, drained with juice reserved
1/2 c. chopped walnuts
4-oz. jar maraschino cherries with stems

Combine flour, baking powder and salt in a small mixing bowl; set aside. Blend shortening in a large mixing bowl for 30 seconds; mix in sugar. Gradually add egg whites, blending well after each addition; set aside. Whisk milk and 1/4 cup reserved cherry juice together; add alternately with flour mixture to sugar mixture, mixing well. Fold in nuts and drained cherries; divide batter evenly and pour into 2 lightly greased and floured 8" round baking pans. Bake at 350 degrees for 25 to 30 minutes; cool on a wire rack for 10 minutes. Remove from pans to cool completely; frost bottom layer with butter frosting. Add top layer; frost. Decorate the top with a ring of stemmed cherries. Makes 8 to 10 servings.

Butter Frosting:

3/4 c. butter, softened
6 c. powdered sugar, divided
1/3 c. milk

1/4 t. salt
1-1/2 t. vanilla extract
4 to 6 drops red food coloring

Blend butter until fluffy; mix in 3 cups powdered sugar. Gradually blend in milk, salt and vanilla; add remaining powdered sugar, mixing well. Stir in food coloring to desired tint.

Crispy Graham Delights

Ginny Shaver
Avon, NY

These are great for putting together when friends drop in or the family needs something yummy fast!

graham crackers
1/2 c. sugar
1/2 c. butter

1/2 c. margarine
1/2 c. chopped pecans or
   walnuts

Line the bottom of an ungreased jelly-roll pan with one layer graham crackers; set aside. Place sugar, butter and margarine in a saucepan; bring to a boil and boil for one minute. Pour over graham crackers; spread to cover evenly. Sprinkle with pecans or walnuts; bake at 325 degrees until golden and bubbly, about 5 to 9 minutes. Cool slightly; remove with spatula and set aside to cool completely. Gently break into squares; store in an airtight container. Makes 2 dozen.

Bake 2 batches of Crispy Graham Delights and wrap several in brightly colored cellophane bags to send home with each guest...a double delight!

Desserts in a Dash

4-Layer Cookie Bars

Angela Hunker
Fostoria, OH

A crunchy and creamy dessert everyone will enjoy.

16-oz. pkg. rectangular buttery
   crackers
1/2 c. margarine
2/3 c. sugar
1/2 c. brown sugar, packed

1 c. graham cracker crumbs
1/4 c. milk
2/3 c. creamy peanut butter
1/2 c. chocolate chips
1/2 c. peanut butter chips

Line the bottom of a buttered 13"x9" baking pan with a single layer of crackers; set aside. Melt margarine in a heavy saucepan; add sugars, graham cracker crumbs and milk. Heat over medium-high heat until sugars dissolve, stirring often; spread over crackers. Arrange another single layer of crackers on top; set aside. Combine remaining ingredients in a saucepan; heat over low heat until melted, stirring until smooth and creamy. Spread over crackers; set aside until firm. Cut into bars to serve. Makes 2 dozen.

Short on table space? Use the kitchen counter for a buffet line, clear off a bookshelf for a self-serve beverage bar and use end tables for desserts.

Easy-Time Dessert Squares

Sharon Murray
Lexington Park, MD

Switch it every time...top with blueberry, strawberry or apricot pie filling.

1-1/2 c. sugar
1 c. margarine
4 eggs
2 c. all-purpose flour

1 t. lemon juice
21-oz. can cherry pie filling
Garnish: powdered sugar

Cream sugar and margarine until light and fluffy; add eggs, one at a time, mixing well after each addition. Blend in flour and lemon juice; spread in a greased jelly-roll pan. Score dough into squares with a table knife; spoon one heaping teaspoon cherry pie filling in the center of each square. Bake at 350 degrees until golden, about 25 to 30 minutes. Cool slightly; sprinkle with powdered sugar. Cool completely; cut into squares along scored lines. Makes 3 dozen.

Paper baking cups are available in many sizes and are a great way to serve individual desserts... especially for those ooey-gooey treats!

Desserts in a Dash

Sunny Lemon Bars

Kris Warner
Circleville, OH

Place cut bars in a freezer bag and freeze up to one month.
Thaw, covered, in the refrigerator before serving.

1-1/2 c. plus 3 T. all-purpose
    flour, divided
2/3 c. powdered sugar
3/4 c. butter, softened

3 eggs, beaten
1-1/2 c. sugar
1/4 c. lemon juice
Garnish: powdered sugar

Combine 1-1/2 cups flour, powdered sugar and butter; mix well.
Pat into a greased 13"x9" baking pan; bake at 350 degrees for
20 minutes. Whisk remaining flour, eggs, sugar and lemon juice
together until frothy; pour over hot crust. Bake until golden, about
20 additional minutes; cool on a wire rack. Dust with powdered sugar;
cut into bars to serve. Makes 2-1/2 dozen.

Strawberry-Banana Sherbet

Linda Nowak
Cheektowaga, NY

So easy to make and serve...just pop a few frozen cubes in a bowl
and add a spoon!

4 c. strawberries, hulled and
    sliced
4 ripe bananas
1/2 c. sugar

1 c. orange juice
3 T. lemon juice
2 c. milk

Mash strawberries in a large bowl; set aside. Mash bananas and sugar
in a medium bowl until smooth; add to strawberries, mixing well. Stir
in orange juice, lemon juice and milk. Divide mixture between 4 ice
cube trays; freeze about 4 hours. Serves 6 to 8.

Brownies à la Mode

Judy Borecky
Escondido, CA

I've been using this recipe since the 1960's and I have revised it over the years into this yummy dessert. It's so simple, but fit for extra-special company.

1-1/2 c. all-purpose flour
1/2 t. baking powder
1/2 t. salt
1/3 c. baking cocoa
2 c. sugar
1 c. butter, softened

4 eggs, beaten
1/2 c. chocolate chips
1/4 c. chopped nuts
vanilla ice cream
Garnish: caramel ice cream
     topping and chocolate syrup

Combine the first 5 ingredients together; toss gently to mix. Stir in butter and eggs; blend well. Spread batter into a greased 13"x9" baking pan; sprinkle with chocolate chips and nuts. Bake at 350 degrees for 30 to 35 minutes; cool to lukewarm. Cut into squares and top each with a scoop of ice cream; drizzle with caramel topping and chocolate syrup. Makes 2 dozen.

Host a pile-it-on ice cream social! Alongside Brownies à la Mode, set out Mason jars filled with yummy toppings like chocolate candies, butterscotch chips, raspberries, cherries, hot fudge and creamy caramel...guests can even bring their favorite to share.

Desserts in a Dash

Chocolate-Peanut Butter Brownies *Jennifer Dutcher*
Lewis Center, OH

Chocolate and peanut butter...two reasons these brownies will disappear fast!

4 1-oz. sqs. bittersweet baking
   chocolate
3/4 c. butter
2 c. sugar
3 eggs, beaten

2 t. vanilla extract, divided
1 c. all-purpose flour
1 c. peanuts, chopped
1 c. creamy peanut butter
1/2 c. powdered sugar

Place chocolate and butter in a microwave-safe bowl; microwave until butter melts, stirring often. Add to a medium mixing bowl; blend in sugar, eggs and one teaspoon vanilla. Mix in flour and peanuts; spread in a greased 13"x9" baking pan. Bake at 350 degrees for 25 to 30 minutes; cool. Blend peanut butter, powdered sugar and remaining vanilla until smooth and creamy; spread over brownies. Drizzle with glaze; set aside until firm. Cut into squares to serve. Makes 2 dozen.

Glaze:

4 1-oz. sqs. semi-sweet baking
   chocolate

1/4 c. butter

Melt ingredients together; stir until creamy.

For a change of pace, try serving dessert around the coffee table...everyone can sit on big fluffy cushions.

Time-Saver Chocolate Cake

Carol Golden
Plantersville, TX

Quick and scrumptious!

2 c. all-purpose flour	1 t. vanilla extract
2 c. sugar	1/2 c. buttermilk
1/4 c. baking cocoa	1/2 t. baking soda
1/2 c. margarine	1 t. cinnamon
1 c. water	2 eggs

Combine flour and sugar in a large mixing bowl; set aside. Add baking cocoa, margarine, water and vanilla to a saucepan; bring to a boil, stirring often. Remove from heat; pour into flour mixture. Add remaining ingredients; mix well. Spread in a greased and floured 13"x9" baking pan; bake at 350 degrees until a toothpick inserted in the center removes clean, about 30 minutes. Remove from oven; spread frosting over warm cake. Cut into squares to serve. Makes 24 servings.

Frosting:

1/2 c. margarine	1/4 c. baking cocoa
6 T. milk	1-lb. pkg. powdered sugar

Place margarine, milk and baking cocoa in a saucepan; bring to a boil, stirring constantly. Remove from heat; stir in powdered sugar until smooth and creamy.

For instant cheer, string 4 to 5 helium balloons and tie them to a small bag filled with marbles or sand. Place the bag in the center of a Bundt® cake and let the balloons float overhead.

Desserts in a Dash

Double Berry Cake

Laurie Park
Westerville, OH

*After baking, fill this cake's center with a variety of fresh berries,
whipped topping or vanilla pudding to spoon over
each slice for an extra-special treat.*

2 c. all-purpose flour
1 T. baking powder
1 t. baking soda
1/4 t. salt
1 c. sugar
1/4 t. nutmeg

3/4 c. buttermilk
1/2 c. egg substitute
1/4 c. oil
2 c. frozen raspberries, thawed
2 c. frozen blueberries, thawed

Combine flour, baking powder, baking soda and salt in a large mixing
bowl; set aside. Stir sugar, nutmeg, buttermilk, egg substitute and oil
together; add to flour mixture, stirring until just moistened. Fold in
raspberries and blueberries; spread in a greased 6-cup Bundt® pan.
Bake at 350 degrees until a toothpick inserted in the center removes
clean, about one hour; cool on a wire rack. Remove cake to a serving
platter. Serves 12.

A piece-of-cake centerpiece! A cake stand does double
duty as a simple platform for chunky candles...wrap a
ribbon around each pillar for added color and charm.

Tropical Cakes

Cindy Colley
Othello, WA

This recipe makes 2 cakes...one to share right away and one to freeze
for unexpected company. Just save the coconut
to sprinkle on right before serving.

18-1/2 oz. pkg. yellow cake mix
3 3.4-oz. pkgs. instant vanilla
   pudding mix
3-1/2 c. milk
1-1/2 t. coconut extract
20-oz. can crushed pineapple,
   drained with juice reserved

8-oz. pkg. cream cheese,
   softened
16-oz. container frozen whipped
   topping, thawed
2 c. flaked coconut, toasted

Prepare cake mix according to package directions; divide batter evenly
between 2 greased 13"x9" baking pans. Bake at 350 degrees for
15 minutes; cool completely. Combine pudding mixes, milk, coconut
extract and reserved pineapple juice in a large mixing bowl; blend for
2 minutes. Mix in cream cheese; fold in pineapple. Spread over cakes;
top with a layer of whipped topping. May freeze up to one month or
sprinkle with coconut and refrigerate for at least 2 hours. Makes
36 servings.

Create a super cool
centerpiece for a dessert
party. Clean an empty ice
cream container (or ask the
local store for extras), fill
with floral foam and tuck
in some bright flowers.

Desserts in a Dash

Peaches & Cream Pie

Sydney Taylor
Roanoke, VA

Bursting with flavor, this dessert is special enough for any occasion.

3/4 c. self-rising flour
2-3/4 oz. pkg. cook & serve
   vanilla pudding mix
3 T. margarine
1 egg
1/2 c. milk

28-oz. can sliced peaches,
   drained with juice reserved
8-oz. pkg. cream cheese,
   softened
1 c. plus 1 T. sugar, divided
1/2 t. cinnamon

Combine the first 5 ingredients; mix well. Pour into a buttered
10" glass pie pan; arrange peaches on top. Set aside. Blend cream
cheese, 3 tablespoons reserved peach juice and one cup sugar until
smooth and creamy; spread over peaches to within one inch of the
edge. Sprinkle with remaining sugar and cinnamon; bake at
350 degrees for 30 to 35 minutes. Serves 8.

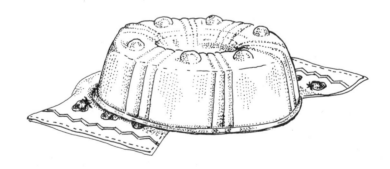

When thinking of centerpieces, remember to use larger,
more showy arrangements on a buffet table and smaller
ones on the dining table so guests can easily talk.

Sprinkle-Swirl Brownies

Rebecca Miller
Union Star, MO

Try sprinkling with chocolate chips, crushed butterscotch candy or peanut butter chips during the last 5 minutes of baking...delightful!

2 c. sugar
3/4 c. baking cocoa
1/2 t. baking powder
1-1/2 c. all-purpose flour

1/2 t. salt
2 t. vanilla extract
5 eggs
1 c. butter, softened

Combine the first 5 ingredients in a large mixing bowl; gradually blend in remaining ingredients. Spread batter in a greased 13"x9" baking pan; drop cream mixture by tablespoonfuls onto the batter. Swirl with a knife through the batter; bake at 350 degrees for 20 to 30 minutes. Makes 2 dozen.

Cream Mixture:

1/2 c. cream cheese, softened
1/2 c. powdered sugar

1 T. all-purpose flour
1 to 2 T. milk

Blend all ingredients together until smooth and creamy.

Tiny bud vases grouped together or used singly make a sweet addition to any dessert table.

Desserts in a Dash

No-Bother, No-Bake Cheesecake

Carla Turner
Salem, OR

Try putting half the filling in the crust, spread a thin layer of jam on top, then add remaining filling.

8-oz. pkg. cream cheese,
    softened
1/3 c. sugar
1 c. sour cream

2 t. vanilla extract
8-oz. container frozen whipped
    topping, thawed
9-inch graham cracker pie crust

Blend cream cheese and sugar until light and fluffy; mix in sour cream. Add vanilla and whipped topping; mix well. Spread into pie crust; refrigerate until set, about 3 to 4 hours. Makes 8 servings.

Yummy No-Crust Cheesecake

Mary Lauff-Thompson
Philadelphia, PA

A pudding-like treat.

2 8-oz. pkgs. cream cheese,
    softened
1 c. sugar
4 eggs

1 c. milk
2 t. cornstarch
1 t. vanilla extract
1/2 t. cinnamon

Blend cream cheese, sugar and eggs together; mix in milk, cornstarch and vanilla. Spread in a buttered and lightly floured 8"x8" baking pan; sprinkle with cinnamon. Bake at 325 degrees for one hour; turn off oven and leave in for 5 additional minutes. Makes 16 servings.

Blueberry-Sour Cream Cake

Kathy Grashoff
Fort Wayne, IN

Homebaked goodness in a hurry!

1-1/2 c. all-purpose flour
1 c. sugar, divided
1/2 c. butter, softened
1-1/2 t. baking powder
1 egg

2 t. vanilla extract, divided
1 qt. blueberries
2 c. sour cream
2 egg yolks

Combine flour, 1/2 cup sugar, butter, baking powder, egg and one teaspoon vanilla; mix thoroughly. Spread batter in a greased 9"x9" baking pan; sprinkle with blueberries. Set aside. Blend sour cream, egg yolks, remaining sugar and vanilla together; pour over blueberries. Bake at 350 degrees for one hour. Serves 9.

Cute on cakes, cookies or cupcakes...stack up 2 or 3 round fruit-flavored candies to use as holders for celebration candles.

Desserts in a Dash

Streusel-Topped Raspberry Bars

Rogene Rogers
Bemidji, MN

Guaranteed smiles!

2-1/4 c. all-purpose flour
1 c. sugar
1 c. chopped pecans

1 c. butter, softened
1 egg
3/4 c. raspberry preserves

Combine first 5 ingredients together in a large mixing bowl; blend on low speed until mixture resembles coarse crumbs, about 2 to 3 minutes. Reserve 2 cups mixture; set aside. Place remaining crumb mixture in a greased 9"x9" baking pan; press to cover the bottom. Spread raspberry preserves to within 1/2 inch from the edges; crumble reserved crumb mixture over the top. Bake at 350 degrees for 40 to 50 minutes; cool completely. Cut into bars to serve. Makes about 2 dozen.

Old-fashioned gelatin molds, tart tins and vintage drinking glasses are just right for filling with bite-size candies...place several around the room for easy snacking.

Slice & Bake Cookies

Kathleen Shockey
Wichita, KS

Make now and freeze...just thaw, slice and bake
as friends drop by.

2 c. butter, softened
2 c. sugar
2 eggs
5 c. all-purpose flour, divided
1 t. baking soda

8-oz. pkg. candied red
 cherries, diced
8-oz. pkg. candied green
 cherries, diced
2 c. chopped pecans

Cream butter and sugar until fluffy; blend in eggs, 4 cups flour
and baking soda. Set aside. Gently toss cherries with remaining flour;
fold into dough. Stir in pecans; mix thoroughly. Divide dough into
5 portions; form each into a roll. Double wrap in plastic wrap, if
desired; either freeze until ready to bake or slice into 1/4-inch thick
slices and arrange on ungreased baking sheets. Bake at 350 degrees
for 5 to 10 minutes. Makes about 8 to 9 dozen.

Quick-Batch Peanut Butter Cookies
Janie Branstetter
Duncan, OK

A favorite, quick & easy cookie...and surprise, no flour!

2 c. creamy peanut butter
2 c. sugar

2 eggs
2 t. vanilla extract

Combine all ingredients together; drop by teaspoonfuls on
ungreased baking sheets. Bake at 350 degrees for 10 minutes.
Makes 3 to 4 dozen.

Desserts in a Dash

Nana's Soft Jam Cookies

Michelle Moulder
The Woodlands, TX

Nana made these for my sisters and me all the time when we were little girls. We would walk down to her house on Saturdays and these mouth-watering delights would be in the oven. Now I often make them for my family...we always have a variety of flavors since you can use all your favorite jams.

1-1/2 c. all-purpose flour	1 egg
1/2 t. salt	1 t. vanilla extract
1/4 t. baking soda	1/2 c. sugar
1/2 c. oil	assorted flavored jams

Combine flour, salt and baking soda in a medium mixing bowl; set aside. Blend oil, egg, vanilla and sugar together in a large mixing bowl; mix in flour mixture. Drop by teaspoonfuls 1/2 inch apart on an ungreased baking sheet; make an indentation with the back of a small spoon in the center of each cookie. Place 1/2 teaspoon jam in the depressions; bake at 375 degrees for 8 to 10 minutes. Cool one to 2 minutes; remove to wire racks to cool completely. Makes 2 dozen.

I am still convinced that a good, simple, homemade cookie is preferable to all the store-bought cookies one can find.
- James Beard

Slow-Cooker Cherry Tapioca

Susan Estel
New Egypt, NJ

Such a fresh taste...friends will love it!

2 qts. milk
10-oz. jar maraschino cherries,
    drained and chopped with
    juice reserved
1 c. pearl tapioca

1-1/4 c. sugar
4 eggs, beaten
1 t. vanilla extract
Garnish: frozen whipped
    topping, thawed

Combine milk, 1/2 cup reserved cherry juice, sugar and tapioca; pour into a slow cooker. Heat on high setting for 3 hours. Blend eggs and vanilla together; add 1/4 cup liquid from slow cooker. Mix well; pour egg mixture into slow cooker. Heat on high setting, uncovered, until thickened, about 15 to 20 minutes. Stir in cherries; refrigerate until chilled. Serve with a dollop of whipped topping. Serves 8.

Who says glasses should be reserved for beverages? Elegant stemmed glasses are just right for serving up desserts like ice cream, tapioca, pudding and mousse...and it's sure to make guests feel extra special.

Desserts in a Dash

Lemon Pudding

Dorothy Baldauf
Crystal Lake, IL

This light dessert recipe has been in the family for years.
The sweet-tart taste makes a great ending to any meal.

1 c. sugar
2 T. butter
2 T. all-purpose flour

zest and juice of 1-1/2 lemons
2 eggs, divided
1 c. milk

Cream sugar and butter; mix in flour. Add lemon zest and juice; blend well. Mix in egg yolks and milk; set aside. Whip egg whites until stiff peaks form; fold into lemon mixture. Pour into a buttered one-quart casserole dish; set in a shallow baking pan filled with 1/2 inch water. Bake at 350 degrees for 35 minutes. Serves 6.

Lemon Vanilla Bark

Deborah Ludke
Glenville, NY

Joining friends for dinner at their place? Take a tin full of this bark
to give to your hostess.

4 1-oz. sqs. white melting
chocolate, chopped

4-oz. pkg. hard lemon candies,
coarsely crushed

Place chocolate in a microwave-safe bowl; melt according to package directions. Stir in 3/4 of the crushed lemon candies; spread in a jelly-roll pan sprayed with non-stick vegetable spray. Sprinkle remaining crushed candy on top, pressing lightly; refrigerate until firm. Break apart and store in an airtight container. Makes about 1/2 pound.

Red Velvet Cake

Jennifer Bryant
Bowling Green, KY

Scrumptiously rich...top with white chocolate curls for a special touch.

1/2 c. butter, softened
1-1/2 c. sugar
2 eggs
2-oz. bottle red food coloring
2 T. baking cocoa
1 c. buttermilk

2-1/4 c. self-rising flour
1/2 t. salt
1 t. vanilla extract
1 t. baking soda
1 T. vinegar

Cream butter and sugar together; add eggs, blending well. Set aside. Stir food coloring and cocoa together to make a paste; mix into creamed mixture. Add buttermilk, flour and salt; blend well. Set aside. Stir vanilla, baking soda and vinegar together; fold into batter. Pour batter equally into 3 greased and floured 8" round baking pans; bake at 325 degrees for 25 to 30 minutes. Cool; place first layer on serving platter and frost. Add second layer and frost; repeat with third layer, frosting top and sides. Makes 10 to 12 servings.

Icing:

8-oz. pkg. cream cheese,
  softened
1/2 c. margarine, softened

1 t. vanilla extract
1-lb. pkg. powdered sugar

Blend all ingredients together until smooth and creamy.

Wrap a wide ribbon around a tall, layered cake and tie a bow in the front. So simple and elegant!

Desserts in a Dash

Classic Carrot Cake

Janet Allen
Hauser, ID

Sprinkle cinnamon and chopped walnuts over top...so pretty!

4 eggs
1-3/4 c. sugar
1 c. oil
2 c. all-purpose flour
2 t. baking soda
1 t. salt

1 t. cinnamon
1-1/2 carrots, shredded
1 c. apple, cored, peeled and
   coarsely chopped
1/2 c. chopped walnuts

Blend eggs, sugar and oil together; set aside. Combine flour, baking soda, salt and cinnamon; mix into egg mixture. Stir in carrots, apple and walnuts; pour into 2 greased and floured 9" round baking pans. Bake at 350 degrees for 30 to 35 minutes or until a toothpick inserted in the center removes clean; cool on wire racks for 10 minutes. Remove from pans; cool completely. Arrange one layer on a serving plate; frost with cream cheese frosting. Add second layer; frost top and sides. Makes 10 to 12 servings.

Cream Cheese Frosting:

8-oz. pkg. cream cheese,
   softened
1/2 c. butter, softened

2 t. vanilla extract
4-1/2 to 5 c. powdered sugar

Blend cream cheese, butter and vanilla together until fluffy; gradually mix in powdered sugar until smooth.

Microwave Chocolate Pudding

Justina Montoya
Belen, NM

The perfect ending to casual meals year 'round.

2/3 c. sugar
1/4 c. baking cocoa
3 T. cornstarch
1/4 t. salt

2-1/4 c. milk
2 T. butter, softened
1 t. vanilla extract

Combine first 4 ingredients in a microwave-safe mixing bowl; gradually stir in milk. Microwave on high for 6 minutes, stirring every 2 minutes. Stir in butter and vanilla until smooth. Divide pudding into 4 individual serving dishes; press plastic wrap directly onto pudding surface in each dish. Chill 3 to 4 hours. Serves 4.

No-Bake Peanut Butter Oaties

Christie Sanders
Grapeland, TX

Oh-so good!

1-1/2 c. sugar
6 T. baking cocoa
1/2 c. margarine, melted
1/2 c. milk

1/2 to 3/4 c. creamy
    peanut butter
3 c. quick-cooking oats,
    uncooked

Combine sugar and cocoa in a saucepan; stir in margarine, milk and peanut butter. Bring to a boil over medium heat; boil for 1-1/2 minutes, stirring constantly. Remove from heat; add oats, stirring thoroughly. Drop by rounded teaspoonfuls onto wax paper; allow to set. Makes 3 dozen.

Desserts in a Dash

Chocolate Chip Cookie Pie

Ann Hess
Bloomsburg, PA

Serve warm with a scoop of ice cream!

2 eggs
1/2 c. sugar
1/2 c. brown sugar, packed
3/4 c. butter, softened

1/2 c. all-purpose flour
1 c. chocolate chips
Optional: 1 c. chopped walnuts
9-inch pie crust

Cream together eggs, sugar, brown sugar and butter; add flour, mixing well. Stir in chocolate chips and walnuts, if desired. Spread in pie crust; bake at 325 degrees for one hour, or until center tests done. Serves 6 to 8.

Really impress guests by serving ice cream cut-outs with dessert. Spoon softened ice cream 1/2-inch thick in a jelly-roll pan; freeze until firm. Use cookie cutters to cut out shapes and serve it on top of a slice of pie!

Oatmeal-Date Cookies

Doreen Dietz
Crystal Lake, IL

A special addition to any cookie platter.

1 c. butter, softened
1 c. brown sugar, packed
2 c. long-cooking oats,
   uncooked

2 c. all-purpose flour
1 t. baking powder
1/4 c. warm water

Mix all ingredients together; shape into forty-eight, 1-inch balls. Press gently with a fork to flatten. Arrange on an ungreased baking sheet; bake at 350 degrees for 10 minutes. Cool. Spread filling on flat sides of half the cookies; press flat sides of remaining cookies on top of spread. Makes 2 dozen.

Filling:

8-oz. pkg. chopped dates
1 c. sugar

3 to 4 T. water

Place all ingredients in a small saucepan; heat until sugar dissolves, stirring constantly. Remove from heat; set aside to cool slightly.

Set up a coffee station for friends to enjoy while nibbling on dessert. Make it extra special by offering flavored creamers, candied stirrers and scrumptious toppings like whipped cream, cinnamon and chocolate shavings.

Desserts in a Dash

Orange-Spice Shortbread Cookies
Karrie Middaugh
Salt Lake City, UT

These cookies melt in your mouth...and they make your kitchen smell wonderful too!

2-1/4 c. all-purpose flour
2/3 c. sugar
1 t. orange zest
1/4 t. nutmeg

1/8 t. salt
1-1/4 c. chilled butter, sliced
Garnish: powdered sugar

Combine flour, sugar, zest, nutmeg and salt; cut in butter with a pastry cutter until coarse crumbs form. Form dough into a ball; divide in half. Press one portion into the bottom of a lightly greased 8"x8" baking pan; prick lightly with a fork at one-inch intervals. Repeat with remaining dough. Bake at 325 degrees for 30 to 35 minutes; immediately remove from pans. Cut into 2-inch squares with a pizza cutter; slice each square diagonally to form 2 triangles. Sprinkle with powdered sugar; cool completely. Makes about 5 dozen.

Cover up a less-than-charming serving plate with a paper doily before arranging cookies on top. Chic and cheap, paper doilies are easy to come by at the grocery or craft store.

Abracadabra Bars

Lisa Johnson
Hallsville, TX

7 layers of heaven!

1/2 c. butter, melted
1 c. graham cracker crumbs
1 c. milk chocolate chips
1 c. butterscotch chips

1 c. flaked coconut
1 c. chopped walnuts
14-oz. can sweetened
  condensed milk

Coat the bottom of 13"x9" baking pan with butter; sprinkle the next 5 ingredients on top in the order listed. Gently pour condensed milk over top; bake at 325 degrees for 25 minutes. Cool; cut into bars. Refrigerate until firm. Makes 2-1/2 dozen.

Don't forget to serve milk with dessert! Wrap printed napkins or bands of oilcloth around tall drinking glasses and secure with a sticker...you can even write guests' names on the stickers so they always know which glass is theirs.

Desserts in a Dash

Cream Cheese Crescent Bars

Lisa Delisi
Bristol, WI

I take this dessert to almost every event I attend...and I always bring copies of the recipe because I get so many requests.

2 8-oz. tubes crescent rolls,
 separated
2 8-oz. pkgs. cream cheese,
 softened

1 t. vanilla extract
2/3 c. sugar
1 egg, separated

Line the bottom of a greased 13"x9" baking pan with one package crescent rolls, pinching seams together; set aside. Blend cream cheese, vanilla, sugar and egg yolk together; spread evenly over crust. Gently place remaining crescent roll dough on top, pinching seams together; set aside. Whisk egg white until frothy; brush over the top of the dough. Sprinkle with topping; bake at 350 degrees until golden, about 25 to 30 minutes. Slice into bars to serve. Makes 2 dozen.

Topping:

1/2 c. sugar
1/4 c. chopped pecans

1 t. cinnamon

Gently toss all ingredients together.

A heaping plate of cookies, bars or cupcakes makes a delightful (and delicious) centerpiece at a casual gathering with friends...don't forget the napkins!

Soft Molasses Cookies

Jenn Vallimont
Port Matilda, PA

The key to softness is to not overbake.

1 c. shortening
1/4 c. molasses
1 c. brown sugar, packed
1 egg
2 t. baking soda
1/2 t. ground cloves

1/2 t. ground ginger
1 t. cinnamon
1/2 t. salt
2 c. all-purpose flour
1 c. sugar

Cream shortening, molasses, brown sugar and egg together in a large mixing bowl; set aside. Combine dry ingredients except for sugar in a medium mixing bowl; mix well. Gradually blend dry ingredients into creamed mixture; shape dough into a ball. Wrap in wax paper; refrigerate for at least 3 hours or overnight. Shape into walnut-size balls; roll in sugar. Place on ungreased baking sheets; bake at 375 degrees for 8 to 10 minutes. Makes about 5 dozen.

Show off your basket collection. Load up several with cookies and bars and arrange on the table. Fill others with fresh flowers, and one with flatware rolled up in napkins. So cheery!

Desserts in a Dash

Peanut Butter Sweetie Cookies

Suzanne Stewart
Trumbull, CT

A tasty cookie I bake with my daughter, Molly...they're always a huge success!

1-3/4 c. all-purpose flour
1 t. baking soda
1/2 t. salt
1 c. sugar, divided
2 T. milk
1/2 c. brown sugar, packed

1/2 c. shortening
1/2 c. creamy peanut butter
1 egg
1 t. vanilla extract
6-oz. pkg. chocolate drops, unwrapped

Combine flour, baking soda, salt, 1/2 cup sugar, milk, brown sugar, shortening, peanut butter, egg and vanilla together; mix well. Shape into one-inch balls; roll in remaining sugar. Arrange on ungreased baking sheets; slightly flatten with the bottom of a glass dipped in sugar. Bake at 375 degrees for 10 minutes; place one chocolate drop in the center of each cookie. Cool. Makes about 3 dozen.

Surprise guests with a simple dessert. Whip up a few batches of homemade cookies and serve them in big glass cookie jars...just set them in the middle of the table and invite everyone to dig in!

Brownie Cupcakes

Robin Moyer
Fremont, NE

Make in mini muffin cups for one-bite brownies.

4 1-oz. sqs. semi-sweet baking
   chocolate
1 c. butter
1-1/2 c. chopped walnuts

1-3/4 c. sugar
1 c. all-purpose flour
4 eggs
1 t. vanilla extract

Melt chocolate and butter; stir in nuts and set aside. Combine sugar, flour, eggs and vanilla; mix until well blended. Add to chocolate mixture; mix until just blended. Spoon into paper-lined muffin cups; bake at 325 degrees for 20 to 25 minutes. Makes 2-1/2 dozen.

Make dessert extra fun for the kids. Bake a chocolate-covered mint patty inside one Brownie Cupcake...whoever gets that one wins a prize!

Desserts in a Dash

Fudgy Chocolate-Raspberry Cake

Brad Daugherty
Gooseberry Patch

This has become the traditional "celebration cake" among my friends & family. Chocolate and raspberry are an unbeatable match, but this recipe works well with strawberry jam too!

18-1/4 oz. pkg. devil's food
   cake mix
1 c. water
1/3 c. oil

3 eggs
1 t. vanilla extract
1/4 c. sour cream
1 c. semi-sweet chocolate chips

Combine cake mix, water, oil, eggs, vanilla and sour cream in a large bowl; beat batter with an electric mixture for 2 minutes. Stir in chocolate chips. Divide batter evenly between 3 buttered 8" round cake pans. Bake at 350 degrees for 25 minutes or until centers test done. Cool cakes in pans for 15 minutes; turn out and cool completely. Place one layer on serving platter and frost; add second layer and frost. Repeat with third layer, frosting top and sides of cake. Makes 10 to 12 servings.

Frosting:

1/2 c. seedless raspberry jam
3 T. butter
3 c. semi-sweet chocolate chips

3/4 c. sour cream
2 c. powdered sugar

Bring raspberry jam and butter to a simmer in a heavy saucepan over medium heat; remove from heat. Immediately stir in chocolate chips; stir until melted. Mix in sour cream and powdered sugar; beat with an electric mixer until smooth.

Before frosting layered cakes, wrap individual layers in plastic wrap and freeze overnight. Remove and frost right away...it's so easy to spread frosting and the cake stays moist longer!

Mom's Slow-Cooker Apple Pie

Sonya Collett
Sioux City, IA

Nothing ends a meal quite like apple pie.

8 tart apples, cored, peeled and
  sliced
2 t. cinnamon
1/4 t. nutmeg
1/4 t. allspice
3/4 c. milk
5 T. chilled butter, divided

3/4 c. sugar
2 eggs
1 t. vanilla extract
1-1/2 c. biscuit baking mix,
  divided
1/2 c. brown sugar, packed

Gently toss apple slices with cinnamon, nutmeg and allspice; place
in the bottom of a slow cooker. Combine milk, 2 tablespoons butter,
sugar, eggs, vanilla and 1/2 cup biscuit baking mix; layer on top of
apple mixture. Mix remaining biscuit baking mix with brown sugar;
cut in remaining butter with a pastry cutter until crumbly. Sprinkle on
top of apple mixture; bake on low setting for 7 to 8 hours. Makes 8 to
10 servings.

Personalize each dessert. Fill a pastry bag with melted
caramel (or chocolate!) and drizzle designs on wax
paper...try hearts, stars and friends' initials. Freeze
caramel until firm, then use to top each
serving of pie, cake or pudding.

Desserts in a Dash

Apple-Nut Cake

Kim Malusky
Twinsburg, OH

An old-fashioned favorite...enjoy with a warm cup of cider.

1-3/4 c. sugar
1 t. salt
1-1/2 t. cinnamon
3 eggs
1 c. oil

2 c. all-purpose flour
1 t. baking soda
1 c. chopped nuts
6 to 8 apples, cored, peeled and
    thinly sliced

Combine first 3 ingredients; blend in eggs and oil. Set aside. Mix flour and baking soda together; add to sugar mixture. Fold in nuts and apple slices; spread in a greased 13"x9" baking pan. Bake at 350 degrees for 50 minutes. Makes 15 to 18 servings.

Fill your home with an inviting aroma. Core an apple, place on a baking sheet and sprinkle brown sugar inside. Heat in a low oven one hour before guests arrive. Also try adding apple pie spice to a pot of boiling water...just let simmer over low heat.

Mocha Brownie Cookies

Linda McTaggart
Ankeny, IA

My Grandma La Velle always had these cookies in her freezer to bring out when anyone stopped by...we couldn't wait to have them, we'd just eat them frozen!

6 T. butter	3/4 c. sugar
1-1/2 1-oz. sqs. unsweetened baking chocolate, melted	1 egg
	1 t. baking powder
6 T. buttermilk	1 t. vanilla extract
1/3 t. baking soda	1 c. plus 2 T. all-purpose flour

Combine all ingredients in order listed; mix well. Drop by tablespoonfuls onto ungreased baking sheets; bake at 350 degrees for 10 minutes. Cool; frost. Makes about 1-1/2 dozen.

Coffee Frosting:

5 c. powdered sugar	6 T. butter, softened
1/4 c. baking cocoa	1/3 c. prepared coffee

Combine the first 3 ingredients; gradually blend in coffee until desired spreading consistency is reached.

Nestle several Mocha Brownie Cookies inside coffee filters...set a few "bowls" around the table for guests to enjoy after dinner. So clever!

Desserts in a Dash

All-Occasion Iced Cut-Outs

Christi Miller
New Paris, PA

*These yummy cookies can even be decorated
and then frozen...this shiny-hard icing stays bright!*

3-1/2 c. all-purpose flour
2-1/2 t. baking powder
1/2 t. salt
2/3 c. butter, softened

1-1/2 c. sugar
2 eggs
1-1/2 t. vanilla extract
1 T. milk

Sift flour, baking powder and salt together; set aside. Cream butter and sugar; blend in eggs until fluffy. Add vanilla; blend in flour mixture and milk. Mix well; cover and refrigerate dough overnight. Roll dough out on a lightly floured surface to 1/4-inch thickness; cut into desired shapes using cookie cutters. Transfer to parchment paper-lined baking sheets; bake at 400 degrees until golden, about 8 to 10 minutes. Cool on wire racks; frost, if desired.

Shiny Hard Icing:

2 c. powdered sugar
4 t. corn syrup

4 t. water
food coloring

Blend all ingredients together until smooth and creamy, add additional equal portions corn syrup and water until desired spreading consistency is reached.

Index

Appetizers

30-Minute Olive Appetizer, 44
Aloha Chicken Wings, 59
Baked Artichoke-Spinach Spread, 53
Baked Onion Dip, 60
Baked Spinach Balls, 66
Basil-Mushroom Triangles, 64
Black Bean Salsa, 55
Brie with Caramelized Onions, 37
Carefree Cheese Spread, 67
Cheesy Potato Skins, 65
Crab-Stuffed Mushrooms, 39
Cream Cheese Terrine, 38
Creamy Artichoke-Garlic Dip, 52
Creamy Crab Dip, 46
Cucumber Canapés, 40
Delicious Dill Dip, 41
Denise's Meatballs, 45
Easy Cheese Sticks, 72
Easy Slow-Cooker Bean Dip, 55
Everyone's Favorite Party Mix, 56
Family Chip Dip, 47
Festive Chicken Enchilada Dip, 43
Flaky Sausage Wraps, 61
Fluffy Peanut Butter Dip, 57
Fresh Pesto Spread, 49
Honey-Glazed Chicken Wings, 58
Jazzed-Up Cream Cheese Ball, 51
Mini Manicotti, 70
Party Cheese Ball, 50
Pepper-Swiss Cheese Log, 51
Pesto Packages, 49
Pizza by the Scoop, 68
Sausage-Cheese Dip, 60
Slam-Dunk Vegetable Dip, 47
Snappy Asparagus Dip, 65
So-Simple Hummus, 48
Spicy Buffalo Bites, 58
Stuffed Jalapeños, 42
Sweet Salsa, 54
Sweet-Tooth Cheese Ball, 57
Toasted Almond Party Spread, 36
Tortilla Roll-Ups, 67
Veggie-dillas, 71

Beverages

Cappuccino Cooler, 12
Espresso Whirl, 12
Fabulous Fruit Slush, 13
Mint Ice Cubes, 63
Pineapple Limeade Cooler, 63
Strawberry-Tea Punch, 62

Breads

Butterscotch Banana Bread, 30
Clover Tea Rolls, 125
Grandma's Biscuits, 114
Hearty Cheeseburger Bread, 69
Herb Biscuits Supreme, 111
Herbed Onion Bread, 125
Kitchen's Best Dinner Rolls, 115
Lemon Biscuits, 136
Parmesan & Basil Pull-Apart Bread, 110
Sunrise Cinnamon Loaves, 7
Tasty Garlic Bread, 110

Breakfast

3-Ingredient Sausage Squares, 32
Baked Garden Omelet, 19
Best Brunch Casserole, 10
Blueberry-Almond Muffins, 17
Blueberry Pillows, 34
Cheese, Please Pie, 24
Chef's Baked Oatmeal, 25
Cinnamon-Apple Pancakes, 31
Crispy French Toast, 20
Crustless Swiss Broccoli Quiche, 33
Early-Riser Breakfast, 14
Frozen Fruit Squares, 16
Fruity Oatmeal Coffee Cake, 29
German Apple Pancake, 9
Get Up & Go Granola, 28
Gooey Caramel Rolls, 21
Jump-Start Pizza, 15
Mini Ham Muffins, 19
No-Eggs Breakfast Casserole, 24
Overnight Coffee Cake, 6
Pear Pancake, 27
Puffy Pancakes, 26

Index

Raisin-Oat Muffins, 11
Sausage & Egg Muffins, 10
Southern Country Casserole, 18
Sticky Buns, 34
Strawberry Scones, 23
Sweet Apple Rolls, 26
Sweet Berry Popover, 22
Whole-Grain Jam Squares, 30
Yummy Caramel French Toast, 8
Zucchini Quiche, 32

Slice & Bake Cookies, 200
Slow-Cooker Cherry Tapioca, 202
Soft Molasses Cookies, 212
Sprinkle-Swirl Brownies, 196
Strawberry-Banana Sherbet, 189
Streusel-Topped Raspberry Bars, 199
Sunny Lemon Bars, 189
Time-Saver Chocolate Cake, 192
Tropical Cakes, 194
Yummy No-Crust Cheesecake, 197

Desserts

4-Layer Cookie Bars, 187
Abracadabra Bars, 210
All-Occasion Iced Cut-Outs, 219
Apple-Nut Cake, 217
Banana Cream Pie, 183
Banana Cupcakes, 183
Blueberry-Sour Cream Cake, 198
Brownie Cupcakes, 214
Brownies à la Mode, 190
Chocolate Chip Cookie Pie, 207
Chocolate-Peanut Butter Brownies, 191
Classic Carrot Cake, 205
Cream Cheese Crescent Bars, 211
Creamy Peanut Butter Pie, 182
Crispy Graham Delights, 186
Double Berry Cake, 193
Easy-Time Dessert Squares, 188
Fudgy Chocolate-Raspberry Cake, 215
Lemon Pudding, 203
Lemon Vanilla Bark, 203
Microwave Chocolate Pudding, 206
Mocha Brownie Cookies, 218
Mom's Slow-Cooker Apple Pie, 216
Mom's Special Occasion Cherry
  Cake, 185
Nana's Soft Jam Cookies, 201
No-Bake Peanut Butter Oaties, 206
No-Bother, No-Bake Cheesecake, 197
Oatmeal-Date Cookies, 208
Orange-Spice Shortbread Cookies, 209
Peaches & Cream Pie, 195
Peanut Butter Sweetie Cookies, 213
Quick-Batch Peanut Butter Cookies, 200
Rainbow Cake, 184
Red Velvet Cake, 204

Mains

Baked Herb Chicken, 173
Beef & Sausage Empanada, 180
Beef Stir-Fry with Couscous, 169
Better-than-Ever Beef Stroganoff, 168
Black Bean Spaghetti Sauce, 151
Bowties & Blush Pasta Dish, 139
Bubble Pizza, 152
Cheddar Ziti Bake, 138
Chicken Casserole Supreme, 158
Chicken Enchiladas, 167
Chicken in Cream Sauce, 159
Chicken Salad Croissants, 142
Chicken with Basil Cream Sauce, 174
Citrus-Cherry Pork & Pasta, 161
Classic Lasagna, 165
Company Spaghetti Bake, 179
Crowd-Pleasing Potato Pizza, 145
Deluxe Chicken Bake, 176
Elegant Chicken Roll-Ups, 177
Easy-on-the-Cook Barbecue Ribs, 170
Feed-'Em-All Casserole, 149
Fool-Proof Homemade Pizza, 144
Ham & Swiss Pie, 157
Make-It-&-Go Ham Dinner, 171
Meatball Sub Casserole, 155
Mom's Stuffed Cabbage Rolls, 175
One-Skillet Chicken & Rice, 149
Oven-Baked Pineapple Pork Chops, 140
Oven-Crispy Barbecue Chicken, 162
Overnight Chicken Casserole, 148
Pantry Ham, 171
Pizza Pasta Casserole, 178
Pork Chop & Potato Bake, 141
Potluck Casserole, 146

Index

Quick Ham & Cheeses, 157
Reuben Casserole, 156
Rose Hill Chicken Spaghetti, 164
Salisbury Steak & Onion Gravy, 163
Santa Fe Sandwiches, 143
Saucy Meatloaf, 147
Scalloped Scallops, 160
Simple Stuffed Shells, 153
Slow-Cooker Steak, 154
So-Tender Barbecue Chicken, 162
Sour Cream Taco Bake, 150
Super Scrumptious Soft Tacos, 166
Taco Pie Delight, 167
Tomato-Olive Pasta, 173
Traditional Sunday Steak, 172

Salads

7-Fruit Salad, 87
Asian Chicken Salad, 83
Colorful Apple Salad, 103
Cool Melon Salad, 102
Country Club Salad, 74
Creamy Potato Salad, 95
Extra-Easy Taco Salad, 98
Fabulous Feta Salad, 82
Family-Pleasing Coleslaw, 94
Frozen Cranberry Salad, 103
Fruity Marshmallow Salad, 104
Homemade Ham Salad, 88
Light & Fruity Turkey Salad, 89
Peanutty Crunch Salad, 79
Picnic Spaghetti Salad, 79
Pineapple-Pretzel Fluff, 86
Spiral Pasta Salad, 78
Thumbs-Up Cornbread Salad, 100

Sides

6-Bean Slow-Cooker Bake, 116
All-Time Favorite Corn Casserole, 107
Asparagus-Onion Casserole, 112
Awesome Onion Casserole, 122
Baked Spinach Casserole, 135
Broccoli-Cauliflower Bake, 109
Buttermilk Hushpuppies, 119

Crispy Wild Rice, 113
Dressed-Up Cucumbers, 99
Easy Scalloped Potatoes, 118
Escalloped Apples, 121
Fabulous Baked Potato Casserole, 106
Garden Skillet, 126
Green Beans in Garlic Butter, 107
Harvest Zucchini Pie, 131
Homestyle Dressing, 124
Impossible Garden Pie, 130
Lemon-Rice Pilaf, 120
Marinated Carrots, 121
Marinated Tomatoes, 99
Marvelous Mashed Potatoes, 118
Microwave "Baked" Beans, 117
New England Baked Beans, 117
Oh-So-Creamy Hashbrowns, 123
One-Dish Macaroni & Cheese, 133
Pineapple-Topped Sweet Potatoes, 129
Potluck Vegetable Casserole, 134
Praline-Topped Butternut Squash, 128
Rosemary Potatoes, 132
Roasted Root Vegetables, 127
Savory Corn, 122
Spinach Mashed Potatoes, 132
Tomato-Zucchini Casserole, 108
Winter Ranch Dumplings, 85

Soups

3-Meat Slow-Cooker Chili, 80
Bean & Ham Soup, 101
Black Bean Chili, 80
Broccoli-Cheese Soup, 77
Cheeseburger Soup, 81
Dutch Oven Stew, 97
Fix-Today, Better-Tomorrow Stew, 90
Hearty Vegetable-Beef Soup, 91
Oh-So-Quick Potato Soup, 76
Pepper Pot Soup, 85
Plaza Steak Soup, 84
Pumpkin Chowder, 92
Slow-Cooker Chicken Chili, 96
Traditional Clam Chowder, 76
Veggie-Cheddar Chowder, 93
Wild Rice & Nut Soup, 75

Send us your favorite recipe!

*and the memory that makes it special for you!** If we select your recipe for a brand-new **Gooseberry Patch** cookbook, your name will appear right along with it... and you'll receive a FREE copy of the book!

Submit your recipe on our website at
www.gooseberrypatch.com

Or mail to:

Gooseberry Patch • Attn: Cookbook Dept.
P.O. Box 190 • Delaware, OH 43015

*Please include the number of servings and all other necessary information!

Since 1992, we've been publishing country cookbooks for every kitchen and for every meal of the day! Each has hundreds of budget-friendly recipes, using ingredients you already have on hand. Their lay-flat binding makes them easy to use and each is filled with hand-drawn artwork and plenty of personality.

Have a taste for more?

Call us toll-free at
1•800•854•6673

Find us here too!

Get the inside scoop when you watch our product videos, read our blog and follow us on Facebook & Twitter!

www.gooseberrypatch.com

PRODUCT VIDEOS

Our NEW **Blog**

Find us on Facebook

Follow us on **twitter**

Marie,

This looks like a fun cookbook with easy stuff.

It's one I might go back and get for myself.

Enjoy